MUSLIMS IN INDIAN DEMOCRACY

MUSLIMS IN INDIAN DEMOCRACY

Ram Puniyani

KALPAZ

Muslims in Indian Democracy

ISBN: 978-81-7835-928-1

Published in 2013 in India by
Kalpaz Publications
C-30, Satyawati Nagar,
Delhi-110052
E-mail: kalpaz@hotmail.com
Phone : 9212729499

Laser Type Setting : Quick Media, Delhi
Printed at : G. Print Process,Delhi

Contents

SECTION–IV

AYODHYA, BABRI AND THE AFTERMATH

SECTION–V

GUJARAT: MUSLIMS AS SECOND CLASS CITIZENS

SECTION–VI

MUSLIM WOMEN: DOUBLE VICTIMS

SECTION–VII

GLOBAL TERROR

SECTION–VIII

PERCEPTIONS AND REALITY

Preface

The political process in India has taken a turn in a very sectarian direction. This sectarianism based mainly on religion has been the dominating phenomenon of Indian political scene. Starting with Ram Janmbhumi temple agitation, it took a center stage and has been unleashing events in which minorities are the direct victims and Dalits, women, Adivasis and workers face the brunt in an indirect way. Even amongst minorities, Muslims, the biggest minority have been bearing the brunt of this sectarian politics. Indian Muslim community has a long history in the country and starting from the coming of Arab traders on Malabar Coast and the invasion of Sind by Mohammad bin Kasim in eighth century, Muslim community came into being over a period of time.

During the rule of many a Muslim dynasties the process of interaction between Hindus and Muslims took another major leap in the syncretic traditions of the country. The partition of the country further led to a tragic process whereby the Muslim community in the area got divided into three major chunks, Pakistan, India and Bangladesh. In India it became the largest single minority community (13.4%) of population and has a significant social presence.

The politics based on religious identity began during the British rule, subtly encouraged by them, and later resurfaced in the decade of 1980s. While confronting this politics, its formulations, its propaganda and its onslaught on democratic ethos, I took up many themes for elaboration through journals, magazines, newspapers and email lists. The result was that over a period of time a total outline, the picture of Muslim minority emerged. This not only deals with the historical background but also the contemporary situations, the once related to daily problems of this minority. Meanwhile the US policies also resulted in the emergence of terrorism, for control over oil resources. US propagated that the terrorism is due to Islam and this was a big tarnishing of the image of Muslims and Islam in the society.

Today while we are grappling to understand the truth, trying to spread it via different mechanisms, the US propaganda and the local (Indian) propaganda against the Muslim minorities has been dominating the social scene. It has split the communities along religious lines and today the very concept of national integration needs to be strengthened to overcome the dark clouds of communalism, moving menacingly in the sky of democracy.

There are multiple efforts which are needed which will help in overcoming the dark period of our history. Dark as the very foundation of our nation. Values of Indian Constitution are being challenged, dark as the principles of our freedom movement. Liberty, Equality and Fraternity are being questioned by those who had no role to play in the freedom struggle. We have to overcome this and to see that the basic idea of democracy, that minorities not only feel safe and secure but are also able to progress as they get equal opportunities, is to be actualised. Struggle for minority rights, the goal of their security and equity is essentially an effort which is the root of democracy.

While engaging with the issue of communalism and threats to national integration, I found affectionate support from very close and dear friends. The list of these is very long but some of them I will like to mention, Asghar Ali Engineer, Shabnam Hashmi, L.S. Hardenia, Digant Oza, Irfan Engineer deserve special mention for their unstinted support in my small endeavour. My family stood by me like a solid rock, and that's what gave me all the courage to venture in this difficult terrain. Grateful thanks to them all.

Ram Puniyani

Introduction

I

India after its independence charted a course for economic progress and democratic Constitution. The struggles for progress, the debates on policy related to paths of progress, rational approach to problems and struggles for human rights had been the major issues occupying the social horizon. There were stray voices calling for identity related issues but they were on the margins and could not affect the main social-political discourse till 1980.

The decade of 1980 was a turning point in many ways. The downslide journey began with coming to the fore of the issue related to Shah Bano case, where a Muslim widow had sought for maintenance after divorce. The court granted this maintenance. At the same time the floodgates of conservative Muslim reaction dominated the scene. The Congress Government, led by the un-experienced Rajiv Gandhi, bypassed the court judgment via legislation in the parliament. The Hindu right wing reaction, as if it was waiting for a pretext jumped in the fray to press for the issue of a Ram temple at the place where Babri Mosque was located. This Ram temple agitation 'succeeded' in whipping mass hysteria in large sections of people, who rallied around different identity related campaigns launched by BJP, VHP and other related organisations, all the progeny of RSS, the supra political organisation, which calls itself a cultural organisation and manipulates its politics through it different progeny.

Meanwhile the clash of political interests between Devilal and V.P. Singh led the latter to implement Mandal Commission report for reservation of 26% of seats for OBCs. This report which was retrieved from the deep freezer gave a new direction to the politics of OBCs and gave them hope and justice in the system. At the same time the Ram Temple forces, saw the Mandal report as a big set back to their social interests and they rallied more firmly around the Ram Temple agitation. This was the turning point for Indian political scenario. Now the whole politics got derailed from the secular issues and discourse to the issues related to identity, to the emotive issues and the policies related to social progress and empowerment of the downtrodden were kept aside from the political arena.

The assertive RSS progeny put together their act and masses started following the Rath Yatras and other campaigns launched for Ram Temple. This also led to a well planned demolition of Babri Mosque and the consequent violence against Muslims in Mumbai in particular and partly in Surat, Bhopal and some other places. The Mumbai violence came as a big shock to the nation as a whole. Mumbai was seen as the most progressive city, a city with composite plural culture, most progressive values backed up by workers movement, literary endeavours and film industry. It was beyond the comprehension of most progressive people as to how Mumbai can be gripped by such a sectarian violence? The second point of importance of Mumbai violence was the whole quality and quantity of the violence. It surpassed all previous riots in its brutality and came close to be called as a pogrom against Muslims.

Mumbai was to change for the worse and for good, the ghettoization, the marginalisation of Muslim community was very blatant and communal party which led the pogrom, a close cousin of RSS-BJP, Shiv Sena romped to power in alliance with BJP.

The Ram Temple issue continued to stalk the national political scenario. The returning Kar Sevaks, from Ayodhya, on 27th Feb 2002, got killed in the train fire near Godhra. The fifty-eight of those burnt included thirty-six women and children. The Gujarat Chief Minister Narendra Modi instantly came to the conclusion that it was an act of Islamic terrorists in collusion with local Muslims and told his administration that there will be a reaction to this; a Hindu backlash will take place, which should not be curbed. This saw a pogrom in its full nakedness. Over 2000 Muslims killed. The pattern of the killings showed that there was a good deal of planning which led to the 'spontaneous' reaction. This anti Muslim killings not only led to the relegation of Muslims as second class citizens but also led to Gujarat being labeled as the First Hindu Rashtra in the Indian nation. The Gujarat Muslims were not only denied proper rehabilitation but also denied justice. Some of these cases are going on, including the SIT's work where the Chief Minister of Gujarat himself had to appear for deposing about his role in the Gujarat carnage.

After Gujarat, the major victims of communal violence were the Christian minorities, the peak of which was manifested in the Kandhamal violence of August 2008. Meanwhile the global phenomenon of terror caught up with the social perceptions and Islam Muslims and terrorism became sort of synonymous words in popular thinking. In India, blasts in Varanasi temple, Ajmer Dargah, Samjhauta Express, Malegaon, Mecca Masjid led to further intimidation and arrest of hundreds of Muslim youths, most of whom had to be let off for the absence of any proof whatsoever barring the fact that those caught were Muslims. The vicious cycle partly broke with impeccable evidence against ex ABVP (an RSS progeny) member Pragya Singh Thakur in Malegaon blast, since then there is some respite in the police swooping on innocent Muslim youths after every blast in the country.

The economic plight of the community had been worsening and Gopal Singh Commission (1981) did highlight the worsening plight of Muslims. The same was reconfirmed with Sachar Committee report (2005). Also the Rangnath Mishra Committee went into the declining percentage of Muslims in employment and recommended 10% of seats for Dalit/OBC section of Muslims. While Sachar committee has been placed in the Parliament and Prime Minister has formulated a 15 point program, the one which is adorning the official papers only, the Rangnath Mishra report has not even been tabled in the parliament. All in all the security of Muslim community is present by its absence and equity related issues are well kept in the freezers. The national process of marginalisation of Muslim minorities is on the rise and their rights as citizens have been heavily compromised by the aggressive political formations and the absence of will power amongst those controlling the levers of state power.

II

India has a rich plural heritage. Even before the Muslim Kings came from the North West, the Islam had arrived from the Malabar Coast of Kerala through the Arab traders. Later many Muslim dynasties established their rule in Delhi and other places. Islam spread in India mainly through the Sufi saints while other factors like fear of Muslim kings, expectation of reward and social interaction also contributed to spread of Islam in India. The Muslim rulers did not change the social structure of the places they ruled and interacted with different castes in different ways. They had Hindu kings as their allies, Hindu upper castes in their administration and soldiers were also drawn into to their army.

While Muslim Kings were belonging to different dynasties, they all were having different policies towards other religions. While Aurangzeb was the most bigoted one, Akbar had more amicable policies towards other religions and he did follow Sulah-e-Kul and also tried to found a new religion, *Deen-e-Ilahi*, without any success. Interestingly the number of Hindu court officials in the court of Aurangzeb was the highest. The kings had alliances cutting across religious lines and the battles were manly for the sake of power and wealth, not religion.

The maximum converts to Islam were from the low caste, Shudras who wanted to escape the caste tyranny of the system prevalent here. They belonged to farmers or artisans. At social level the interaction between Hindus and Muslims gave rise to syncretic traditions and the culture prospered during this period mainly due to this interaction. While music had great contribution from Muslim Ustads, Hindus contributed to the language, picking up Persian for use in the court. Urdu developed through this interaction and is one of the highest symbols of interaction.

Same way clothing, food, poetry, other literary forms enriched during this period. Muslim kings became the part of this social system and the plunder of earlier Kings was replaced by stable Muslim rule here. Muslims also got affected by the native systems, the most glaring one being social adoption of the caste practices. Religious traditions intermixed and led to the development of Bhakti and Sufi traditions, which were very popular with the middle and poor sections of is society.

This period of Indian history while a beautiful mix of Islamic and Hindu traditions was deliberately misrepresented by British historians as the tyrannical Muslim rule, to pursue their policy of divide and rule. The 1857 rebellion was the high point of Hindu Muslim unity. This shook the British and they resorted to the communal historiography to ensure that such rebellions don't take place in future. Hindutva ideologue Vinayak Damodar Savarkar, before his becoming the ideologue of Hindutva upheld this Hindu Muslim unity. Later on the lines of British, Hindutva ideologues started demonising the Muslim Kings. While pre-Hindutva Savarkar sees virtues in the role of Hindus-Muslims in 1857, RSS ideologue M.S. Golwalkar sees this as the problem. According to him since Bahadur Shah Zafar, the Mughal Emperor was leading the rebellion, it failed to inspire the Hindu soldiers so the rebellion failed.

This is also the period of history, the misrepresentation of which is currently used by RSS combine to spread hatred against Muslim minorities, they label it as dark period in contrast to the ancient "Hindu' period, the period of *Manusmriti* as the Golden period of Indian History.

This medieval period is also presented by the Muslim communalists as a period when Muslims ruled India. This is as distorted a presentation as that by RSS combine. The rule of Muslim dynasties cannot and should not be equated with the rule of the community. It was only the handful of elite Muslims, who were kings or courtiers, while majority of them were poor peasants or artisans. To think that it was Muslims who were ruling and British should have handed over power to Muslims as they had snatched it from Muslims is fairly convoluted argument. Neither today's Muslims a uniform monolith, nor they the legal heirs of the Mughal dynasty, and finally the era of dynasties is over and we are in a democracy where the elected representatives of people should be in the seats of power with full answerability to the people who are Sovereign.

III

The British rule sowed the seeds of sectarian politics. The British 'plunder project' initiated some changes which led to the emergence of industrialists-businessmen, workers and the educated middle classes. From these the democratic tendencies, the political streams representing the interests of workers, dalits came up. While the old sections of landlords and Princes' power declined and in the face of democratisation of politics and social norms they threw up communal organizations. Later some educated elements joined these landlord and related sections and gave birth to communal streams. They assisted the British designs of divide and rule in an indirect way, they talked of Muslim Nation and Hindu nation according to their religion.

After 1857, British had held Muslims as the chief culprits of rebellion and bypassed them from privileges. Muslim community as such was fairly downtrodden, and could really never catch up as far as education and jobs were concerned. This got worsened after Independence where the discrimination of the rulers kept them away from the jobs and other social and economic opportunities. While Partition was the outcome of British ambitions in the subcontinent, they were helped by Muslim and Hindu communalists in their goals and India was partitioned, Pakistan in the name of Islam and India on the grounds of Secularism. Pakistan was predominantly for Muslims. Muslim majority areas were carved out to form Pakistan. The same Pakistan also later broke into Pakistan and Bangladesh.

While the majority of Muslims who stayed back had no role in the demand of Pakistan, the communal elements in the state apparatus and the communal organisations gradually strengthened the propaganda that Muslims belong to Pakistan, they are loyal to Pakistan and the communal propaganda started getting stronger after every communal violence. There were campaigns to humiliate them, Indianisation of Muslims', and the anti-cow slaughter campaigns also targeted Muslims in a subtle fashion.

The communal violence was mainly spearheaded by the RSS and its progeny, but Congress leaders also used communal violence for their pragmatic goals. There is a crucial difference between the communalism pursued by RSS combine and the one resorted to by Congress off and on. The net result has been the marginalisation of Muslim community over a period of time. Their exclusion from economic, social and political space. This got firmed up in the decade of 1980s with the Ram temple campaign coming up. It was also a period when the dalit and Adivasi struggles were moving up along with the women's rights struggles. The anti Muslim campaign became the overarching one and other movements for rights became undermined.

As such the decade of 1980s had lot of global changes which were to strengthen the conservative politics here. The bipolar world started changing and Socialist economies came under the cloud and ultimately collapsed. The rise of US changed lot of equations. It is during this period that United Nations as the potential World Government got a setback and US-Israel axis bypassed the United Nations deliberately to enhance their political and economic interests. The US intervention in Afghanistan, the US encouraging/supporting Madrassas to train All Qaeda-Taliban was the main turning point in the global history. This was the period after which the global politics veered more and more to the identity issues, and "Clash of Civilisations" became the cry of US policies of attacking Muslim countries. The real interest was to control the oil wealth but the language was that of religion and civilization. From here on the conservative values all over the world started going up and the hard earned rational/democratic space started shrinking all over.

Economically, the globalization started becoming more oppressive to the poor of the world and less powerful countries. It led to pauperisation of large sections of the oppressed who were fed the opium of religiosity by all section around. In India the rise of God men, in thousands became the norm and the leading one's amongst them started rubbing shoulders with the political powers and at the same time influencing the social thinking in conservative direction. All in all, the potion of global changes and national rise of communal forces supplemented each other and the rights of weaker sections came under the chopping block of the interests of the elite. The US sponsored Al Qaeda became the hallmark of "Islamic Terrorism", a word coined by US media and lapped up by the media at large, this had adverse impact on the perception of Muslims in the country.

Media played its own role in the demonization of Muslim community. This can easily discern in the Mumbai carnage and the Gujarat Pogrom. The Mumbai carnage witnessed over 1000 dead, 80 per cent of them being Muslims. It also saw the gutting of nearly 10000 crores of property, mainly of Muslim minority. This was followed by bomb blasts in Mumbai. Interestingly the media played a dynamic role in ensuring the punishment to the perpetrators of bomb blasts, correctly so. At the same time it treated the culprits of carnage with kid gloves. The result was that all the culprits of bomb blasts were punished while most of the culprits of carnage got off lightly, some of them got promotion and some others became politicaly formidable forces.

Gujarat pogrom is no different. While Bannerjee Commission affirmed that it was an accident, long before that the state chief minister ensured unleashing of the pogrom on the ground that Muslims have burnt the train. All the suspects of Godhra train burning were arrested under draconian acts while most of the culprits of pogrom are having a field day in social and political life. Large section of media has been playing the role being hand in glove with the communal forces. The role of demonizing the Muslim community.

IV

This volume divides the theme of Muslim minorities in to eleven sections. These thematic sections deal with one aspect each of the issues related to the Muslim community. Section I deals with the historical background of the nation, its plural traditions, its freedom movement, and the rise of communalism, the one which is the major tormentor of Muslim minorities. One must point out here that the major problem is due to the absence of land reforms, secularisation process, the reduction in the hold of clergy due to which communalism could come up and resurface in the decade of 1980 due to the global changes and due to the national changes which have thrown up vested interests in strong measure. This section also deals with the concept of democracy and the place of minorities in a democracy, the rights due to minorities in a plural country. Also how do we understand who is a minority, as times and again there is a further demonisation of Muslims on the grounds that they are bang appeased, or they are not a minority.

The economic deprivation, exclusion is the major outcome of communal politics, seeped in the state apparatus or openly stalking on the streets. The already poor section of Muslims got further marginalized during last sixty years of development. This is the theme of Section II, which takes up the socio-economic exclusion of Muslim minorities. Whether they have been appeased or marginalised is something to be given a serious thought. The popular notion suggests that under the influence of communal propaganda Muslims have been appeased. This fact has been brought out by different commission/committee reports, Gopal Singh, Sachar and Rangnath Mishra. It takes up the issue of Government paying lip service to this large section of population and merely paying lip service to the economic issues of this section of the nation.

Section III deals with the communal violence, how this community has been subject to regular repetitive violence? How violence has been used as a political tool by communal forces to strengthen their political ground comes out in this section. Various inquiry commission reports have highlighted the culprits, the political outfits behind them, the role of police-the state machinery is outlined in this section. These inquiry commission reports blast the perception that Muslims start the violence. In a way, the manufactured perception is the best defense for the attackers. It also brings forward the fact that the communal violence creates a social thinking due to which conservative elements become strong in the society and liberal elements in the community are bypassed. The next step in this is that the process of ghettoisation becomes all pervasive and then even the prominent people from that community are unable to buy houses in mixed localities.

Ayodhya has been the major transformer of the level of communalisation in the national scene. What was the story behind the mosque; how demolition of the mosque changed the national scenario is brought out in Section IV. This section also deals with the local efforts by the peace groups to bridge the divide between communities created due to the demolition. Also the report of much awaited Liberhan Commission confirmed the role of RSS combine-BJP etc., in demolishing the mosque in a planned manner, and figured out the guilty of the crime. What can be the solution to this vexed issue? Probably Mosque can be restored, the criminal act can be undone and Ram Temple built nearby to appease the communal elements.

Section V takes up the case of Gujarat, which has been called Laboratory of Hindu Rashtra for the right reasons. It began as the laboratory and by now it is a Hindu Rashtra in one nation. Here the state of minorities has been relegated to that of the second class citizens. It all began with the projection of Godhra train burning as an act of Muslims; the truth of this was brought forward by the Bannerjee Commission, which pointed out that all evidence shows that it was an accident. The communal atmosphere by the state is very obvious here as the wedge between communities is deepening due to the assertion of the communal politics by the state and para state actors who have a very respectable place in the state by now. The result is that the democratic norms have been given a go by and right from top to bottom a dictatorial atmosphere exists here to the detriment of the minorities.

Section VI takes up the sensitive case of Muslim women, who are double victims of communal violence. On the one side during the communal violence they are subjected to physical violence, sexual violence and all brutal acts targeted at their reproductive organs. After the violence they suffer a great amount of insecurity which leads them to come under the spell of maulanas and are made to adopt burqa as a matter of imposed social practices. Many a women who are earlier not wearing hijab, head scarf or burqa come under the pressure to adorn these. Which is very symbolic of the totality of the condition of minority women?

Section VII is devoted to the issue of terrorism as it became a prominent phenomenon after 9/11, 2001. Since it was linked to Islam's teachings and Muslims, this section tries to demonstrate the real truth behind the phenomenon of terrorism. The politics of cold war era lead to the series of events leading to setting up of Madrassas in Pakistan by US, where the meaning of jihad and kafir were distorted to indoctrinate the Muslim youth to train them to the path of insane violence. They were also supplied with money and arms with the help of which they joined anti Russian forces, leading to the defeat of Russian army. Later these indoctrinated Muslim youth took to different acts of terror. US media at this time popularised the word Islamic terrorism and that did the trick of demonizing Islam and Muslims all over the world. This section goes to the history of Islam, its role in Middle East and its core teachings. It also demonstrates how some youth take to the path of terror and how on the one hand there is demonisation of Islam, and on other hand there is phobia about this religion. The investigating agencies generally operate on the ground that if there is some act of terror, some Muslim youths must be the culprits, and accordingly in India many an innocent Muslim youth have been victimized at regular intervals.

There are various misconceptions about Muslims and Islam in the popular mind and this affects the social thinking and also the attitude of media towards this community. The myths about

Muslim community are constructed around Indian medieval history, around the illiteracy and poverty, around Muslim personal laws, size of their families and of course around the phenomenon of terrorism. The Section VIII takes this up along with various contextual themes like those related to the nature of Madrassas and RSS run single teacher schools (Ekal Vidyalaysa). While Madrassas teach Koran, RSS run schools dish out hate minority syllabus, and this has resulted in the new crop of youth who are indoctrinated to hate the minorities, Muslims and Christians. A lot has been made about singing of Vande Matram, and the so called Love Jihad, the section takes these issues also.

Section IX deals with Indo Pak issues. A lot of politics has been done here by inciting hate against Pakistan. The terrorism emerging from Al Qaeda type outfits has been attributed to being sponsored by Pakistan. The truth of the matter is that many of these terror outfits are no more controlled by the civic leadership of Pakistan. It is true the military regime was partly hand in gloves with the terror outfits, but to think of Pakistani people and the civic regime in the same light will be fallacious. Pakistan society has been a bigger victim of the terror groups. Good relations with Pakistan will be the best path to curb terrorism in the long run. The acts of Taliban are crude and defy any sensibility, their imposing Jazia on Sikhs and beheading them is horrible for example. Taliban has been creating obstacles in the path of Peace between the two countries, India and Pakistan.

Section X deals with the terrorism done by different groups owning their allegiance to Hindutva groups. This got detected with two Bajrang Dal workers getting killed in Nanded in Maharashtra while making bombs. The series of blasts took place in front of mosques, dargahs, at times when maximum crowd is there, Ajmer, Malegaon, Mecca Masjid were few amongst these. The Malegaon blast case was investigated with success and ex-member of ABVP, an RSS affiliate was the major turning point. This led to the link of all those, Swami Dayanand Pande, Swami Aseemanand, Lt Col Prasad Shrikant Purohit and with this the earlier firmly held belief that all terrorists are Muslims was quashed for good. The murder of Ishrat Jahan a student of Mumbai College turned out to be a fake encounter. The attitude of police in arresting hoards of Muslim youth after every act of terror creating a sort of pathologic fear amongst the Muslim community. The question started being asked, Is it a crime to be born a Muslim in India? Also the question of eradicating terrorism remains a million rupee question. The Al Qaeda variety on one side and the Sadhvi variety on the other.

Section II, the last section, takes up the life story of Prophet Mohammad and the teaching of Islam, the messenger of peace. It also presents the UN sponsored High level committee's report which quashes the theory of clash of civilisation and talks that human civilisations have always been collaborating with each other, there is a constant and ongoing alliance of civilizations. That is what we need to promote and nurture. With this as the base we have to talk of overcoming sectarian violence, we need to find the path for peace, to bring the communities together, cutting across religious lines, to promote dialogue, to ask for democratic values being firmed up to create an atmosphere for progress in all the fields of life.

V

Today we as a nation are sitting on the horns of dilemma. While our constitution is secular-democratic, our society is turning more and more religious. The result is that parties with religious appeals, the forces with religious imageries become more acceptable. How do we carve out a niche for secular society, relegating religion to the private space of individuals?

The global situation of hegemony of a single super power has to be substituted by the democracy amongst the nations. That requires that the superpower comes around for the democratic dialogue with all the nations.

In India the society and state has to ensure that all communities are able to live in peace and thrive. As society and state we need to curb the sectarian political tendencies. We need to implement affirmative action for weaker sections of society, minorities included. Last three decades have shown us the worst of our travails and sorrows, more so for the minorities. We need to reverse this process and talk of times where all of us are able to intermix without any fear. The spirit of freedom movement, the moral values of religions have to be promoted.

The leaders of minority community need to focus more on the issues of equity, education, employment, self employment, etc. They also have to take up the issues related to security of the community, the baseless demonisation and harassment to see that community can mobilise all its resources to pull out through these troubled times.

SECTION–I

INDIAN DEMOCRACY AND MINORITIES

1

Indian Muslim Minority: A Prelude

Formation of Muslim community in India took place in various stages. To begin with it started emerging along Malabar Coast when the Arab traders used to come for trade during Seventh Century A.D. Later a section of untouchables converted to Islam to form bulk of Muslim population. The Muslim community was not a monolithic one. There were different economic strata, majority being low caste poor peasants, and another group belonging to traders, and a very small number of landlords. The difference in interests of elite and poor was very vast.

After the great rebellion of 1857, British held Muslims responsible for the revolt and punished them severely, tried to keep them out of government jobs and other facilities. The newly introduced modern education and government jobs were initially filled mainly by Hindus. Later with Sir Syed's the matters changed slightly but the difference in the status of Muslims and Hindus as communities continued. Muslims had more of poor, uneducated sections, while section of Hindus was able to take good advantage of the educational and employment related opportunities.

The perception of interest between elite and the poor Muslims was: elite shared different cultural values, had aspiration for higher number of jobs and wanted to make a compromise with ruling powers for their social and economic aspirations. Upper and middle class aspirations, the pro-imperialist ones' got channelised through the politics of people like Sir Syed Ahmed and Jinnah, while the aspirations of lower castes were anti-imperialist and were represented through the politics of people like Badruddin Tyabji, Khan Abdul Gaffar Khan and Maulana Abul Kalam Azad.

Electoral franchise was restricted to 10% elite of the community only, those owning property or having higher education were the one's having voting right. In 1945 elections, the results of which formed the basis of partition, not more than 4% Muslim elite decided the fate of the country. "Out of 10% who had right to vote, not more than 60% voted and out of these 60% about 40% voted against Muslim League. Thus, ultimately less than 4% Muslims voted for Partition plan, Muslims had played no role at all in determining the future of India. They either had no right to vote, or did not vote or voted against Muslim League (Asghar Ali Engineer, 'Secularism in Indian Context' CSSS Sept. 1-15, 96).

India's tragic partition (1947) left a deep scar on the South Asian polity. While Pakistan was formed on the basis of Islam, India was formed on secular grounds. That time undivided India had 25% Muslim population. Of this India was left with 11.6% Muslim population, while 13.4% were in Pakistan. Meanwhile a large affluent section of Muslims left for Pakistan. Today Muslims constitute 13.4% of India's population and are 138.18 millions in total population. (2001 Census) The sporadic but regular occurrence of the violence against this community has left it with a feeling of insecurity and has resulted in ghettoisation. A large section of this minority was on the lower rungs of socio-economic levels, which went on worsening with time due to the social and political discrimination. This has been put forward by various indices as presented by Gopal Singh Commission in 1982 and by Sachar Committee, 2006. The findings of this committee are very disturbing as this section of India's population has been constantly sliding down.

Muslims have not been able to take advantage of various government schemes, one of the reasons being that they are mainly small farmers, marginal farmers, agricultural laborers, landless laborers, city based artisans and petty workers. Amongst other reasons one of the main causes for this is the discrimination and indifference on the part of planning and implementation authorities. "Consequently, the limited progress that some sections of Muslims have been able to make in recent years owes almost wholly to their own efforts. Overall the economic conditions of most Indian Muslims are unenviable, to say the least. Most of them eke out a hand-to-mouth existence either by way of self-employment in petty trade or by working in the unorganized sector. They are engaged mostly as construction laborers, rickshaw, taxi and truck drivers, handcart pullers, coolies, barbers, tailors, carpenters, pavement hawkers, or at best as mechanics, fitters, plumbers, electricians or welders." (Report AA, JMI, ISI, Indian Social Institute 2006)

"As far as education is concerned figures of Sachar Committee suggest that Muslim men and women are less educated than their non-Muslim counterparts. In fact, a large number of Muslims do not even possess basic reading and writing skills. At the national level, the number of literate Muslims is less than non-Muslims. Based on the figures of the 2001 census, only 55 per cent Muslim males are literate as compared to 64.5 per cent non-Muslims, while only one among 41 male graduate as opposed to one among 19 non-Muslims. The condition of the Muslim women is much worse, with only one among a hundred being a graduate." (DNA, Mumbai 4th October 2006)

Their representation in the jobs in the government offices, public sector and private sector is abysmal, more the higher jobs, lower their representation. Since the decade of 1980s India has seen the unprecedented political phenomenon, the one related to Communalism, i.e. religious identity based politics. This phenomenon uses the religious identity for political mobilization, which in turn forms their route to coming to political power. The agenda of communal formations is essentially to suppress the human rights of weaker sections of society. It begins by spreading hate against the people of 'other religion', this hate propaganda in turn vitiates the social atmosphere and aids in the precipitation and intensification of communal violence, This violence over a period of time intimidates the minority communities, ghettoising them.

Today India is seeing this ghettoisation of Muslim minorities, and an equal intimidation of the Christian minority. Muslim minority has been subjected to repeated communal violence followed by arrest of large number of Muslim youth on the pretext of their being terrorists, while the Christian community has been intimidated due to the attacks on the nuns and priests in remote places and due to the horrific violence, which is gradually becoming more intense. Globally we are witnessing a period of Islamophobia, which has increased the insecurity of the Muslims World over, more so after the events of 9/11/2001, the attack on

Afghanistan and Iraq. In South Asia one has witnessed this as a simmering problem right from the decades of 1940s, the partition of India, and migration of Hindus from the then West and East Pakistan. To add to the problem the issue of Kashmir over a period of time has come to be seen as a Hindu-Muslim issue while it is the result of ultra nationalism of India and Pakistan and the US design to keep a foothold on this strategically important region through its proxy, Pakistan. The result is aggravation of the anti Muslim sentiments constructed around the memories of partition and the imbroglio which continues in Kashmir.

2

Religious Pluralism, Peaceful Coexistence and its Efficacy in Democratic Polity

During the last three decades worldwide in general and in India in particular, there has been a great deal of intolerance for others' religious tradition. Globally the theory of clash of civilizations is based on the clash between religious traditions, and locally the politics of RSS combine, the Hindutva also builds itself on the dislike, demonisation and hate for others religious traditions.

Medieval Times

As such India has been a country with multiple religious and cultural traditions living and interacting peacefully in the society. While kings had been fighting with each other for the sake of power, the average people interacted with each other, cutting across religious lines and created the humane syncretic traditions.

The diversity of Indian society has been a rich source of strength and resilience of the community. Though it is true that kings fought amongst each other for larger control of territories, the average people, the toilers, the downtrodden of both the religions celebrated the interaction with each other. While the kings had bigger preoccupations with expansion or preservation of their kingdoms for their material benefit, the large chunk of society derived the pleasure from their social and community life. While different sectors of nobility were more interested in consolidating their political powers and humiliating the other, different creative layers of society: poets, laureates, architects, performing artists, folk artists and painters integrated the other streams into their art, and went on to enrich the art itself in the process.

Religion

Biggest synthetic trends are discernible in the popular religions, Bhakti from Hindu side and Sufi from the side of Islam are the major religious trends to have come up in this period. Kabir, Nanak and Tulsidas reflected the synthetic trends and the influence of both religions in their lives and works teachings spread amongst vast sections of weavers and others, cutting across both the religions.

Kabir rejected Sanskrit, the language of elite Brahmins and communicated with people in simple Hindi and reflected the building of bridges between the two communities. In one of his *Sabda* he goes on to say that just as ornaments are different manifestations of same basic product, gold, so Allah, Ram, Rahim, and Hari were all different names of the same god. *Puja* offered by Hindus and Namaz offered by Muslims are just different methods of adoration of the same God. Kabir was a harsh critic of institutionalised religions and the religious traditions which divided people. He was a critic of the mullahs and pandits in equal measures, and the social evils which had infested the society in the name of religion like caste system and untouchability: his teachings spread amongst vast followers of major religious trends to have come up in this period.

Tulsidas another poet sage of this time in an autobiographical couplet shows how the religious synthesis was operating at this time:

A slave of Ram is Tulsi,
What ever they say let them say.
On alms I live, the mosque is my refuge,
my give and take with the world is done.
(Tulsidas: from Kavitavali)

One of the biggest Ram bhakts of the time was living in a mosque, from where most of his devotional works for lord Ram emanated. Guru Nanak was for peace in the society, influenced by ideas of Kabir and was a strong proponent of syncretism. He tried to unite Hinduism and Islam by adopting beliefs from both these religions. Borrowing from Islam, it believes in one God and prohibits image worship. From Hinduism it adopted the theory of reincarnation and karma according to which a persons actions determine his fate in future incarnations. It was against the caste system. Sikh's holy-book, *Adi Granth,* draws extensively from Kabir and Sufi saints like Baba Farid. Also one of the Sufi saints Mir Miyan was requested to lay the foundation stone of the Golden temple.

Sufis attracted a large following among the lower classes and castes. It was their unorthodox and simple lifestyle which attracted large number of low castes to convert to Islam. Their majors (holy places) were open to all irrespective of their religious following. Sufis were basically upholding the spiritual side of Islam, and it can be said that it was a revolt against the rigidities of Islam, propagated mainly by the Ulema. One of the great Sufi saints Muhiuddin Ibn Arabi founded the doctrine of Wahahdat-al-wujud i.e. Unity of being, which promoted spiritual universalism, in turn demolishing the barriers of caste and creed. The Sufi doctrine states that the real being is One and we are all its manifestations, this brought in harmony amongst followers of different religions.

It is interesting to note that Sufi saints' writings were very close to the people. Baba Farid wrote poetry in Punjabi and his writings are a part of *Granth Sahib,* the holy book of the Sikhs. Baba Farids' most distinguished follower was Nizamuddin Auliya, who proudly used to say that there were as many ways of worshipping God as there are particles of sand. He was very fond of listening to bhajans, being touched equally by bhajans and quavallis. His respect for local traditions was tremendous. One small story will illustrate as to how he was away from Islamic orthodoxy and had great respect for local traditions.

"One day he was passing through the bank of Jamuna in Delhi, along with his disciple, the famous poet Khusrau, and saw some Hindu women bathing in the Jamuna and offering prayers to the sun. To this Hazrat Nizamuddin said, "O Khusrau, these women are also praying to Allah; they have their own way of prayer"; and then he recited a verse from Quran: "And every one has a direction to which one turns, so vie with one another in good works" (from A.A Engineer, Sufism and Interfaith Harmony: Institute of Islamic Studies, March 4, 95)

Asghar Ali Engineer points out "Ulema often denounced all those who followed religions other than Islam as kafirs, whereas

Sufis respected similar spiritual practices in all other religions and showed utmost respect for them." (A.A Engineer, above paper). Similarly Mazhar Jan-I-Janan was a Sufi theologian of repute who was again a great upholder of respect for others traditions. Dara Shikoh, the heir of Jahangirs throne, who was murdered by his own brother for the sake of power was a great Sanskrit scholar who had studied the Hindu scriptures at depth and had written a book called as Majmaul Baharayn (The meeting of the two great oceans, Hinduism and Islam). In this book he compared the Islamic and Sufi Phraseology and that of Hinduism and shows that there is much in common between the two.

The interaction of the practice of these two religions has been very well summarised by well known scholar Dr. B.N. Pandey, "Islam and Hinduism which appeared at the start so antithetical, at last intermingled, each one stirred the profoundest depth of the other and from their synthesis grew the religion of Bhakti and Tasawwaf, the religion of love and devotion, which swept the hearts of millions following different religions and sects in India. The current of Islamic Sufism and Hindu Bhakti combined into a mighty stream which fertilised old desolate tracts and changed the face of the country. It was this spirit of India which achieved apparently an impossible task of reconciling the puritanical severity and awe inspiring transcendence of Islam into luxuriant fullness and abundance of form and the intuitive perception of there immanent unity with Hinduism, and created those monuments of art, literature, painting, music and poetry and love, inspired religion which are the heritage of Indian History' during the middle ages.".

Culture

Due to interaction of the Muslim kings, Islam and local culture there developed a whole stream of synthetic culture in all walks of life, in music, *khayal*, *ghazal* and *thumri* are outstanding contributions of these interactions. North Indian classical music as known today, is a thorough blend of Hindu and Muslim elements achieved over 500 years. Ibrahim second Adishahi of Bijapur (1580-1626) had 300 Hindu singers in his court. To popularise this music among Muslims he himself composed *Kitab-e-Naurang* in Urdu (a book containing 59 poems) and of those the first one is an invocation of goddess Saraswati). Chaitanya Maha prabhu and most of the Vaishnav saint poets influenced many Muslims to write in their idiom. Rahim and Raskhan are among the very popular Hindi poets who have written in Brij-bhasha in praise of lord Krishna. Syed Wazid Shah wrote Hir and Ranjha the greatest classic of medieval times. Sheikh Mohammed has greatly contributed to Marathi literature and Shivajis guru (saint teacher) Ramdas had special words of praise for him.

Mixture of Persian dialect with Western Hindi spoken in and around Delhi produced a new language which later on came to be called as Urdu. There were great Hindu scholars who took to Urdu not only as administrative language but also wrote and contributed to Urdu literature. Hindu architecture was masked by profusion of intricate sculptured detail, while Islamic architecture was notable for elegance and lightness. The fusion of the two got manifested in different architectural marvels which came up during this phase. This fusion is seen in Jodhabais palace in Agra fort, in Fatehpur Sikri, and in arches of Kuwat-ul-Islam mosque. The influence of this mixture is discernible far and wide in the havelis of Rajasthan and Madhya Pradesh and the Indo-Saracenic architecture of Jodhpur, Bikaner and Jaisalmer. Similarly fusion of Persian techniques and brilliant Hindu colors resulted in the type of miniature painting marked by beauty and lyricism.

One of the most valuable relics of the harmony of mediaeval society which has survived the onslaughts of different communal forces is Sufi dargah (shrine). These dargahs are scattered in many a cities, managed by Hindu or Muslim families and visited by people of all religions, unmindful of the communal venom being poured by practitioners of communal politics. Right near Mumbai, Haji Malang shrine is a very good expression of syncretic ethos of medieval times. The hereditary trustee of the shrine is the Kailashnath Gopal Ketkar (a Brahmin). The offerings given at the shrine are a mixture of Hindu and Muslim traditions. Devotees offer chaddars, coconuts, flower and sheets of flower. To add on to this the Christian churches also became a place of pilgrimage for people of all religions like Mount Mary Church in Mumbai, amongst many others.

Such examples are numerous and scattered all over. Today there is a conscious attempt to downplay such a valuable tradition and to harp upon the differences of the elite and the rulers. There is a need to observe the richness of these syncretic traditions which are a rich tribute to our communities love, respect and tolerance for each other.

3

Communal Fascism in India

During last three decades India has witnessed a strange political scene. The language of political interaction has been made to shift away from the struggles and travails of the poor and exploited i.e. those revolving around bread, butter, shelter, housing, health and education (the problems of this world). It has been made to take up the issues supposed to be related to 'faith'. We are witness to newer dangers to society, to democratic and secular values in the form of communalism, communal violence and rise of new social political forces basing themselves on 'Religion' in the political arena. We have been hearing a new word called Hindutva from last two decades or so. Though this Hindutva ideology was rooted in certain social segments from last many decades, its social visibility has been much more in the last decade. On first thought it gives the impression as if it is some sort of religion. As we will see it derives its name from Hindu Religion but it is a political ideology akin to the Islamist political ideology. This political ideology has raised afresh, the questions of nationality, community, identity and host of other issues in the social space. The Hindutva movement presents itself for building a strong nation based on the tenets of `Hindu Dharma', Hindu Rashtra (Hindu Nation). There are many notions attached to this word and we need to understand the meaning of this. But this is a newer set of value system, which has found sympathy amongst a section of population. We need to understand as to which segment of society is behind this political movement.

While pursuing its political agenda, the Hindutva movement has brought to fore a number of precepts, which have found acceptance amongst some sections of society. It has popularized a new version of History, which looks at the past through the parameter of religion alone. Also the major political force, which is the vehicle of Hindutva politics, the RSS has been spreading this version of history from last many decades. Today large section of media does accept this version of History. It in a way has become part of 'social common sense'.

Hindutva movement is being spearheaded by a plethora of organisations, the patriarch of which is Rashtriya Swayam Sevak Sangh (RSS), the real controller of all other organisations. It was founded in 1925. It was founded in the backdrop which needs to be understood in detail. In 1920 with the entry of Mahatma Gandhi into the political arena, the dynamics of the anti-British movement got tremendously galvanised. He brought in to the struggle people of all religions, castes and creed. The Brahminical domination in the Congress started declining. At this time the upper castes, and the Brahmins, supported by *Jamindari* elements and *bania's*, in order to reassert their hegemony on the social political and social scene came up with the idea of a Religion based National organisation, the RSS.

'Slightly prior to this Savarkar put forward the idea of 'Hindutva as the basis for politics, which stood for Nationalism based on Hinduism.' (Puniyani, 2000, 51) At that time the Non-Brahman movement was peaking itself and was threatening to shake the very social power of Jamindar-Brahmin nexus. At international level the race based Nationalism of Nazis (Germany) and Fascists (Italy) was on the ascendance. This was the main inspiration for the ideas 'Nationalism' of RSS. "German National pride has now become the topic of the day. To keep up the purity of the nation and its culture, Germany shocked the world by her purging the country of the Semitic races-the Jews. National pride at its highest has been manifested here. Germany has also shown to the world how well nigh impossible it is for races and cultures having differences going to the roots to be assimilated into one united whole, a good lesson for us in India to learn and profit by." (Golwalkar,1938, 27)

Marzia Casolari, an Italian researcher who has done work on roots of Hindu Nationalism concludes that

"(a) the main historical organisations and leaders of Hindu Nationalism had a distinctive and sustained interest in fascism and nazism;

(b) fascist ideological influences on Hindu Nationalism were present and relevant;

(c) to a certain extent, these influences were channeled through direct contacts between Hindu nationalists and members of the Italian fascist state."

(Casolari, 2000, 37)

RSS decided to keep aloof from day to day to day political struggles and began to train the young boys into the doctrine of Hindu Rashtra. As per this core ideology of RSS "Hindus and Hindus alone, constitute the Indian Nation, since they are the original inhabitants and sole creators of its society and culture. Hinduism is uniquely catholic and tolerant and hence superior to other faiths, ...The subsequent entry and takeover by foreigners created an illusion that India was a land of many different and equal cultures....Only a 'truly secular' Hindu Rashtra will afford protection to non- Hindus."(Basu, 1993, 37)

Bharatiya Janata Party (BJP) is its political wing, Vishwa Hindu Parishad (VHP), is the organisation translating Hindutva political agenda on the emotive, religious ground, Bajrang Dal is a group of youth, who are active on the streets. Vanavasi Kalyan Ashram is engaged in promoting 'Hindu norms' amongst Adivasis, and Rashtra Sevika Samiti is its women's wing. In addition there are other organisations like Saraswati Shishu Mandirs, which inculcate the young minds with its social, cultural and political understanding. These all are collectively called as Sangh Parivar (SP).

The initial concern of Hindutva movement (RSS and Hindu Mahasabha) was to counter the politics of Muslim League and to influence the Congress in pro-Hindu direction. RSS was mainly focusing on Shakhas, training volunteers for Hindutva movement and Hindu Mahasabha was taking part in electoral politics. After independence the number of cadres of RSS increased, Hindu Mahasabha gradually went into oblivion. One of the ex-pracharak of RSS, Nathuram Godse, murdered Mahatma Gandhi in 1948, following which RSS was banned for some time. Meanwhile RSS volunteers kept on infiltrating in army, bureaucracy, media and educational institutions. The number of RSS volunteers went on increasing and multiple RSS controlled organisations started coming up.

RSS undertook mainly the campaigns of ban-cow slaughter in earlier period (1960s) but the response was lukewarm. It became very visible with its anti-communist noises during India- China war and projected 'Nationalist, Patriotic' fervor. Its political wing Jan Sangh undertook the campaign 'Indianise Muslims' (late 1960s). Meanwhile the ideology spread by RSS and the increasing urbanisation process were the key factor in the increasing intensity of communal violence.

RSS gained higher respectability JP movement (1974), its political wing joined Janata Party, and came to power, got vital ministries (External affairs, Information and broadcasting etc.) and used the opportunity to further enter the bureaucracy. It left the Janata Party on the issue of duel membership, there was a demand from other components of Janata Party that former members of Jan Sangh leave the RSS. And so either they should leave RSS or the Janata Party. (It did not want to leave the RSS), Janata Party broke and Jan Sangh re-merged as BJP on the plank of 'Gandhian Socialism'.

The period of early 80s saw a great turmoil in the society. Initially the event of conversion of some Dalits to Islam was given a great projection as the threat of Islam engulfing India. In 84 the operation Blue Star (Indian army entering Golden temple to evacuate the temple from the occupation of Khalistani militants, was followed by the assassination of Indira Gandhi by her body guards. This was followed by massive anti-Sikh pogrom in which many a Congress workers lead the assaulting mobs. During this pogrom the RSS ideologue wrote a document subtly supporting Rajiv Gandhi's turning blind eye to the ongoing anti-Sikh pogroms (Nanaji Deshmukh, 1984). Later to appease the Muslim fundamentalists Rajiv Gandhi got a bill passed in the Lok Sabha to reverse the Shah Bano verdict granting maintenance to her by the Supreme court. In the same superficial and opportunist style he went on to get the locks of Babri masjid opened. Both the fundamentalist streams, Hindu and Muslim were on the ascendant. The opening of the locks emboldened the Hindu Fundamentalists and now the sections of Muslim leadership started feeling insecure on the Babri masjid issue. Opening of the locks of Babri Masjid gave a fillip to the SP and BJP decided to take up the Ram Janmbhumi issue.

In 1990 due to his own compulsions vis-à-vis the politics of Devi Lal, V.P. Singh cleaned the dust of Mandal Commission report and decided to implement it. This implementation of Mandal Commission recommendations intensified the backlash of upper castes, who rallied around SP (Sangh Parivar) in a big way and the Rath Yatra got a tremendous response from these sections of society. With the Kar Seva of Dec. 6, the SP's political wing became politically more powerful getting more seats in the Lok Sabha and also coming to power in various state assemblies.

The presence of religion in social and political space was not significant in first few decades of India's independence. The political formation of religion in politics is RSS which "was conceived primarily as the egalitarian vanguard of the 'Hindu Rashtra'(Hindu Nation), its leaders' conception of ideal society continued to be based on the varna (caste) system. (Jaffrelot, 1998, 23). RSS remained a fairly insignificant formation till quite late. Through its 'quiet' work it did keep on training young boys into the Hindutva doctrine. Hindutva doctrine is the crystalised ideology of Hindu Communal politics. Historically development of concept of Hindutva...comes in succession on the construction of Brahminism as Hinduism and this Brahminical Hinduism then forming the base for Hindutva politics. Savarkar began to articulate the ideology of Hindu elite (Zamindars and Brahmins, kings) by integrating Brahminical Hinduism with nationalism, calling it Hindutva which further showed the way to building the Hindu Rashtra. His key sentence was 'Hinduise all politics and militarise all Hindudom' (Ram, 1998). This ideology asserts that India is a Hindu Nation and here Christians and Muslims are aliens. There is no place of 'Western' concepts like secularism and democracy in Hindu nation as Hinduism itself is the most 'secular' and tolerant religion. This ideology aims to bring in Hindu Rashtra in India and so far it has been consolidated on the hatred of Muslims, Christians and 'Western concepts'.

It did go in to create a number of 'children' organisations, meant to bring in the Hindu Rashtra by working in different fields of society. Before independence this ideology was the rival to Muslim communal ideology. After 50s it kept communalising the social space, receiving due provocation's from either the remnant Muslim communalism here or from the assertive postures of Pakistan on Kashmir issue, from across the border. The communalisation of society resulted in the communal riots, which began in a big way from 1960's and these riots went on assuming more menacing proportions over a period of time. The most ghastly of which were to be seen in the decades of 80s, post Babri demolition riots being amongst the worst as for as their impact on the psyche of minorities is concerned. Talking in the same breath one has to take note of the 'new' enemy of this ideology. From 1996 this ideology's followers have been paying 'special' attention to another minority about which they were 'just theorising' so far, the Christians.

The 'real' strength of this ideology started picking up in the social and political arena after the development model pursued so far resulted in the rise of vast sections of middle classes. The lopsided development on the one hand resulted in the rise of rich farmers and on the other, of vast mass of landlesss peasantry totally bereft of any support system. In cities it got compounded by the rising unemployment and under-employment due to rise of small-scale industries, which act as suppliers and subcontractors to the main industries. These type of industries result in the proliferation of small but prosperous industrialists on one hand and that of the workers whose living conditions are abysmal and wages are very close to the poverty line, on the other. It also results in the rise of affluent professional groups. These middle sections have the peculiar type of existential anxieties; they are the one who have been the strongest supporters of the communal ideology. This is the sector, which has shown strong presence in the social space since the 80s.

Hindutva : What is it?

Hinduism is a collation of multiple religious traditions developed in Indian sub continent. While the religious streams were diverse in themselves, the culture of people was equally diverse. Religion is only one of the markers of culture of the people while there are so many other components of culture which are similar amongst people of different religions in the same region. We can not equate relgion with culture. This is so very well exemplified in the cultural similarities between Hindus and

Muslims for example, in Kerala. Also the culture of a Kerala Muslim and a Bangladesh Muslim is so very different.

Hindutva as a term came in usage mainly from the second decade of 20th century. There is some vague mention of this term in 19th century as well, but it did not have a broad usage. This term began in the backdrop of consolidation of Brahminism into Hinduism. Savarkar was the one to initially formulate the politics of Hindutva, "the Aryans who settled in India at the dawn of history already formed a nation, now embodied in the Hindus ...Hindus are bound together not only by the tie of the love they bear to a common fatherland and by the common blood that courses through their veins and keeps our hearts throbbing and our affection warm but also by the tie of the common homage we pay to our great civilisation, our Hindu culture" (Savarkar; 1923, 94). Thus "Hindutva according to him rests on three pillars: geographical unity, racial features and common culture." (Jaffrelot, 1993, 26). He further went on to elaborate the criterion for who is a Hindu? According to him all those who regard this land as their fatherland and holy land are the only ones who are Hindus and thereby the people to whom this land belongs. This led to the automatic interpretations that the Christians and the Muslims, whose holy places are in Jerusalem and Mecca are not on par with the 'Hindus' who own this country. Initiating the theorising of the 'doubting of patriotism of Muslims', Savarkar posits, "but besides culture the tie of common holy land has at times proved stronger than the chains of a motherland. Look at Mohammedans: Mecca to them is a sterner reality than Delhi or Agra" (Savarkar 1923, 108). This development of the concept of Hindutva comes in succession to the construction of Brahminism as Hinduism and this Brahminical Hinduism then forming the base for Hindutva politics. Savarkar began to articulate the ideology of Hindu elite (zamindars, Brahmins, kings) by integrating Brahminical Hinduism with nationalism, calling it Hindutva, which further showed the way for building the Hindu Rashtra.

These concepts were further refined and given the parallel projection by M. S. Golwalkar the second supremo (*Sarsanghchalak*) of RSS, an organisation formed in 1925, ostensibly aimed to train young boys in 'Hindu Culture'. Its ideology was based on Brahminical Hinduism; Hindutva and it aspired for the formation of Hindu Rashtra. This body which began as exclusively upper caste Hindu male organisation (and continues to be so despite some sprinkling of low castes and a rare show piece in the form of a Muslim or a Christian) concentrated in indoctrinating adolescent boys in the 'hate other' (Muslim) ideology and began slowly consolidating in different parts of cow belt to begin with. Golwalkar drawing heavily from Nazi ideology went on to elaborate the ideas on Nation, Hindu Rashtra, in his books '*We or our Nationhood defined*' and '*Bunch of Thoughts*'. He was forthright in his criticism of Nationalism of Congress, and its 'amazing' theory that the nation is composed of all those who for one reason or the other happen to live at the time in a country. For Golwalkar racial factor in nationhood is crucial and he goes on to propound, "To keep up the purity of Race and its culture, Germany shocked the world by her purging the country of Semitic races, the Jews. Race pride at its highest has been manifested here. Germany has also shown how well nigh impossible it is for races and cultures having differences going to the root, to be assimilated into one united whole, a good lesson for us in Hindustan to learn and profit by." (Golwalkar, 1938, 27). He is very candid in showing the other races and those belonging to 'foreign' religions their place, "The foreign races in Hindustan must either adopt the Hindu culture and language, must learn to respect and hold in reverence Hindu religion, must entertain no ideas but those of glorification of the Hindu race and culture or may stay in the country wholly subordinated to the Hindu nation claiming nothing, deserving no privileges, far less any preferential treatment not even citizens rights." (Golwalkar, 1938, 52)

Thus Hindutva is a political and not religious category. Hindutva is a brew of (Brahminical) Hinduism with Nationalism i.e. politics of Hindu Religious Nationalism i.e. Political movement for Hindu Rashtra.

Hindutva and Culture

The politics of Hindutva asserts that the Hindu nation has existed for 8,000 to 10,000 years and Hindustan has been in possession of Hindus for at least that length of time. Also, that in India for its proper running the majority community, the Hindus, should have a dominant role. Both these assertions are at the root of Hindutva movement and both of these contradict the Indian ethos and culture. Despite various theories about the origin of Aryans one can roughly say that their original abode was somewhere in the northwest, from where they migrated to different areas and on way they went on interacting with different cultures in Iran, Afghanistan and Indian subcontinent. The flowering of social life was a product of interaction of the Aryans and the native tribes. Though this also resulted in the caste system and other social evils, the interaction mainly resulted in growth of interactive culture.

As a reaction against many social evils, Buddhism came up as a religion, which had wide popularity amongst the untouchables and some other sections of society. This development came as a corrective to the uninhibited growth of social evils, and went a long way to enrich Indian culture. This culture was further enriched by arrival and spread of Islam (through Arab merchants in South and Mughal rulers in north) and Christianity (through traders again, through Malabar coast and through missionaries coming during the British rule). Thus, India had been a vast social field developing, progressing and marching forward with the interaction of multiple cultural streams. During the rule of Mughals the syncretic culture reached its heights with development of Bhakti and Sufi sects. Both these were very popular amongst the people for the simplicity of their appeals, and unity of their message. People like Kabir, Nanak and Tukaram contributed their soul to the richness of the life of society. All this is a part of Indian ethos, which in nutshell can be ascribed to different facets of Indian syncretic culture, which stands on the principles of love for all fellow beings, respect for others faith, tolerance for others' religion and equal treatment to followers of different paths.

In contrast, Hindutva politics is based on upper caste ethos, and aims at the hegemony of one section of society, one type of religion over the whole society. It theorizes the subjugation of minorities to the upper caste ethos. It does away with the affirmative action needed for the protection and furtherance of the interests of disadvantaged sections of society. Hindutva contradicts the Indian ethos and syncretic culture and is a total break from the 'spirit' of Indianness.

Table 1.1 : Comparing the concepts of Hinduism and Hindutva

Hinduism	*Hindutva*
(1) A collation of multiple traditions Brahminism- Shramanism-Tantra, Kabir, Tukaram, Nanak	(1) Politics of Hindu elite, drawing from Brahminical Hinduism.
(2) Brahminism is based on ethos of Caste system	(2) Brew of Brahminical Hinduism and Nationalism
(3) Brahminism was projected as the Hinduism initially in 6-10 century, Then in early 19th century, Brahminical Hinduism was projected to be synonymous with Hinduism.	(3) Aims at Hindu Rashtra based on Brahminical Hinduism
(4) Shramanic traditions: there were constant rebellion: attempt to escape the clutches of Brahminism: Conversion to Buddhism (early times and now after the lead given by Ambedkar).	(4) Led initially by Brahmins: Banias: even now dominant leadership is from upper castes.
(5) 'Dharma' is caste based religious duties.	(5) Political expression through Sangh Parivar now, earlier Hindu Mahasabha and RSS.
(6) Semitisation process being spearheaded by SP— Holy deity: Ram, Holybook: Gita, clergy: Shankaracharyas etc.	(6) A mix of fundamentalism and Fascism (see later table)
(7) Its proponents claim it to be tolerant and catholic. cf: earlier it's attitude to shudras cf: Now it's attitude to Muslims	(7) VHP bring in the stink of fundamentalism in the essentially fascist politics of RSS, BJP and Bajrangdal.

Hinduism and Hindutva are not the same. As we have seen above Hinduism is a religion which has multiple streams the most dominant of which is the Brahminical one. While Hindutva includes not only religion, race, language and geographical territory. In practice it was the politics of feudal elements in pre-independence times and now it represents the political agenda of upper caste/upper class elite.

Table 1.2 : Similarities and differences between Hindutva and Fascism

	Hindutva	*Fascism*
Similarities:		
(1)	It got strengthened in post-Mandal period: after fearing the assertion of lower castes.	Came up and became strong in the wake of powerful workers movement
(2)	Projects 'National' interests over The interests of the people.	Same
(3)	Has the seeds of expansio-nism; Concept of 'Akhand Bharat' (undivided India, including Pakistan, Myanmar, Bangladesh and Sri Lanka)	Expansionist: attacked neighboring countries on the ground that they were part of earlier German empire
(4)	Targeting Muslims as the cause of the ills of the country	Targeted Jews as the cause of ills of the country.
(5)	Glorification of the past.	Same
(6)	Oppressive to workers (produce for nation, don't bother about your Rights), Dalits (oppose Mandal In a subtle way of demand for Meritocracy), women (they should be ideal wives and mothers), minorities (they should subjugate themselves to Hindu culture).	Oppressive to Jews, (subjected them to physical elimination), Communists/ workers (physical violence to reduce their strength), women (their place is in the kitchen, church and they primary role is in rearing children).
(7)	Post Babri demolition resulted in social space full of terror and anti-human rights, 'pro'-national hysteria.	The regime implemented its Pogrom through creation of mass hysteria.
(8)	Urbanised middle class and rich peasants/upper castes and some backward castes: the main support base.	Urban middle class and landed Aristocracy: the main social base.
Differences:		
(1)	Long gestation period: Successful communalization of Social space in 'cowbelt' region; Success in polarisation of upper castes only after implementation of Mandal Commission.	Quick ascendancy to power on the anti Jew plank.
(2)	Medium range social crisis from mid 80's : rising unemployment, increasing poverty.	Severe post World War economic crisis.

Table 1.3: Comparing Hindutva and Fundamentalism

Hindutva	*Fundamentalism*
(1) Targeting against liberal ethos of the society	Same
(2) Imposition of retrograde social values selectively culled out from religious texts.	Same
(3) Swadeshi is the "economic policy"	Anti imperialist noises
(4) Built around (Gita, Vedas), Ram and Acharyas	Based on Semitic religion-Holy book, Holy daily and clergy
(5) Harping on traditional orthodox beliefs	Same
(6) Projection of women as ideal mothers	Women under patriarchal control of father, husband and son
(7) Claim that Vedas are created by Brahma, the God	Claim that 'Our' creed based on divine law: holy book coming from God himself
(8) Golden past of religious rule is shown to be the ideal goal	Same
(9) Demand homogeneity of Hindu culture	Abhor pluralism
10. Political onslaught to impose interests of elite, middle class, upper caste on whole society	Creates hysteria (against Shah of Iran, in Iran, against women in Saudi Arabia)
11. Creates hysteria against internal enemy, the Muslim	Hysteria against Women, Imperialism, neighboring country
12. Great importance to women's dress Code	Same
13. Built around emotive appeal of religion	Same

Hindutva's Goal

Hindu Rashtra is not a religious state; it is a 'modern' phenomenon to impose the pre-modern social hierarchies on all sections of society. It is the goal of a section of society, which is the major beneficiary of current social privileges, the section of society, which have gained in the process of development of last few decades. It was the goal of section of society which was threatened by the social changes in pre-independence times (*Zamindar-Brahmins*) and who were champions of status quo and were allies of British at economic and political level. The Hindu Rashtra which is threatening to engulf the society from last two decades is the battle cry of the sections who again are upholders of a status quo vis-à-vis social position of women, workers, Dalits and Adivasis. It is the offence of the section of society, which has benefited maximum by proliferation of middle classes-small industries, petty business and agriculture of the 'Green Revolution' type and of the professional and bureaucratic cadres. Indian Nationalism as an encompassing concept based itself on secular grounds and attempts to strive for formal liberty, equality and fraternity supplemented by the liberal space to struggle to convert these formal concepts into reality. Indian Nationalism is a positive concept, incorporating different religion's, ethnicity's and culture's and is an integral part of world economy and emerging global village.

The chronicity, i.e. slow speed of this movement has its inherent problems. Whereas, on one hand it can capture the social space, on the other it can also elicit a reaction to itself. This reaction to it from dalits, workers, women, section of middle class that is secular, is a big obstacle to the march of Hindutva. Big capital, the major industrial houses have a unique relation with Sangh Parivar. Whenever faced with crisis to their own existences, the socially terrorising atmosphere created by Sangh Parivar helps the bourgeoisie to wriggle out of the compulsions of liberal ethos. The conservative movement of Sangh Parivar helps the needs of capital to keep thriving in an uninterrupted way. Thus, this chronic, resilient, thriving Fascism, expressed through the vehicle of Sangh Parivar continues to throw up different shades of its existence, sometimes terrorising (to the poor and the minorities) sometimes aggressive (to the neighbouring 'enemy' countries), and sometimes even appearing to collapse under the weight of its own contradictions. But the march, at the moment is on. The social roots of Hindutva are all for the support and continuation of the repressive capitalist regime; sustaining the bourgeoisie aspirations, while continuing to pursue its own project.

Hindutva onslaught draws some support from fundamentalist concepts also. It culls out from the past-selective values to impose them on present. It uses religious imagery, glorifies the 'golden past' of rule of Hindu kings, sees women primarily under patriarchal control dictating their way of life, dress code etc. It co-opts all and sundry religious professionals and personnel to strengthen its political base and it uses religion in a very effective way to create the nationalist hysteria. At present the situation is fairly in balance. The onslaught has achieved mammoth proportions in the north, but south and east are comparatively unaffected by its paranoid aggression. The reaction of Dalits, though fragmented is definitely going to retard the march of the *rath* (Chariot) of Hindutva.

The apparent target of Sangh Parivar, the Muslims are in a bind. On one hand, they have been battered so much by Hindutva that they cannot afford to lie quiet any more. Secondly unlike the Dalits they lie in sub-critical zone of backwardness where they find it difficult to come out of the grip of their own 'religious leaders', 'the Muslim obscurantists' posing to be speaking on behalf of their community. Thus, they face a double attack from both Hindu Fascism and Muslim fundamentalism. Probably the suffering of the 'poor Muslims' is so great that they will be forced to come out and resist the 'bears hug' of Sangh Parivar and by side-tracking their 'obscurantist leaders' will pose definite obstacle to the march of 'Trishuls of Hindutva'. How Sangh Parivar overcomes this 'problem' and which new 'velvet gloves' it discovers to remove this obstacle remains to be seen. The response of Christian community though mixed to a great extent has been that of responding in a strong secular manner, to defend the Human rights of different sections in general and to defend the secular rights of minorities in particular. This is an ongoing phenomenon set into motion due to the attacks on Christians by different wings of SP directed by the ideological formulation of the RSS.

References

Chritopher Jaffrelot, *The Hindu Nationalist Movement and Indian Politics, Viking* 1993.

Marzia Casolari, 'Hindutva's Foreign Tie Ups in 1930s: The Archival Evidence, *Communalism Combat*, March 2000, p. 37.

M.S. Golwalkar, '*We or Our Nationhood defined*', Bharat Publications 1939.

Nanaji Deshmukh, 'Moments of Soul Searching', *Pritipaksh*, Delhi, Nov. 25, 1984.

Ram Puniyani, *Fascism of Sangh Parivar*, Media House, Delhi, 2000.

Romila Thapar, '*History of India*' Vol. I, Penguin, Delhi, pp. 39-40.

T. Basu, P. Data, S. Sarkar, T. Sarkar and S. Sen, '*Khaki Shorts Saffron Flags*, Orient Longman, Hydrabad', 1993

Vinayak Damodar Savarkar, '*Hindutva, Who is a Hindu?*', Nagpur, 1923.

4

Minorities and Human Rights

As such in a democray no body should need a minority identity. But as the democracies have evoloved from complex backgrounds there has been prevalence a certain sections of citizenary, which belongs to this category on the grounds of religion and culture. In order that they feel free and non-intimidated, various provisions have been set by the United Nations conventions to take care of their special needs and feelings. A society can be judged by how free the minorities of that country feel. The religion-based nationalism has the primary agenda of suppressing the inner groups, caste and gender, and they project the external group, minority, as the real culprit for the ills of the country. In a way the minorities are collateral victims of the onslaught of the Religion based nationalism. This type of nationalism relegates the rights of minorities to secondary position and through browbeating them tries to seek their submission and ghettoisation through violence.

The majoritarian politics achieves this by spreading myths and stereotypes against them. These form the base on which communal violence rides, this in turn creates the feeling of insecurity and other consequences follow the major of which is emotional alienation.

In India, Hindutva politics has identified Muslims, Christians and Communists as the 'Internal threats' to the Hindu nation. It is no coincidence that Muslims were the first targets, Christians are coming under the chopping block from last one decade and communists, are a constant threat to Hindutva and so they have been in various ways all through. One does not know what lies in store for them in the future.

All minorities do not have a similar social and national situation. The Muslims are a discriminated against lot, and

Christians are currently being hauled to the coals for the 'sin' of conversions. It is the sign of times that during the ascendance of Hindutva party BJP some Governments came up with anti conversion laws. Tamil Nadu's Jayalalita is an interesting example; she came up with anti conversion legislation during BJP regime and scrapped the same once BJP lost power at the center. Currently some other states, where BJP is ruling, anti-conversion legislations are being contemplated. Gujarat, which is called the Laboratory of Hindu Rashtra and currently is the example of 'Hindu Rashtra in One-State' came up with the census monitoring of minorities for the purposes, which are anti democratic. It also came up with norms for monitoring inter-religious marriages.

The Political and Social backdrop of the Minority Problem

India inherited the problem of minorities right since Independence. The whole partition process was seeped in the majority-minority discourse. The process of partition was the outcome of the interaction of the three major forces: Muslim Communal politics, Hindu Communal politics and British policy of divide-and-rule, while the process of Pakistan formation had the patronage of the Jagirdari and salaried class of Muslims. The discrimination against the Muslims in jobs was prevalent right from the beginning and the anti-Muslim riots became a regular phenomenon. The culmination of these resulted in the demolition of Babri Masjid and after sometime the focus of majoritiarian communal forces shifted to persecution of another minority, the Christians. The anti-Christian violence is currently being witnessed in a sustained fashion.

Modern Democracies: Melting pot or Mosaic model

The very concept of democracy is based on Liberty, Equality and Fraternity. The state grants equal status and citizenship rights to all its citizens irrespective of their caste, creed, color, gender or religion. The initial idea in the democracy was that since people interact on different facets of life the societal interaction will act as a melting pot bringing in uniformity in the language, dress code, social values and different other aspects of life. But the experience of most of the democracies has shown that this is only partly true and the mosaic of different shades persists for long time. This pluralism is healthy as it encourages the values of tolerance. Accordingly most of the good constitutions have endeavored to incorporate this in their statuettes.

Despite these provisions, the reality of the situation has not been very satisfactory. "An ideal pluralist society demands that all citizens irrespective of their caste, creed, class, ethnicity and sex shall enjoy not only equal rights, but also security of life, property and avenues to promote their religion, language and culture while enjoying the fruits of economic development in an equitable manner. The Constitution of India does guarantee all this but there are serious and complex problems as far as their implementation is concerned." One of the main reasons for eruption of resistance to the pluralism is from the vested interests who fear that the democratic processes will change the status quo, which will go against their interests. This brings into the open the conflict of interests of different social groups disguised as communal, ethnic or language conflict. And if one of the communities is too dominant it is likely that it can trample on the rights of others.

How to define Minorities

Generally minorities are defined by numerical weakness or socio-economic vulnerability. But this term requires lot of qualifications. Also modern state has to deal with individual rights and group rights and with internal democratization in social communities. Another catch is that the reform process in the communities is to be expedited without hurting the sentiments of the people of the community. This is one of the goals of the state, which has to be executed in a very balanced way.

The problem of Minority-Majority crops up due to the vested interests in the course of which the elite of numerically dominant community assert and try to usurp the social privileges for themselves. "Generally it is used to denote those non-Hindu minorities whose members are for one reason or another inclined to assert their distinctiveness in relating to Hindu community. Members of the Scheduled Castes and Tribes whose members are in many ways more severely disadvantaged, are hardly ever characterized as minorities. On the whole therefore the word 'minorities' seems to have been narrowly defined and denotes religious communities whose members project themselves as being different from majority community." Apart from the popular notion of minorities the minorities can also be on the basis of language, ethnicity and race.

Formation of Minorities

Minorities have been formed in the history due to multiple reasons. As the world is interacting more and more through transmigrations it results in different communities locating themselves in far and distant countries. Large number of Indian communities have emerged as minorities in America, South Africa, Britain, Canada and many other countries as these communities emigrated in search of work and business. Migration of labour force in plantation and other types of work has been one of the most important factors in the initial part of 20th century. Spread of religion has been another major cause, because of which Muslims, Christians and Buddhists are minorities in different places.

It is worth recalling that all minorities are not disadvantaged. Jews in Germany, Parsis, Jains and Christians are a good example of this. Amongst these Jews were targeted in Germany and Christians are being targeted in India in pursuance of the political agenda of the fascist-fundamentalist forces. In India, Nepali's have a very different status, while Sikhs are also not regarded as minorities per se!

In this presentation for the sake of brevity we will be focusing only on Muslims and Christians as the minorities.

State and Minorities

The democratic constitution of ours gives equal rights to all the citizens irrespective of their caste, creed or religion. Since minorities are disadvantaged in these societies they are provided with affirmative actions to strive towards substantive equality. State is committed to protect their social and political rights. Despite the provision for protection of Minorities, the state apparatus is heavily infiltrated by the communal elements who ensure the protection of the violators of the human rights of minorities.

Indian Constitution and Minorities: Indian Constitution's being secular gives right to freedom of conscience and religion and it is also duty bound to preserve the composite culture of the country. Article 15 ensures that there is no discrimination on the grounds of religion. Article 29(1) gives the right to preserve language, script and culture. Article 30 (1) gives the right to establish and run educational and other institutions, while Article 30 (2) ensures that there should be no discrimination against minority institutions. Also Article 25 gives the Freedom of conscience, free profession, propagation and practice of one's religion.

Rights of Minorities under the Constitution of India. Article 29(1): "Any section of the citizens residing in the territory of India or any part thereof having a distinct language, script or culture of its own, shall have the right to conserve the same." Article 29(1): "No citizen shall be denied admission into any educational institution maintained by the State or receiving aid out of the State funds on grounds only of religion, race, caste, language or any of them."

Article 30(1): "All minorities whether based on religion or language, shall have the right to establish and administer educational institutions of their choice."

Article 30(1A): "In making any law providing for the compulsory acquisition of any property of an educational institution established and administered by a minority, referred to in clause (1), the State shall ensure that the amount fixed by or determined under such law for the acquisition of such property is such, as would not restrict or abrogate the right guaranteed under the clause."

Article 30(2): "The State shall not, in granting aid to educational institutions, discriminate against any education institution on the ground that it is under the management of minority, whether based on religion or language."

U.N. Declaration of Human Rights of Minorities

This declaration is based on Democratic, Humanist model. Thereby it prescribes multiethnic states with equal rights to all. It prescribes all the member states to protect the existence and identity of minorities. The member states are obliged to create conditions for promotion of their identity. India is a signatory to this declaration.

The U.N. Declaration of Minority Rights (3):

ARTICLE 1

1. States shall protect the existence and the national or ethnic, cultural, religious and linguistic identity of minorities within there respective territorial, and shall encourage conditions for the promotion of that identity.
2. States shall adopt appropriate legislative and other measures to achieve that ends.

ARTICLE 2

1. Persons belonging to national or ethnic, religious and linguistic minorities (hereinafter referred persons as belonging to minorities) have the right to enjoy their own cultures, to profess and practice their own religion, and to use their own language, in private and in public freely and without interference or any form of discrimination.
2. Persons belonging to minorities have right to participate effectively in culture, religious, social, economic and public life.
3. Persons belonging to minorities have right to participate effectively in decision on the national and, where appropriate, regional level concerning the minority to which they belong or the regions in which they live, in a manner not incompatible with national legislation.
4. Persons belonging to minorities have right to establish and maintain their own associations.

Persons belonging to minorities have right to establish and maintain, without any discrimination, free and peaceful contacts with other members of their group and with persons belonging to other minorities, as well as contacts across frontiers with other citizens of other States to whom they are related by national or ethnic, religious or linguistic ties.

Problems of Muslims in India

Muslim community has been the victim of different biases

and prejudices because of which they have been kept out of the Govt. and private sector jobs. Their representation in these has been very low. Also the 'social common sense' has been against them and regular and repeated violence against them has taken a heavy toll of their psyche. After partition the elite of Muslim community left India for Pakistan, and mainly poor Muslims and only few professionals and traders were left behind further worsening the status of Muslims. Muslim fundamentalist leadership came to the fore, unconcerned about the 'real' material problems of community, and today the community remains poor, backward and in the grip of orthodox elements.

It is propagated for political goals that successive governments have pampered and appeased the community. The facts are in total contrast to this. Their status in employment and other parameters are a good index of their social status and appeasement.

The discrimination against minorities is glaringly obvious and different committees have confirmed this time and over again (Gopal Singh, Sachar, Ranganath Mishra). This has occurred due to the biases against them. The popular myth that Muslim Kings destroyed Hindu Temples (truth is that both Hindu and Muslim kings destroyed temples and mosques sometimes in pursuit of gold and sometimes for other political motives). Islam spread on the point of sword mainly under the influence of Sufi saints, who were away from the seats of power, and primarily Sudra's embraced Islam to escape the tyranny of Brahminism). Muslims are polygamous (as per the census figures the percentage of polygamy amongst Muslims and Hindus is more or less same), they produce more number of children and that shortly Muslim population will overtake the Hindu population has been the major propagation of the communal politics (the Muslim population has shown a minor increase during last nearly fifty years; 1947-11.4, 2001-12.6). These myths have been the foundation on which the anti-Muslim violence stands.

Minorities in India Today

The onslaught of communal politics is intimidating the minorities while the state is extremely insensitive towards their protection. As we have seen above the ghettoisation of Muslim community is very strong. Also the present intimidation of Christian community has reached intolerable limits. The provisions for their protection are on paper but the ground reality is something else. The rise in social power of SP has been the bane for the Human rights of weaker sections of society, in general and those of minorities in particular. The State being infiltrated by communal elements has been unable to protect the minorities and has been fairly insensitive to their plight. It is only through the struggles for their rights and alignment with the struggles of other weaker sections of society that they can try to preserve their democratic and Human rights.

References

Asghar Ali Engineer, "Some thoughts on pluralist model of Nation Building", Minorities in India, Conference papers, Rajiv Gandhi Institute For Contemporary Studies (RGISS), 1996, p. 27.

Imtiaz Ahmad, 'Indian Minorities', Minorities in India, RGISS, 1996, p. 27.

Iqbal A. Ansari, Readings on Minorities: Perspectives and Documents, Institute of Objective Studies , New Delhi 1996.

Vinayak Damodar Savarkar, 'Hindutva, Who is a Hindu?', Nagpur, 1923.

M.S. Golwalkar, 'We or Our Nationhood defined', Bharat Publications 1939.

Chritopher Jaffrelot, *The Hindu Nationalist Movement and Indian Politics,* Viking, 1996.

5

Defining Minorities

Allahabad High Court ruling (April 2007) that Muslims have ceased to be a minority in UP as their percentage in population is 18.5% totally defies the logic of Indian Constitution, the legislatures understanding and the pronouncements of the Supreme court on the issue. No wonder it has been stayed by a two judge bench. This verdict gave a lot of ammunition to many to feel jubilant, and pen pushers of right wing ideology got extra boost to spew their anti minority sentiments. It is argued that by retaining the concept of minority these sections are reminded about their being 'different' and that sows the seed of divisiveness. They even point out that Africans-Americans were/are considered a minority as there was systematic injustice against them, they were discriminated against. But in India there is no such case for Muslims so they should not be considered as minorities, neither should there be any affirmative action for them.

There have been similar sentiments by a large section of ideologues that belong to Right wing politics. It is also noteworthy, that these are precisely same sections who celebrate when the quota for OBC is questioned and reservations against dalits are opposed.

Is there a place for minority concept in democracy, and who should be called a minority? These questions were settled by the Constituent assembly and samples of the debates around these issues indicate the national thinking on that. The attitude of the founders of Indian Constitution, who were themselves echoing the values of freedom movement, indicates a lot on the matter. It was pointed out in Constituent assembly debates that numerical weakness and soci-economic vulnerability should be the major criterion in defining the minority. Even the United Nations charter of Human rights went on to recommend the affirmative action towards minorities of all types. India is a signatory to many a UN declarations on minority rights.

All minorities are not disadvantaged. We can see that Brahmins are also a minority within Hindu religion, but the prevalent caste system gave them inherent advantage. There are people who try to find a 'poor' Brahmin as a ground to show that caste based reservations are not valid. But surely the social connections of Brahmin minority, ensures that poor and deprived Brahmins, is more a matter of exception. In India the minority generally boils down to religious minority. This is more of a legacy of India's policies and politics which were prevalent before Independence, and this, while prevalent all through, has got re-strengthened after the rise of religion based politics from the decade of eighties. This identity politics has rolled back many a conceptual developments which were in progress during the decades immediately after the independence.

The affirmative action for dalits and OBC itself has come under heavy criticism from the same social sectors. Also the thought of development programs for Muslim sends shivers of discomfort amongst many. We have witnessed that a particular ideology which is solidly against this affirmative action for dalits and minorities, was at the root of riots against dalits and OBCs, in Gujarat in the decade of 1980s. This ideology suits those whose children are in the category of 'economic reservation' as they can openly 'buy' education, knowledge and degrees by shelling out the bagfuls of money.

One wonders how the condition of Indian Muslims is different from that of African Americans for whom affirmative action is being accepted and recommended. Have Muslims found a decent, tolerant atmosphere here? Let's recall that 'social common sense' has been against them all through. The policy of subtle discrimination against them was in operation all through. Private sector dominated by the non Muslims kept them out deliberately. As communal violence was unleashed from sixties, it went on rising and went to critical limits from the decades of 80s. Various statistics coming from Home ministry Government of India, compilation of data on riot victims shows that over 80 per cent of riot victims are Muslims. The violence has ghettoized large sections of this community. The progressive norms which were being picked up by the community despite economic odds got a set back after the Babri demolition and massive anti Muslim violence which followed. Later after the Gujarat carnage, this process of ghettoisation got intensified. Today irrespective of whether communalism, communal violence is visible or not, most of the states are witnessing an atmosphere where minorities feel intimidated and stifled.

It is true that minorities should not perpetuate their condition. They should try to come out of minority psyche and feel like anybody else. But what happens if the political climate is very adverse to your progress. What happens when the social thinking demonises you time and over again, in every aspect of social existence, on any or every pretext? The earlier slogan of Jan Sangh, the previous avatar of BJP, had launched campaign called "Indianise Muslims"; giving a clear message that they are not Indians and so they must be Indianised. This is a 'catch twenty-two' situation. On the one hand, minorities are excluded from the process of social development, as they are the 'other' and at the same time a demand is made to them to subordinate to the dictates of dominant political stream which is trying to assert as to what should be the social norms. This exclusionary religious tendency is presenting their religious symbolism as the national symbolism.

Every study and data has been pointing to the worsening position of Muslim community. First the Gopal Singh Committee and now the Sachar Committee has shown this marginalisation and exclusion. How does one become part of so called mainstream when one feels excluded and jeered upon? And if for bringing them on par with others, some efforts are undertaken to protect their interests, to support them breathe freely, is it divisive factor or is it only way to strengthen our society? Some ideologues are used to the image of society in the past 'glories' where the Shudras, in their ghettoes, lived to serve the upper caste masters. Is it that which is being presented as the ideal nation? The tendency which is trying to dominate in the name of religion, essentially wants to bring back that state of society and so they oppose the efforts which will empower the ghettoized masses.

The criticism against Sachar committee is that it is creating myth that Muslims are disempowered, and so this committee report should be ignored and bypassed. What are the parameters for assessing the level of empowerment or otherwise of a social group? Surely the socio-economic and political representation should be the main parameter. One knows that not only that Muslim community has seriously been excluded from the development process, they were also forced into low level self employment, that's why some surveys may find that rate of their employment is better than others. Here the definition of employment has to be kept in mind. As such the type of self employment which a large section of Muslim community had to resort to was the last option and not a preferred choice. It has become the norm because of the exclusionary policies adopted by the sections of society, who have a powerful say in the matters, and in the running of the state. It by no means is a symbol of empowerment of minorities.

One is sure that the two judge bench's superseding the 'Muslims are not a minority judgment' will be upheld by the due process of law. In the overall political scenario and the economic perspective, a radical change has to take place where suitable employment for every person is the norm. The size of cake is also a problem. The type of economic development being pursued has to be superseded by one which aims at giving employment to all, and in the interregnum the affirmative action for different disadvantaged sections has to be pursued to unite the society. The definition of minorities needs to be recalled from the Indian constitution and understood in the context of constituent assembly debates.

6

Majority Report: Who is a Minority?

Indian democracy was the outcome of the freedom movement, which in turn was based on the values of Liberty, Equality and Fraternity (community). During the freedom movement there were marginal streams which did not subscribe to these values and they stood out as Muslim League on one side and Hindu Mahasabha and RSS, on the other. The Indian nation inherited the celebratory ethos of pluralism and diversity. Few sections whose interests stood to be threatened due to democracy and accompanying social and political relations did raise voice about their religion coming under threat. Indian constitution, like most of the progressive modern constitutions provided the concept of affirmative action for weaker sections of society (SCs and STs) and certain other type of provisions for security of minorities (religious, linguistic and ethnic). Later to keep in tune with the concurrent developments and articulations in the concepts of human rights, India did endorse the recommendations of various UN bodies on this issue.

The idea of these was that the religious, ethnic or linguistic groups which are numerically smaller should not feel intimidated, should not feel out of place and should feel free from the fear of being swept aside by the dominance of majority community. Indian constitution while giving the minority status to the religious denominations did recognize most of the religions with smaller following as minorities. The base of this provision was numerical weakness and social disadvantage due to various reasons. Accordingly Muslims, Christians, Buddhists, Parsis and Jews amongst others were logical religious minorities. Some religions, like Jainsim, were initially denied this minority status as the dominant political forces asserted that it is not an independent religion but is a mere sect of Hinduism. The statement by Sudarshan that Sikhism is a sect of Hinduism did create turmoil in large sections of Sikh community.

Whatever be the position of Indian Constitution, RSS, which does not subscribe to the values of Indian Constitution, naturally stands opposed to that. It is in this context that RSS Chief K. Sudarshan, who earlier had asked for doing away with this Constitution and bringing in the one based on Holy Hindu books, has gone on to lay down a new basis of the concept of minorities. As per him, (Indian Express Sept. 30, 2005) Parsis and Jews are the only religions, which are minorities, as these are the only people who have come from 'outside'. By doing this, through a clever maneuver the whole notion and basis of minorities is turned upside down, its purpose is thrown to the wind and 'insider-outsider' duo is used to define and label the minorities.

This is a dangerous terrain. The concept of outsider-insider is problematic on several scores. To begin with what is the cut off date of this label? As per the ideas of founding fathers of our state, all those living here are insiders, the lawful, equal citizens. History has witnessed different communities migrating from one part of the globe to the other and making that its home. In case of India, despite the 'intellectual' jugglery performed by Golawalkar and later Hindutva ideologues the current understanding is that Aryans came here in the series of waves of migration. Tilak began with the theory of Arctic home of Aryans, Golwalkar went to change it to state that Arctic home was right here in Bihar and Orissa region and later this landmass shifted northwards, leaving behind the Aryans as the original inhabitants of India. To substantiate this intellectual feat by modern techniques, one computer scientist, who also duplicates as Hindutva ideologue, N.S. Rajaram, went on to manipulate the seal of bull found in Mohanjodaro. The head of bull was substituted by the head of horse; the animal associated with Aryans, so as to prove that Aryans were the natives of this land and so are the logical owners of this land. All this has been done Golwalkar onwards to prove that Aryan Hindus are the real natives, so the real natives the Adivisis are called as Vanvasis in this scheme of things. Constitution, and in turn the Indian nation has given the minority status not on an insider-outsider basis, nor it has gone into the past to give th deifintion of this. The date of India's birth here is 15th August, and matters regarding as to who is an Indian begin from that date and not from the vague amorphous past, which has been constructed by some for their the sake of their political agenda. If Sudarshan's definition is to be believed, which incidentally has no legitimacy as per the Indian ethos, as the Aryans are the immigrants, then Hindus are the minority, whatever that means.

One should not blame Mr. Sudarshan beyond a point. As he and his RSS do not subscribe to the Indian Constitution and have the goal of Hindu nation, Hindu Rashtra, running in their blood. We need to ensure that such illegitimate ideas have no place in our modern democracy. The whole concept of minority is essentially meant to provide security to numerically vulnerable groups. Again it cannot be taken in the straightjacket manner. Democracy has to give paramount importance to the individual rights. Group rights come in only as a defense in certain situations and also for the reason that minorities are not subjugated by the dominant communal streams. Unfortunately in India due to the prevalence of communal violence, due to bringing to fore the issues related to religion and the identity politics, the threat perception amongst religious minorities has gone up and many of them may be seeking further strengthening of these group identities. Ideally such group identities have to loosen up and become secondary over a period of time, with the Indian national and Human identity taking precedence over the other one's. Dr. Ambedkar tried to overcome this dilemma by suggesting that majorities should create a situation where the minority does not have to seek shelter under the minority tag and minorities should try to overcome that label and avoid taking recourse to being a minority.

The onus seems to be on the state, which ideally should not let the majoritarian discourse sweep away the democratic agenda and norms, while providing the assurances and proper protection to the minorities. In this direction the conduct of Indian state has been abysmal. It has let the dominant tendencies run riot, its components, police, bureaucracy and even at times judiciary have compromised with the norms of democratic conduct as per the law, resulting in the violence against minorities and the consequent strengthening of minority identity to the extent of ghettoisation of minorities at places.

By asserting that only Jews and Parsis are minorities, Mr. Sudarshan, true to his Hindu Nation theory, wants to do away with the safeguards for weaker religious denominations, especially Muslims and Christians, who are the major victims of RSS progeny's *trishuls* and *lathis*. Doing away the provisions for Muslims in particular be exrememly harmful as the community has been thrown back on the scales of human development, be it socio-economic status or education, housing, jobs and what have you, the Muslims are lagging behind. The clauses which can improve their condition are already being opposed tooth and nail by majoritarin tendencies and on the top of that the very clause of minority will be removed if Mr. Sudarshan's Hindu nationalism is to be accepted. Such anti minority designs need to be curbed so that we can have the flowering of democracy in a more egalitarian manner.

SECTION–II

SOCIO-ECONOMIC EXCLUSION

7

Appeasement or Maltreatment: Muslim Demographics, Education and Employment

No community can be seen as uniform, homogenous entity. We have to first understand the criterion of 'appeasement' of a community. What are the parameters for pampering a community? What information will enable us to judge whether a community is discriminated against or pampered? Though these are a fairly complex questions, one can say that level of education, employment and socio-economic status can give us a rough picture of appeasement or otherwise of the community. Also, rather than generalising the demographic common sense, it is necessary to have a look at the statistical figures to arrive at some understanding about this.

Due to historical reasons the current profile of employment and education amongst Muslims is very different than amongst Hindus and Christians. This is not a static picture and things are changing constantly. During the colonial period there was a great divergence in the education and employment status of Muslims in different parts of the country. Two contrasting examples will be able to throw much light on this. In the regions of West Bengal most of the converts came from, sections suffering from poverty and illiteracy. Most of these were artisans from cities and landless peasants from villages. Their representation in the Government was also very poor. This stands in contrast with the Muslims in the UP, where Avadh, the major princely state was ruled by Muslim *nawabs*. Here, though the Muslim population was 15-16% their representation in services was close to 20%. In Bengal, the numbers of Muslims in primary education was very low, while in Avadh it was around 30%. Thus, in the area corresponding to present UP, the representation of Muslim population in education and services was much higher than their ratio in the population.

The causes of backwardness in education and employment seem to be more social than religious.

There are many who assert that "Independence can not be achieved only through the efforts of Hindus, so Gandhi wanted to take Muslims along at any cost. And that is the beginning of Muslim appeasement." ('Sangh and Muslims' p.16, Rashtra Jagran Abhiyan 2000, RSS Pune). They add it up saying that this appeasement of Muslims has continued by the successive Governments in Independent India.

As a matter of fact, status of Muslims in employment and other socio-economic parameters are the real parameter for judging their social condition, and 'appeasement'. Let us see where they stand in these parameters.

In *Government sector* in higher cadres their representation is very small (Class I: 3.19%, Class II 4.30%. In Class IV is just 8.16%, while in private sector this figure is much lower). As per Gopal Singh Committee compilation (Discrimination against Minorities in India, Satya Saran, National Meet on the status of Muslims, 2009) shows that there is a gross under-representation of Muslims in All India Services, there are just 3.04 % representation of Muslim in All India Services, (IAS, IPS, IFS). As per Sachar Committee report in Raliways and across the board Government services they are 4.9%.

In High Courts out of 310 judges as on 1.4.1980, only 14 were Muslims. In All India Services (IAS): In decision-making posts Muslim representation was (1984 figures) 2.14%, in Indian Police Service 3%, Central Secretariat Service 1.43%, and only 0.72 of them were Section officers.

In Industry: Among the country's top industrial houses, not many are owned or controlled by a Muslim. As to participation in fresh growth of industries, the situation of industrial licenses issued for units between Rs. 3 crores and Rs. 20 crores during the year 1979 is as follows: Total No. 260, Muslims: 5 (1.9%), 1980 Total 386, Muslims 6 (1.5%).

Muslims are predominantly in the handicraft sector as skilled artisans. A countrywide survey, which covered 31 districts, from 12 States indicates that out of 12.68 lakh artisans employed in the Sector, 51.89 per cent were Muslims. But Muslim ownership accounted for only 4.4 per cent. In terms of financial assistance, Muslim borrowers were 4.3 per cent, and the volume of loans paid out to them was 2.02 per cent. The total financial sector disbursed only 3.76 per cent differential interest rate credit to Muslims. The average per capita income of Muslims is 5 per cent less than average of Rs. 4,247.

As far as *education* is concerned according to the survey of the Planning Commission, 87-88, the average literacy rate among Muslims was 42 per cent, which is less than the national average of 52.11 per cent. In the case of women, only 11 per cent Muslim women were literate compared to the national average of 39.42 per cent. Let us take a holistic view of the social, economic and historical reasons for the high level of illiteracy among Muslims. Though this backwardness has nothing to do with the Islamic tenets, the role of a section of mullahs in perpetuating this backwardness has to be recognised. It needs to be re-emphasised that most of the converts were already from the disadvantaged sections of society. They embraced Islam in the hope of joining the egalitarian religious order. This conversion did change their religious status, but their counterparts, the Dalits, stagnated even in the newer setup as *ajlafs*.

The educational levels amongst Muslims have remained low due to multiple factors. They have been discriminated against in jobs and other social facilities all through. Most of the scholars on the topic have come out with immaculate statistics on the topic. Omar Khalidi analysing the National sample survey data, round 43rd, of 1987-88, the later data is worse, shows that there are 53.4% self employed amongst Muslims vis a vis 35.9% amongst Hindus. While 46.7% Hindus are on wages/salaries, 28.9% of Muslims are on salaries. (Khalidi, Indian Muslims Since Independence, Vikas, Delhi 1996, p. 66) Apart from trade, the places where one can find employment is the jobs in Government, public sector and private enterprises.

According to Table 7.1 There representation in jobs also is very low, in 1981, amongst the total of 3883 IAS officers only 116 (2.99%) were Muslims (Hasan, 282) same was the pattern in class I jobs in most of the sectors while in lower categories, Class II, to IV the situation was marginally better. Data cited by Robinson shows that the percentage of Muslims in police force was roughly

4-5 % in most states, much less than their ratio in population. (Robinson, Rowena; Tremors of Violence, Sage 2005, p. 92).

Table 7.1: Muslims in Public employment: All Indian Central Services

Service	Year	Total	Muslims	Percentage
IAS	Total in 1981	3,883	116	2.99
Income Tax I	Total in 1981	1,753	50	2.85
Railway Traffic and Account Services	Intake during 1971-80	881	27	3.06

Source: Mushirul Hasan, Legacy of a divided nation, p.282 from Muslim India June 1983, pp. 261-63

These data show high rate of self employed amongst the Muslims, the reason being their discrimination in the employment. "Muslims are marginalised from more prestigious domain of regular and salaried employment. There are 46.7% Hindus involved in regular wage/salaried employment in contrast with just 28.9 per cent of Muslims. Muslims are but marginally more represented than Hindus or Christians in the category of casual labour. Later data (Shariff Abusaleh; India Human Development Report: A Profile of Indian States since 1990s, Oxford University Press 1999) also shows that Muslims continue to get their share from artisanship and petty trade as compared to other social groups; in contrast their income is far below the national average and less than that earned by Hindus from this source. NSS data (Rounds 50 and 55 for years 1993 and 1999-2000) reveal the unsettling trend of increasing disparity between Hindus and Muslims during 1990s with respect to the consumption, education, employment and landholdings, though literacy rates of both communities showed gradual improvement. (Hasan, 2000:248)" (quoted in Robinson, p.67)

Gopal Singh Commission appointed by Government of India in 1980s showed that only 3.41% students in Engineering colleges are Muslims, only 6.77% of them are registered at the employment exchange, in private sector they are 8.16%, borrowers under bank loan schemes-9.41% getting 3.37% of borrowings, poor representation in judiciary (Gopal Singh Commission, Quoted in Puniyani, Communal Politics, Sage 2002, p.145).

Sir Syed Ahmed, was the great modernizer and the one to advocate modern secular education but his effort was mainly for the enhancement of the feudal nobility. According to him, higher education was meant for scions of noble families, while children of artisans deserved only elementary education. Again the hold of the ulema was strong amongst the poor sections of society and they were against modern education.

On top of this, came the tragedy of partition, an outcome of the communal politics of elite's of both the communities, (Hindus as well as Muslims), and it affected the present Muslim community in the most adverse way. Muslim communal politics projected Pakistan as the solution for the Muslims problems. In the terrorizing atmosphere of prepartition days, most of the Muslims who could leave for Pakistan tried to go, and these were sections of rich businessmen, bureaucrats, landlords and the educated middle class. And those from the lower rungs of the social ladder, the artisans, poor peasants and the like, who even in earlier times could not take the advantage of modern education, continue to be poor and illiterate even in Pakistan.

There is a misconcption that the rate of population rise is higher amongst Muslims, they marry four times and shortly their population will overshoot the population of Hindus and this country will become a Muslim state. Some say 'Muslims don't practice family planning, indulge in polygamy to increase their population' (RSS and Conversions, Booklet by Rashtra Jagran Abhiyan 2000-RSS)

The truth is that the dominant communal forces over the years have propagated these myths. The communalists have on purpose projected the fear of Muslim population growth to consolidate their own electoral majority and towards this strategy they have effectively combined half-truths, ideological concoctions and rumour spreading techniques to entrench these myths in popular psyche.

We will like to begin with the myth that the rise in Muslim population is tremendously high and so they will outnumber the Hindus. The census surveys by religion totally negate this firmly held popular belief. Religion is one of the markers used in these surveys. As per 1971 survey Hindus constituted 82.7% and Muslims 11.2% of the population. The corresponding figures for

1991 census are Hindus 82.6% and Muslims 11.4%. (Malayalam Manorama, 1992) The marginal difference in the growth pattern as we will see a bit later has more to do with socio-economic factors rather than the religious ones. Over all, this statistics shows a reasonably 'stable' (religion wise) population. That apart, even if the current differentials persist, it is not only unlikely, but impossible for Muslim population to overtake the Hindu population for the next century or so. On the contrary, if the prevailing growth rates are analysed, it will be clear that between 1961-71 and 1971-81, Hindu population increase went up from 23.71% to 24.42%, while between the same period Muslim population increase went down from 30.85% to 30.20%. If these rates of growth are frozen at same level hundred years from 1981 Hindus and Muslims will record a decadal growth rate of 30.71% and 30.55% respectively i.e. growth rates of Hindus will be higher.

The social common sense that Muslims do not practice family planning because of their religion is also very fallacious like other perceptions about Muslims.

It is true that a section of Islamic fundamenatalist clergy does pass occasional *fatwas* to disapprove family planning, but a section of clergy can neither be equated to Islam, nor to Quran, nor to emerging Islamic practices as such. On the contrary, many Ulemas of different countries have actually favoured temporary forms of family planning. In his book '*Family Planning and Legacy of Islam*' Islamic scholar A R Omran of Cairo dispels the myth that Islam is inherently against family planning, as per him there is no text in Koran prohibiting prevention of pregnancy. In Islamic countries like Turkey and Indonesia family planning methods are quite popular. In Turkey for example 63% of the population in the reproductive age group uses contraception and in Indonesia the figure is 48%. In India the number of Muslim couples in the child bearing age practising family planning in 1970 was 9% (Hindus 14%) and in 1980, 22.5% (Hindus 36.1%) (Operation Research Group, Baroda 1981). Thus, the number of additional Muslims taking to family planning is keeping pace with the number of Hindus doing the same. Like all other social programmes, family planning is also linked with socio-economic status, level of general social awareness, etc. We will be repeatedly encountering this fact that a large number of Muslims being in the low socio-economic strata share these statistics more with other socially disadvantaged sections of society.

Is it true that Muslims marry more number of times, indulge in polygamy as Islam permits the men to have upto four wives?

The myth of polygamy amongst the Muslims is also very firmly rooted in popular mind. The correlation of polygamy with increase in population is the most simplistic concoction to have taken grip of our psyche. Overall the number of children born depends on the number of women in the reproductive age group and is limited by that. On first count it is immaterial whether a man is having one or more wives as the total number of children depends on the number of women, which does not get influenced by polygamy. If at all, this number of women has more to do with the prevalence of social practice of female infanticide and 'bride burnings' in the areas where the practice of extortion by parents of 'grooms' called dowry is prevalent. Secondly, the male/female ratio cannot permit the 'luxury' of four wives to the Muslim males unless three-fourths (75%) of them go without marriage. As per 1981 census the male/female ratio for Muslims was 1.068 and for Hindus 1.072 i.e. for every 1000 Muslim females there are 1068 Muslim males. One has to conceive of gigantic mental acrobatics, in the light of these statistics, to believe that all Muslim males can have four wives.

As such a slightly earlier but relevant statistics of polygamy (1961 census report) totally smashes the myth of Muslim polygamy, unless the social trends have worsened drastically, which obviously have not. As per this the incidence of polygamy is highest among the Adivasis (15.25) followed by Buddhists (7.9), Jains (6.72) Hindus (5.80) and lo behold, followed by Muslims (5.70). Research carried out by Mallika B.Mistry of Gokhale Institute of Pune, concludes "there is no evidence that the percentage of polygamous marriage (among Muslims) is larger than for Hindus". A comparison of nuptiality patterns for Hindus and Muslims shows great similarity, the incidence of polygamy has been declining among both Hindus and Muslims.

From the above it will be interesting to draw the religion based fertility patterns. These patterns differ within Muslim community itself, they vary from region to region as per the socio-economic and educational levels of the community are concerned. Those in the better socio-economic and educational ladder have lesser population increase, while those on the lower rungs of socio-economic educational ladder have higher rate of population growth. This conforms to regional, urban and rural distribution as well. Birth rate in Malabar region of Kerala, whose Muslim population is 40%, is significantly lower than those in Uttar Pradesh with a Muslim population of 15%. The contrasting case is that of Kashmir, a Muslim majority state. Here the fertility rate of Hindus is almost twice that of Muslims. Here again the birth rate was lower 31.4 (per thousand) than in U.P (36.5), MP 36.4, Bihar 34.8 and Rajasthan 33.4.

Can we bother to realise that the overall rate of population increase in educationally and socially advanced states like Kerala, Tamilnadu and Karnataka, is lower, both for Muslims and Hindus, compared to the rest of the country. Also let us have a look at Urban rural divide. More than one third of the Muslim community is concentrated in the peripheral and decaying areas of urban economic life. Incidence of urban poverty is higher among them by 17% (vis-à-vis Hindus). The number of Muslims living below poverty line is close to 45%. They are generally living in older areas of modern cities, which are well known for poor sanitation, lack of health facilities and basic amenities. On top of this the repeated outburst of communal violence against them is 'ghettoising' them with the result that improvement in their lot is becoming more and more difficult.

Overall, one observes that there are multiple factors determining the rate of population growth, religion being very low on weightage scale, if at all it counts at all. Socio-economic betterment and education are the foremost factors helping in the control of population growth. Feeling of insecurity and poor socio-economic status counter the efforts to promote family planning, (nee, welfare, which is the term conveying the goals of this exercise more precisely), and these two factors transcend the religious factor by number of times. In such a complex scenario, propaganda machine of the Sangh Parivar has done a 'remarkable job' by making' *Ham do, hamare do: Woh panch, unke pachees* (We (Hindus) practise two children norm, they (Muslims) practise four wives, twenty five children norm), a part of social common sense'.

One has to 'complement' the Gobbelsian methods of Hindu right, which have concocted this offensive slogan, which is far removed from the truth.

References

Guide for Secular Action: Vikas Adhyan Kendra, Mumbai, 1998.

Omar Khalidi, *Indian Muslims Since Independence*, Vikas Publishing House, Delhi, 1995.

Mushirul Hasan, *Indian Muslims, Towards Secular India*, CSSS, Mumbai, Jan. 95.

8

Myth of Minority Appeasement

While the opposition to reservation is on its peak, another front has been opened by those opposed to affirmative action of any sort. It may be a common observation by now that the most 'consistent' political and social force opposed to any sort of affirmative action is the communal politics, the politics of RSS affiliates. Surly there are other elite affluent sections who also are diehard opponents of affirmative action and reservation, but for communalists, reservation/affirmative action is a red herring. So it was not much of a surprise when Rajnath Singh, the BJP chief, came down heavily against the 15 point scheme for minorities, which aims at all round upliftment of the minorities, more so the economically deprived sections of minority. Singh, (26th June 2006), went to label the cabinet decision to allocate 15% of the funds for social welfare schemes for minorities as the 'appeasement' of minorities, an oft repeated allegation of this political outfit.

The central cabinet in its meeting approved Dr. Manmohan Singh's new 15 point programme for minority welfare, including ways to prevent communal riots. In a comprehensive proposal the prime minister has asked for introduction of ways to enhance the living conditions, and allocation of 15% of funds from welfare budget for minorities. The aim of the proposal is to upgrade the facilities for minority education, modernize madrassa education and to provide scholarships for meritorious students. The program lays emphasis on equitable share in economic activities and employment. It also touches on different facets of lives including the rural housing schemes.

Before we take up the issue whether all this is appeasement or is a much needed measure to ensure that minorities also are able to progress like any other community, it is imperative that we have a brief look at the implementation of National Rural

Employment Guarantee Scheme (NRES) in Gujarat. Reports indicate that Muslim minority is not able to take the benefit of this scheme as the Sarpanchas and concerned officials have been preventing Muslims from registering for this scheme. They are sent back couple of times, after which they get a subtle message and keep away from approaching the authorities.

Rajinder Sachchar committee initiated a report about the status of Muslim minorities in India. What ever one could glean from the parts of report, and from the document prepared by a voluntary organisation for presenting to the Sachchar Committee, (National Study on Socio-Economic Condition of Muslims of India, Indian Social Institute, Delhi, May 2006) Makes one sit up with deep sense of anguish. The current socio economic status of Muslim minorities in particular, has slipped down in the human development indices. Also their abysmal representation in jobs, the more of them living below poverty line and more of them being illiterate, leaves no doubt in one's mind that without serious affirmative action, this community will go on being deprived more and more. The additional problem of post communal violence and ghettotization is adding salt to the wounds, as in the ghettoes the living conditions go down and threatened psyche, fuels the conservative ideology.

Earlier, Gopal Singh Commission Report had also brought to our attention a similar fact in the decade of early 1980s. It showed that only 3.41% students in Engineering colleges are Muslims, only 6.77% of them are registered at the employment exchange, in private sector they are 8.16%, borrowers under bank loan schemes-9.41% getting 3.37% of borrowings, poor representation in judiciary. No action was taken based on this report, which has been gathering dust since. Later data (Shariff, India Development Report, OUP 1999) also shows that Muslims continue to get their share from artisanship and petty trade as compared to other social groups; in contrast their income is far below the national average and less than that earned by Hindus from this source. NSS data (Rounds 50 and 55 for years 1993 and 1999-2000) reveal the unsettling trend of increasing disparity between Hindus and Muslims during 1990s with respect to the consumption, education, employment and landholdings, though literacy rates of both communities showed gradual improvement.

While the charges of appeasement abound and have been made part of the social common sense the reality is the contrary. No doubt the earlier governments have appeased the Mullahs and conservative sections of society for electoral purpose; it is also true that the Muslim community has been getting marginalized by the day. Right after partition, the elite Muslims left for Pakistan and majority of the Muslims remaining here were the poorer one's, coming from Shudra background and now living as *ajlafs* with Islamic identity. They were bypassed in the social development process so the percentage of their representation in jobs, bank loans, higher education and other social benefits has been declining constantly. During the past when communal politics has been on the rise their situation is worse off, and without a determined effort they can in no way come close to the national averages of social and economic indices. The problem is not that, they are being appeased. In spite of that most of the development schemes for minorities have been too few and even those few, have not been implemented properly.

Communal outfits, irrespective of which religion they derive their identity from, generally stand for status quo, so any measures which can lead to social transformation are shirked and opposed, some times upfront, sometimes in a subtle way. Since the opposing to reservation for Dalit/OBC will be an electoral hara-kiri, so Mandal is not opposed directly, instead Kamandal (Rath yatra for Babri demolition) is engineered. To oppose the Mandal II, 'Youth for Equality' or some such forum is created. In case of Muslims where talking of reservation, barring at few places, is not a rewarding electoral strategy, the opposition to this can be upfront under the banner of Minority appeasement. As such, communal forces are opposed to minorities' welfare and have been opposing it right since the formation of Congress in 1885. At that time Congress was charged with appeasing Muslims as Congress regarded Muslims as a part of Indian nation. The most ghastly manifestation of this came up when a Hindutva trained volunteer, Nathuram Godse, killed the father of the Indian nation, Mahatma Gandhi on the same charge of Muslim appeasement. And Later Mr. Rajnath Singh of BJP opposed the welfare measures and labeled these overdue measures as minority appeasement!

9

Communalism or Affirmative Action

Prime Minister Manmohan Singh's statement to the National Development Council that we need "to devise innovative plans to ensure that minorities, particularly the Muslim minority, are empowered to share equitably in the fruits of development, these must have first claim on resources" was backed up by the statement in Parliament by the minister of minorities affairs that Government will implement the recommendations of Sachar Committee. This has on the one hand acted as a ray of hope for the 'discriminated against' Muslim minorities, while on the other hand', RSS combine has started crying fowl, BJP asserting that it is rank communalism, its ideologues saying that these steps of the government are in the footsteps of Jinnah. BJP has raised a serious question mark on the very formation of this committee calling it unnecessary and it being against the interest of the nation.

Just to recapitulate, Sachar Committee submitted its report (November 2006). The Committee after extensive home work found that the Muslim minority is way behind the national averages in most of the parameters of social development, its economic status has been sliding seriously, its representation in jobs, bank loans is abysmal, and its representation in the political process has been very poor and worsening on top of that. In sum and substance, Muslim community is under-represented in most of the arenas of society barring the jails. One also recalls the report of Gopal Singh Committee of 1982 which also had found the poor status of this minority. Gopal Singh Committee report kept lying in the deep freeze while the issues like Ram Temple kept hogging the national attention. To add up one can say this community's representation as riot victim is way above its percentage in population. The committee has recommended that an Equal Opportunity Commission should be set up, a national data bank should be started, a nomination procedure should be started to ensure their participation in public bodies, in order to promote religious tolerance by a procedure to evaluate text books for appropriate social values, so on and so forth.

Whatever one could glean from the yet to be initiated policies being reflected in the statements of the government functionaries, it seems to be taking it seriously. Steps are being contemplated, short of reservations to improve the lot of the Muslim minorities. It is a matter of conjuncture whether this government is really serious about it or is it a mere replay of the earlier broken promises during last several decades. During last several decades while governments after governments have been promising to look after the problems of Muslim minorities, nothing much came out. This includes not only the longest reign of Congress party but also of the one's of formations in which BJP was an important component or supporter. Amongst multiple reasons of this neglect of this minority one was the aggressive propaganda of Hindu right that Government is out to 'appease' the Muslims so that they can be used as vote banks. One does not know whether this aggressive anti minority propaganda did contribute to the policies of the government, but one can say for sure that this 'appeasement of minorities' had become a part of 'social common sense' in the face of the worsening situation of Muslims.

It is during last two decades that not only Muslim minority was battered through the post-Babri demolition violence and Gujarat carnage, it was during the same period that another big minority, the Christians also started being attacked, especially in the remote Adivasi areas. Where do we go from here? Was the commissioning of Sachar an act of appeasement? Will the implementation of measures to alleviate their plight be communalism, as claimed by RSS combine?

India has inherited a negative legacy of partition. While the major part of the country was for democracy and secularism, the communalists, Muslim League and Hindu Mahsabha, RSS were for Islamic Nation and Hindu nation respectively. Their ideologies served the British 'divide and rule' policy very well. With partition tragedy, the communal propaganda here went on getting sharper over a period of time, saying that Muslims have been responsible for partition, the subtle nuances and policies which led to partition were deliberately underplayed and put under the carpet. The role of elite of both communities in partition tragedy was put aside and the process to blame the whole Muslim community for this tragedy started, and this identity of Muslim minorities started becoming a negative one.

This was in contrast to the dalits, who were also underprivileged but their identity came in as a positive one and the reservations, which came for them came to be accepted to some extent. Even in their case the Hindu right and their followers did sabotage the whole reservation process in order to keep the status quo of Brahminical system, in newer garb though. That's how while the reservations were subtly sabotaged, the implementation of Mandal was countered by the Babri demolition, Mandal opposed by Kamandal. Essentially the RSS combine is against any affirmative action which can lead to social transformation towards substantive equality. In the case of Muslims, to demonize them is no big deal for this formation, RSS combine. The propaganda is simpler; 'they' created Pakistan now through such measure for their uplift, foundation for another Pakistan is being laid down.

In democracy, the concept of Liberty, Equality and Fraternity (community) remains at a formal level unless one does proactive action to undo the inherent infirmities of sections of society. One notices this in most of the advanced democracies including the United States where serious proactive steps were initiated for the African Americans. The politics of right wing and more so, right wing in the name of religion is against affirmative action. For them, democracy itself is not an acceptable concept. Today they pay lip service to democracy so that they can use it to subvert it, to bring in a Hindu nation based on refined values, social relations, from *Manu Smriti*. Democracy is neither their goal nor the cherished value system. They nurture the hope to have Hindu Rashtra and inherent hierarchies of caste and gender. And any affirmative action cannot be tolerated by them.

What is being called rank communalism is essentially a bit of affirmative action. Surely even the reservations, which were brought in for Dalits have improved their conditions slightly, so now a full fledged opposition to those polices in different language has been unleashed. While in the case of minorities not only the condition is bad as of today, the bigger worry is that it is sliding towards worse very rapidly. We need to distinguish abuse of community identity for politics and the bowing to the institution of religion from the concrete economic steps, social actions to support the weaker sections of society. Will the community identity become strong due to this? Will the community become crippled due to this?

If one notices amongst the dalits who have slightly benefited from reservations, their community identity has loosened up. It is a contradictory process, as such, if you bring a community to economic level, the religious or caste identity becomes weaker and other identities start becoming stronger. When a community is so helpless due to political reasons, how can this affirmative action cripple them? As such, a lack of such an action will cripple them forcing more of them to go in the aberrant way. Already a large section of youth from them is being targeted on any small pretext, the number of them in jails is appalling. Surly that's what RSS combine wants and any hindrance to the measures meant to uplift them will worsen their condition.

To revoke Jinnah at this stage is deliberate. The idea is to frighten and polarize the upper castes/middle sections of society around the politics of Hindu right. While Jinnah played the card for Muslim elite, the current efforts, if at all they come through, are for the poorer sections of society, which in no way can be labeled as communalism. As such had there not been the fear of backlash of RSS combine, reservations for Muslims would be the ideal solution out of this impasse. In the present scenario all steps short of reservations should and need to be taken to work towards the democratic goal of equality.

10

Fate of Gopal Singh Commission and Sachar Committee Report

There may be various parameters to judge the prevalence of democratic spirit in a country. One of them may be how well the minorities are doing, how safe they feel, how aligned they feel, how much at home they feel. Whatever was the answer to these questions couple of decades earlier, today it seems the answer to these questions is becoming more and more negative and the quantitative worsening of these parameters is leading to the qualitative transformation of social scene towards abysmal social scenario.

One has been hearing the aggressive propaganda that minorities are being appeased in this country for the vote bank politics. This was being 'successfully' injected to the societal consciousness despite Gopal Singh Commission, which portrayed the grim picture of the socio-economic condition of the Muslim minority. Close to two decades later Rajinder Sachar Committee, on the basis of a thorough inquiry has not only confirmed what Gopal Singh Commission found but also that trends are in the direction of further worsening of the socio-political indices of Muslim minorities. The data shows that Muslim community is at the bottom of economic indices, being worse than even the SCs, STs. They are worse off in education, and are far behind OBCs in employment. Their representation in judiciary, bureaucracy is very poor compared to their percentage in population, and more so in Class I and II jobs, they are very low down in landholdings, and much worse in employment in private sector. The number of MLAs and MPs coming from this community has also been declining over a period of time. Of course there is one place where they are over-over represented and that's in prisons. One may add there is other data which tells us that their representation amongst the riot victims is also very heavy, more than 80% riot victims being Muslims and not to be left behind most of the POTA detainees also happen to be Muslims!

The biases against them abound in all spheres; the police machinery in particular is the biggest victim of these biases and prejudices. This becomes apparent in their role during the riots and after the riots. The latest in the series is of course the pattern of investigations followed by them. By now most of those in the police machinery have come to firmly believe, and this is the basis of their 'professional conduct', that Muslims are criminals. The propaganda emerging from some rumour manufacturing factory that 'all Muslims are not terrorists but all terrorists are Muslims' is not only becoming part of social common sense but also the core guiding principle of investigation authorities. This makes their complex job also very easy. Recently the investigation of Mumbai bomb blasts and later Malegaon blast investigation has seen the targeting of Muslims through and through. Right on next day of Mumbai blasts, Muslim youth were detained in hordes, to be released only when a section of the community went on protest. But the pattern remains the same.

While someone from top leadership of police issued a formal appeal that they want to play a fair game and are open to listen to the innocents if approached. Some social workers of repute were also taken in by these formal appeals and narrated through newspaper columns as to how approaching police authorities are 'working' in getting the innocents released. What levels of democracy we have reached that police will nab the innocents for the crime not committed by them, then they will ring up the top police officials or the reputed social worker/s to get themselves released. What if the immediate *havaldar* decides that you cannot use the mobile now, what if you are intimidated beyond your wits to be able to contact these worthies? The question remains how many from the community can have access to these socials workers, whatever be the levels of their accessibility. How many from community can contact the top leadership of the police which makes these claims? In the face of such massive goofs, which have been committed in such cases, mostly due to biased and prejudiced approach of authorities, is there not a need for training the police in the lessons of pluralism removing their biases and prejudices if that be possible. Does a help line exist for an average person? Does not a need exist for creating an effective help line?

There are media reports telling us how innocents are being trapped in different ways during interrogation, what do we do for that? Do the people know their rights in the face of being apprehended by the Khaki uniforms? Is it not the responsibility of the state to let the people know their rights also when they are being booted and tortured to extract 'confessions from them? Do we not need to have provisions that without the legal help to the one arrested the arresting authorities will not proceed with their various 'degree' methods of increasing levels of torture to force the accused speak what Khaki uniformed one's want to hear to make their job easy. Incidentally that also fits in to the scheme of their line of preformed opinions?

The system is so insular, and by now becoming so self righteous that the appeal from Prime Minister, not to target the particular community fell on deaf years of the hardened stiff collared khaki machinery. In Malegaon the limits of police bias are openly apparent. And being disgusted with that the local Muslim community had to resort to day long peaceful bandh to vent out their frustration and anguish. The partisanship of the investigation is crystal clear to those who have been following the incidents in Maharashtra. The Bajrang Dal, whose activists died while making bomb in Nanded, is totally protected by the other type of bias, 'affirmative bias' to be applied to some sections and political streams of society. The bomb shells and RDX which were found in Shanker Shelke shop in Ahmadnagar seems to be of no relevance and it does not give any clues to our professionals in uniforms. The sketch of the person who bought the cycle on which bombs were kept has been relegated to the background and the thesis that SIMI activists have done this to kill exclusive Muslim crowd near Bada Kabristan seems to be the central point of investigation as far as our agencies are concerned.

Is it that the sectarian ideology has already completed its task of ensuring that the half truths, half lies spread by it are the core operating principles of the large section of bureaucracy and police? The insecurity of the other minority, the Christians, especially in Adivasi areas knows no bounds and through organizations like Vanvasi Kalyan Ashram the divisive and intimidating role is being carried to the full extent in remote places. The news of attacks on Christian nuns and missionaries have become a matter of routine and no more has any 'news value' as per the parameters of our media. At social and cultural level the Freedom of Religion Bills in various BJP ruled states are an open threat to the Christian missionaries working in the area of education and health in deep interiors. Madhya Pradesh government like other BJP governments has been manipulating the things at cultural level. It has been naming most of the social schemes in Hindu imageries, like water irrigation projects as Jalabhishek, marriage support to the poor as Kanyadan, and so on. Gujarat as a Hindu Rashtra has already relegated the Muslims out into refugee camps away from the main areas. Is it a return of old untouchable ghettoes?

It seems the democratic ethos is under severe threat and the state of alienation of minorities is a pointer to that. It seems that even without being in power, the BJP-RSS agenda of Hindu Nation is already unfolding itself in a threatening manner in BJP ruled states and in a subtle and overt fashion in other states where BJP is not in power. In those states due to the communal attitude of some of those in power and the communalisation of state apparatus, police and bureaucracy, the restrictions on liberal democratic spaces are mounting. Is it time for celebration in RSS headquarters or is there time still for it to be taken as a warning signal by those who wish to preserve and strengthen democracy. A lip service to minority welfare and security will not do. Those in leadership who are committed to the values of Liberty, Equality and Community (national) need to wake up and take stock of the all round intimidation and alienation of minorities. If Rajinder Sachar Committee Report and Malegaon bandh do not wake them up, what will?

SECTION–III

VICTIMS OF VIOLENCE: GHETTOIZATION

11

Communal Violence, Inquiry Commissions and Deliverance of Justice

Communal violence is the festering wound on the body politic of Indian society. The post partition riots were followed by a period of relative peace till 1961, when the Jabalpur riots brought to fore the unresolved problems of majority-minority relations. This was followed by many a riots in different parts of the country. These went on increasing in intensity over a period of time. The decade of 80s not only saw the intense communalisation of society, but it also witnessed the worst ever communal violence, shaking the society down to its core. The communalisation of society, intensity of communal violence and the rise of 'Hindu Right' run parallel to each other and every communal violence saw the strengthening of the electoral outfit of Hindu Right, earlier Jan Sangh and later BJP. This dastardly process saw its peak in the post Babri demolition riots, which also ushered in the upswing of BJP in the electoral arena, leading to formation of BJP's 13 day govt. in 1996, and later a coalition led by it.

In pre-independence period, the communal riots were a sort of reciprocal violence between Hindus and Muslims with the police (mainly British officers) intervening to restore peace. The nature of these riots after independence has changed in a significant way. First, the number of victims are more from Muslim community, second, the loss of property is also more of Muslims and third, police plays a heavily partisan role in favour of the majority community. Initially it used to be mainly the poor Muslims who were the major victims, but lately even the middle and upper class Muslims have also been drawn into this vortex. The post partition riots were followed by a period of comparative calm, in the decade of 50s, barring the one episode in eastern India and East Pakistan in 1950. This calm was broken in 60s when in 1962 and 1964 Jabalpur, Jamshedpur and Rourkela riots broke out. "Of the bloody pogroms in sixties, the ones at Ranchi, Bihar (1962) and Ahmedabad, Gujarat (1969) stand out as the major events. In seventies the Turkman Gate massacre of 1976 perpetrated by police...., the riots in Moradabad (1980), Nellie, Naogaon, Assam (1983), Bhiwandi (1984) and Meerut (1987) have been the major ones in which more than a thousand lost their lives" (Khalidi, 1995). The Ramjanmabhumi campaign left a big trail of blood in which more than thousand people lost their lives in 1989. The massacres of Bhagalpur, Hydrabad and Aligarh heralded the onset of bloody 80s, which has seen the peak of communal violence. Advani's Rath Yatra and post Babri demolition riots were one of the worst, the country has suffered so far. The post demolition riots gripped Mumbai, Surat, Bhopal in a major way and many other places in a significant way. From 1960 to 1995 the incidents of riots have been on an upswing. A big proportion of these have been taking place in six states UP, Gujarat, Rajasthan, Bihar, Madhya Pradesh and Andhra. Significantly in four of these BJP has been the ruling party off and on and has generally a sizeable electoral presence. These riots' occurrence is mainly in cities, but involvement of villages is also there and has been in the rise.

Mechanism of Riots

A perception has been manufactured and rooted amongst people that it is Muslims who start the riots. It is far from true. The perception that Muslims start the riots and later Hindus retaliate has no basis. The mechanism of riots is very complex and we need to understand the backdrop of the same.

1. ***Background:*** There are some of the factors from pre-independence time which have a strong bearing in creating a situation where communal violence is possible. As a backlash to the secular National movements, there came up Muslim and Hindu communal reactions, mainly supported by the Zamindars (Landlords) and traditional tradesmen. In the complex unfolding of events, where the secularisation movement was week, the communal reactions were encouraged by the British imperialists. Most of the Muslim elite from India migrated to Pakistan. Those remaining behind were subtly discriminated against in

government jobs, industrial employment and other social facilities. The ideological build up against them continued, accusing them to be 'foreigners' etc. They were also accused of enforcing partition of the country, and social biases against them 'flourished' with leaps and bounds. One should remember that a big chunk of Muslim elite and leadership left for Pakistan and over a period of time Fundamentalist leadership came to the fore. It is in this background that different contingent causes could be effective, resulting in the catastrophes witnessed by us.

2. *Communalisation of Social Space*: It is possible for the small incidents to get converted into riots for two major reasons operating at two levels: The first of these is the communalisation of social space and second is the communal organisations and their network which can spread the 'message' in no time, by word of mouth. The communal ideology, which began over a century ago has been systematically nurtured by the vested interests. They take advantage of 'pre-modern' identities, gloss over the inner contradictions of the supposedly 'homogenous groups'. And with the motive of strengthening pre-modern social rigid hierarchies and value systems, plough in the field of semi-secularised society and reap the harvest of blood, and destruction. The Muslim communalism became fairly deflated after the partition, but Hindu communalism has been going from strength to strength, duly being provoked by Muslim communalism. "The Hindu communalist argument asserts that the riots are caused primarily by Muslim extremists acting on behalf of Pakistan to damage India and to create conditions leading to further dismemberment of the country. Riots according to Hindu right, are precipitated by Muslims throwing rocks on the peaceful Hindu processions, on places of worship, or Muslims attacking the police and the defence personnel" (Khalidi). Khalidi's personal interview with cross-sections of Muslims leads him to conclude. "Anti-Muslim violence is planned and executed to render Muslims economically and socially crippled and as a final outcome of that economic and social backwardness, assimilate them into lower rungs of Hindu society..... assimilating them through physical terror and social-economic deprivation may be only way of achieving their final solution." Communal violence is an outcome of multiple factors operating in the society.

This communalisation process goes through various levels, beginning from 'the Muslims are aliens', 'responsible for partition of the country', 'have spread Islam on the strength of sword' and 'are loyal to Pakistan' to the last and one where the slogans like 'Musalman ka Do hi sthan, Kabristan ya Pakistan' (Muslims can have only two places to live: Pakistan or Kabristan), Pahle Kasai Phir Isai (first Muslims and then Christians) etc. In between these two there are various subtle conveyor belts which ensure the translation of this ideology into the action. Which in this case means a violence in which poor Muslims are the biggest victims and a section of poor Hindus, mobilised by activation of communal identities also loose their lives and properties. It goes without saying that Hindu communalism (expressed through Sangh Parivar : RSS, BJP, VHP and Bajrang Dal) is the main player in this game in today's scenario. It keeps getting stimulation and provocation from the remnants of Muslims communalism whose acts of commission, though feeble in social intensity are pretext enough for Hindu Communalism to pounce on the Muslim community with full intensity. We will come back to some of the contingent reason and actual dynamics for occurrence of the riots after having seen some of the major, riots which have occurred in our country.

3. *Pre Riot Mob Psychology* : Build up of group psychology occurs on the communalised social space, which has been actively vitiated by Hindu communalists, duely provoked by Muslim communalists. The group or mob is mobilised on the communal ground and systematic projection of 'fear' of impending attack from the other side. The 'forthcoming attack on our temple', 'build up of weapons in the mosques' are few of the major threats employed by the communal forces. In most of the riots, the majority communalism is well assisted by the state and police machinery and on occasions the police itself takes over the total execution of riot. Religious frenzy is the fodder of such a group and rumours, communalised media are the major forces in broadening the extent of violence. Apathy of state administration thoroughly infiltrated by the Hindu communal elements comes in as a big help to these forces. The communal build up is aided by slogans, some of which have found a permanent place in the dictionary of communalism and some of which are manufactured and propagated as the contingent measures.

Mob psychology is built upon 'projected fears', 'Bangladeshi infiltration' and the like. Organised activities like processions (Maha - Aartis), inflammatory speeches, writings etc., fan the flames. As pointed out before from here on the rumours take over as the engine of mass psychology, 'cow slaughter', chopping of the breast of Hindu/Muslim women. 'They have poisoned the milk, 'Huge number of arms are being accumulated in the masjid as the preparation', 'Temple is going to be attacked', 'Pakistanis are landing on the shore with the arms' are the commonly employed rumours with great effect. Riots break out with the processions raising provocative slogans, desecration of temple/ mosque, music before mosque, throwing colored water, gulal on mosque, elopement of Hindu woman with a Muslim or vice-versa.

4. ***Who starts the riots*** : Teesta Setalvad (Who Casts the First Stone, Communalism Combat, March 98) by citing the extracts from five commissions of inquiry shows the truth behind the start of communal riots.

(i) Ahmedabad 1969 : "There was deliberate attempt to suppress the truth from the commission especially the active participation in riots of some RSS and Jan Sangh leaders" (Jana Sangh is the previous political *avatar* of present of BJP) (from Justice Jagmohan Reddy Commission).

(ii) Bhiwandi, Jalagaon 1970 : "In his report to his superior the SP, Thane district has stated, "I found that a section of Hindu elements, particularly RSS and some PSP men, were bent upon creating mischief. Their idea in accompanying the procession was not so much to pay respect to the Great Shivaji but to establish their right and, if possible, to provoke and humiliate Muslims.

The villagers shouted provocative anti-Muslim slogans, behaved aggressively, threw on the Moti Masjid at Bangad galli Hyderi mosque situated at the junction of Dargarch Road and Sutar Ali aided by passive police." (Justice D.P. Madon Commission).

(iii) Tellichery 1971 : "In Tellichery Hindus and Muslims were living as brothers for centuries... It was only after RSS and the Jana Sangh set up their units and began activities in Tellicherry that there came a change in situation. Their anti-Muslim propaganda, its reaction on the Muslims who rallied around their communal organisation, the Muslims league.... the communal tension that followed prepared the background for these disturbances".

(Report of Justice Joseph Vithyathil (Commission)

(iv) Jamshedpur 1979 : From Report of Commission of Inquiry : "In the run up to the communal build up before the elections prepared by the Intelligence branch, Jamshedpur (March 23, 79) there was a special mention made to the divisional conference of the RSS scheduled to be held on March 31 and April 1, in which among others RSS Sarsangh Chalak was to participate.

The dispute on route of the procession became sharp and agitated reactions from a group of persons who called themselves Samyukta Bajarang Bali Akhara Samiti, who systematically distributed pamphlets to heighten communal feeling and had organisational links with the RSS. A call for defiance of authority and administration when it refused permission for one of the routes led to violent mob protesting and raising anti-Muslim slogans. Thereafter incendiary leaflets doing rounds of Jamshedpur (issued on behalf of Sri Ramnavmi Kendriya Akhara Samiti), that is nothing short of an attempt to rouse the sentiments of Hindus to a high pitch to distort events and show some actions as attacks on Hindus that appear to be part of a design".

(v) Kanyakumari Riots (1982): Justice Venugopal Commission:

"RSS methodology for provoking communal violence is:

(a) Rousing communal feelings in the majority community by propaganda that Christians are not loyal citizens of this country.

(b) deepening the fear in the majority community by a clever propaganda that the population of minorities is increasing and that of Hindus is decreasing.

(c) training young people of the majority community in the use of weapons like daggers, swords, spears;

(d) spreading rumours to widen the communal cleavage and deepen communal feelings by giving a communal colour to trivial incidents.

5. *A Police Officer's Research:* V.N. Rai, a fellow of National Police Academy has dealt with this point very well (Combating

Communal Conflicts). He breaks the myth of Muslims starting the riots by analysing the riot data and demonstrates that in the riots between 1968 and 1980 (Govt. data 3949 incidents occured in which out of 2289 victims 530 were Hindus and 1598 were Muslims. Let us keep in mind that Muslims are 12% of the population but in the riots more that 65% victims are Muslims. The police machinery is extremely biased and all the police action during and after the riots is also concentrated against the Muslims. The preparation for communal violence goes on for a long time before it erupts and a trivial incident sparks off deep lying hatred to the surface. Many a times business rivalry and land disputes are also made to be solved through such a violence. The 'first strike' may be made by the frightened community which is anticipating the attack from the other community. In a very perceptive observation Rai adds "very often the way in which the first stone is thrown or the first hand is raised in aggression, suggests an outside agency at work, an agency that wants to create a situation in which members of the minority community commit an act which ignites severe retribution for themselves. In order to guard themselves against external criticism and to preserve their self righteousness, violence is projected to be started by Muslims. It is as if a weaker person is pushed into the corner by a stronger, forcing him to raise his hand so that he may be suitably punished for his 'attack'. Before the punishment is meted out a suitable hue and cry can be made about the fact that because the person cornered is naturally wicked and violent, he is bound to attack first" (pp. 56-57).

6. *Case Study of Mumbai Riots:* The example of Mumbai riots can be taken to demonstrate the role of Hindutva organisations.

In Mumbai as a spontaneous protest against demolition few local Muslims came out and threw stones on public property: this was not an organised response.

Phase I: On 7th December some Muslims: attacked police station to show their anger against government's failure to protect the mosque. Police undertook effective firing in which 90% of those killed were Muslims: due to bullet wounds in abdomen, chest and head.

(From Shri Krishna Commission Report: "the irresponsible act of Hindutva Parties in celebrating and gloating over demolition of Babri structure was like twisting a knife in the wound and heightened the anguished ire of the Muslims. The celebration rally organised by Shiv Sena in Dharavi jurisdiction is an example" it further continues, "The Muslims protested, angrily on the streets. Large number of Muslims congregated near Minara Masjid in Pydhonie jurisdiction at about 2320 hours on 6th December 1992 and came out protesting. Even at this stage, if the mobs had been handled tactfully and with sensitivity and by accepted leaders of both communities, the protest would have been peacefully blown over." But according to the Commission, "the police mishandled the situation and by their aggressive posture turned peaceful protests into violent demonstration during which the first targets of the anger of the mob became the municipal van and the constabulary, both visible signs of establishment." Justice Shri Krishna further observes in his report, "it is significant that the mobs were not armed, not even with stones and sticks, though they were just angry and wanting to vent their spleen against anyone in authority. The situation was misdiagnosed, mishandled and turned messier." (Vol. 1 P. 4)

Celebrations were organised by Shiv Sena with mobs chanting provocative slogans: Musalman Ka Do Hi Sthan: Pakistan Ya Kabristhan (Muslims can only be in: Pakistan or Graveyard). In retaliation Muslims shout: *Jo ham se takarayega: Mitti me mil Jayega* (Those who attack us will be decimated). Shiv Sena procession threw cow dung on mosques, in retaliation Muslims stone the temples. Riots in Dharavi: Hundreds of houses were destroyed of which 80% were Muslim Households. Riots spread to South Bombay and other suburbs.

As per the survey of riot victims by Nirmala Niketan's College of Social Work students, of the 690 households affected 86% of victims were Muslims, mostly from poor socio-economic strata, daily wage earners, petty self employed etc. They fell to police bullets, were stabbed or burnt. During this time Safiya Hospital was attacked and its ambulance was burnt. Muslim journalists and those writing against Hindu communalism were preferred targets. Mobs attacking Muslims left was generally left unharmed by police.

Phase II: Initial quietness after Phase I was marked only by occasional bouts of violence. This phase was preceded by intense 'anti Muslim rumours: e.g. Muslims are preparing to attack with the help of Pakistan and Muslim countries, milk has been poisoned, they are using AK 47s to attack police; A shipload of terrorists are going to land at Dadar Chowpatty, with arms and ammunitions etc. Maha Arti was invented and started to mobilise Hindus, Maha Artis aggravated communal tension. Many a times Maha Artis were followed by communal violence and exodus of Muslim families of the area. Between 26-12-92 to 5-1-93, 33 Maha Artis were organised. Schedule of Maha Arti was announced in Shiv Sena mouthpiece 'Saamna'. In this phase Shiv Sainiks procured the electoral lists and marked the Muslim households and establishments in different areas.

(Extracts from the Shri Krishna report: "The Maha Artis were started from 26th December 1992 and kept adding to the communal tension and endangering the fragile peace which had been established. Some (were used to deliver) communally inciting speeches and the crowds dispersing from (them) indulged in damage, looting and arson of Muslim establishments in the vicinity." (Volume 1, page 13) On 1st January 1993 there was an article in *Samna* under the caption' *Hindunni Akramak Vhayala Have'*, (Hindus should become aggressive now) openly inciting Hindus to violence." (Volume 1 page 13) On 4th January 1993 a big mob of Hindus led by Shri Gajanand Kirtikar, Shri Ramesh More and other Shiva Sena activists took a Morcha to the Jogeshwari police station complaining of lack of security for Hindus. Some of the people in the *morcha* attacked Chacha Nagar Masjid and the Muslims in the vicinity and injured them. Several Muslim huts in Magdum Nagar in Mahim jurisdiction were set on fire by the Hindus." (Volume 1 pp. 13-14)

[On 7 January 1993] A taxi in which two Muslims were travelling was set on fire in Pratiksha Nagar Antop Hill jurisdiction, resulting in two Muslims being burnt alive." [Volume 1, p. 15]

[On 8 January 1993] some Hindu residences in Radhabai chawl in Jogeshwari jurisdiction were locked from outside and set on fire by miscreants. One male and five female members of a Hindu family and their neighbours were charred to death and three other Hindus sustained serious burn injuries. This incident was sensationalised by the media in giving exaggerated and provoking reports." [Volume 1 p.15]

From Shri Krishna Commission report "From the conversation which could be heard [by Yuvraj Mohite, Mahanagar Reporter, at Thackray house during the riots], it is clear that Thackeray was directing Shiv Sainiks, Shakha Pramukhs and other activists of Shiv Sena to attack the Muslims, to ensure that they give tit for tat and ensure that 'not a single Laundya would survive to give the evidence' [Vol. ii, Page 173-174]. The Commission does not accept the theory that the January phase of rioting was merely a backlash of the Hindus because of the stabbing, Mathadi worker incidents and the Radhabai Chawl incident. "There were attacks going on in the 12 December 1992 to 15 December 1993 period against Muslims and their properties...Several stabbing incidents carried out by professional criminals with the intention of whipping up communal frenzy in which the majority of the victims happened to be Hindus... the communal passions of the Hindus were aroused to a feverish pitch by the inciting writings, particularly in *Samna* and *Navakal*." [Vol. 1, pp. 21-22]

Low scale, sporadic violence against Muslims continued all through. Two events, blamed on Muslims, in which Hindus were killed, gave the much-needed "legitimacy" to the unleashing of full-fledged anti-Muslim pogroms:

(a) 5th Jan. murder of two Hindu Mathadi workers (probably a case of union rivalry) any way there was no proof of being killed by Muslims except the fact that those killed were Hindus.

(b) Jan 8: Bane family's house in Radhabai Chawl: Jogeshwari was burnt: family burnt alive: Probably a 'real estate' dispute'.

In both these cases since the victims were Hindus 'it got attributed to Muslims; and the much-needed pretext, legitimisation for wholesale violence was available to the Hindu communal forces. Police was very supportive to rioters, Shiv Sena mobs went on rampage. On the pretext that they have been criticised for their 'shooting sprees' in Dec., police justified its soft attitude to anti-Muslim rioters by saying, 'so now we will not indulge in shooting'. It was another way of saying that Shiv Sainiks are doing the job, let them carry on.

In Dec.: Victims Muslims 86% of bullet wounds.

In Jan: Majority Muslims were victims of stabbing and burning. On Jan. 2 & 3: Some people posing as people from housing board marked the Muslim houses in Pratiksha Nagar.

6b. A Case Study of Gujarat Carnage

Godhra Train Burning: On 27th of February the bogey S-6 of Sabarmati train got burnt, the fire killing fifty-eight unfortunate lives. There are different conflicting versions of the episode. The minimum, which can be inferred before the true facts come out from the inquiry commission report are that the bogey was full of Ram Sevaks returning from the pilgrimage to Ayodhya where different rituals around Ram Shila Puja were going on. Many reports pointed to the provocative behaviour of Bajrang Dal volunteers traveling in the train. (Jan Morcha, 25th Feb. 2002). On Godhra platform also the Muslim tea stall vendor was humiliated. One Muslim girl was being forcibly taken by the Kar Sevaks but was rescued. The district collector Jayanthi Ravi stated that the tragedy was unplanned. Soon Narendra Modi the Gujarat Chief Minister stated that it was a pre-planned act of terrorism and linked it to global terrorism and ISI. He also called a meeting of top Gujarat officials late on 27th and told them that the Godhra act will be taken revenge of and that they should not try to prevent any local retaliation. (Outlook, August 19, 2002)

The burnt bodies of victims were brought to Ahmedabad and communal temperature was raised by slogan shouting mob of VHP and Bajarang Dal. It was said that the local Ghanchi Muslims living near the station and Signal Falia had poured the inflammable material from outside and torched the bogey. Later the Forensic Laboratory report came to the conclusion that the coach was burnt from inside only as the amount of inflammable liquid needed could not have been sprinkled from outside, the lower part of compartment was intact from outside and the maximum damage due to fire took place on the floor of the coach from inside. (Malekar, The Week, July 7, 2002) Local 62 persons including seven boys were arrested under POTA.

Bannerjee Commission on Godhra Train Burning

Two and a half years after the tragic incident, Justice U.C.

Bannerjee came out with the truth of Godhra. According to the interim report of this Commission this tragedy was a mere accident and was not a preplanned one as claimed by Narendra Modi and the RSS and its progeny. During the NDA regime, dictated by the RSS combine, the mandatory commission to inquire this major accident was not appointed.

It is wrong to say that the Gujarat riots were spontaneous act of revenge by Hindus. Immediately from the next day, 28 February, massive riots, nay genocide of Muslims began in different cities of Gujarat. Ahmedabad was the major city to be affected. Out of 24 districts of Gujarat, 18 were involved in the violence. Mobs generally comprised of two to three thousand and sometimes to the extent of 10,000 also. They were armed with swords, trishuls (trident) and agricultural implements that could kill, "the manner of arson, hacking and killing was chillingly similar, all this suggested a well laid out plan behind the attack. It is only trained cadres who can spill out in such an organised fashion," (Communalism Combat, March 2002, p. 18). The household and business establishments of minorities which were burnt during the violence were those whose lists were available with rioters. Even the business establishments, which had Hindu sounding names but had Muslim ownership, came under the attack. Majority of business establishments owned by Muslim community were destroyed. The household and business establishments were burnt by using gas cylinders and special powder, which raises the temperature to a great extent. In the loot of business establishments large sections of middle classes merrily participated and the looting was coordinated on mobile phones, people came even in their Mitsubishi lancers to do their bit in the service of Hindu Nation by looting the Muslim establishments. In the industrial area of Ahmedabad, 43 people including ex-MP Ahsan Jaffery were killed by a mob of over 10,000 and same evening a mob of over 15000 killed 84 people in Naroda area. The victims of violence are estimated to be over two thousand. It was not just killings; those who were killed were subjected to extreme torture. Women and children were special targets. Women were humiliated and then burnt. Also under the attack were places of religious worship more so Dargahs, the symbols of syncretic culture. Many a holy places were destroyed and overnight roads were built on those sites. At places Hanuman temples came up overnight where the mosques or Dargahs were located. Dargah of famous Gujarati Sufi saint and poet, Wali Gujarati was also not spared. The loss due to burning of business enterprises is estimated to be close to 3800 crores. Hotel, transport, Industry and textile came under special attack.

The brutality towards children and women was sparked off by the rumour that Hindu women were molested in Godhra, the rumours were found to be totally baseless by numerous investigators. But by that time the newspapers contradicted the news in small columns, the intended 'aim' was achieved. "The handiwork of mobs is recorded in chilling detail in women's panel report. The women's testimony is perhaps most devastating and damning accounts of brutality in any riot in independent India. However, the inaction of police and administration speaks for itself." (**Times of India,** Editorial, 26th April 2002).

Godhra incident was propagated as the planned attack by terrorists and even before society could realise what is happening the bodies of the victims were brought to Ahmedabad with great amount of publicity. The report of railway police debunks the theory that Godhra incident was pre-planned and executed by the hawkers and the residents near the Naroda station who mostly are Ghanchi Muslims. On the contrary, the report of Forensic Science Laboratory is clear that the bogey was burnt from inside, leaving many a question marks about as to, "Who started the Fire"! The Govt. had failed to act, it deliberately did not take any precaution in the context of Ram Sevaks traveling by the train and raising provocative slogans. The report of Jan Morcha where the Kar Sevaks had done mischief at stations on way was ignored.

During the carnage, from the word go, the complicity of State Govt. was obvious all through. Statements of Modi (Gujarat Chief Minister) were the key igniting factors. His instructions to the top officials to keep aloof from the anticipated retaliation were very significant. Also the trained volunteers led the rampaging mobs and most of them knew no action would be taken against them. Since there was systematic erosion of the rule of law in maintaining state 'neutrality', the anti-Minority bias had come to become part of the state policy. During the uninterrupted BJP rule, RSS had ensured that Gujarat becomes the laboratory of

Hindu Rashtra. While Modi propagated that Godhra incident was a preplanned act by terrorists, his Home Minister Gordhan Zadafia saw the hand of 'enemy country' Pakistan in the whole episode. This laid the base for the attack on Muslims as in the popular mind the link between International Terrorism, Pakistan and Muslims is a simple and straight one by now.

The VHP called bandh was fully backed by the BJP and the State. Modi in tune with his being the RSS Pracharak was keen to see the consolidation of large section of Hindus behind Sangh Parivar. In response to the rising anti-Muslim pogrom he said that there is a reaction to every action, and this statement of his went on to encourage the rampaging mobs to no end. In addition, despite evidence to the contrary, he kept on repeating that situation is under control. In the initial period he even went on to claim that the violence has been brought under control within 72 hours. Nobody bought this claim but his fellow Swayamsevaks sitting in the Home ministry in Delhi patted his back for his 'efficient' work. All the criticism of his policies was deflected by him by asserting that people are defaming the five crore people of Gujarat.

Many ministers of Gujarat personally went to the police control room to ensure that the rioting mob let free to do what it is doing, to ensure that the mob is not controlled in any way. Many of them led the mobs, "Gujarat ministers Nitin Patel and Narav Laloo Patel allegedly led violence against women in Kadih and Unja in Mehasana respectively. (CC, March 2002, 109). The government's callous attitude towards this also manifests from the fact that Modi visited the biggest camp, Shah Alam, only when Vajapayee paid visit to Gujarat, a good two months after the whole tragedy began. Close to a lakh persons living in the camps braved it without bare minimum necessities. The examination centers of majority community students were shifted away from the minority dominated areas while such a 'care' could not be taken for the students of minority community who had to appear in the examination in such a traumatized state of mind. The distinction of communities was not spared even in death. The victims of Godhra were to be paid a compensation of Rs. two lakhs, while the one's of 'retaliatory violence' were to be paid Rs. one lakh. After popular protests and media criticism it was uniformed at one lakh. The appointment of Justice Shah to investigate the episode also revealed the intentions of the Govt. Justice Shah has the 'reputation' of delivering an anti-Minority judgement in TADA, Dabgarwad- Laliwala, case, which was later reversed by Supreme court. The apex court questioned the very reasoning of the TADA court in convicting the accused.

The attitude of the Government filtered down to the Civil Service. A former Cabinet Secretary, TSR Subramanyam (Indian Express April 10, 2002) went on to say, "There is no Civil Service left in Gujarat...Over the years, Civil Service has changed from steel frame to non-existent." This was equally evident in the partisan attitude of police, which not only assisted those conducting the pogroms, but also refused to register the FIR's. Harsh Mander, a Civil Servant on deputation to Action Aid, was so disgusted after seeing the role of his professional colleagues that he decided to quit the Civil Service. Also to quit the disgraced service were 20 Muslim officers of ONGC who could tolerate it no longer. P.C. Pandey summarized the attitude of Civil Service very well, "These people also, they somehow get carried away by the overall general sentiment. That's the whole trouble. The police are equally influenced by the overall general sentiment". (CC, March 2002,115). If one wants to make a list of the honest law abiding Civil Servants, one should just make a list of officials transferred during this phase. Modi transferred all those who defied the unspelt command of aiding and abetting the violence. Also due to the infiltration of RSS cadres in different wings of bureaucracy and due to the assistance provided by the state Government the whole process has been deeply intensified and a deep nexus between the Sangh Parivar and bureaucracy has developed over a period of years which has been the major cause of violation of rule book by the civil servants.

Sahmat report pointed out that it would be wrong to call this as a riot. "People who tried to help were actively prevented from doing so by the police who were seen in the company of the mobs."(Rajlaxmi, Frontline, April 26, 2002) The new features of this carnage were that Muslims were attacked by their neighbors not only in middle class areas but also in upper middle class localities; seemingly urbane Hindus also participated in looting. Muslims were also attacked in areas where they constituted majority. This carnage saw the outcome of the work of communalisation of Sangh Parivar as it could 'use' Dalits and Adivasis as its foot soldiers carrying out the job on the streets. The rampage, which has been turned, as an upsurge of Hindus by VHP and other RSS affiliates was not spontaneous was proved by the fact that cranes, trucks and shovels were used extensively for the whole operation. Also the extensive use of gas cylinders, the lists of Muslims household and business enterprises and the import of trucks of swords and dangerous chemicals used commonly also point to the fact of extensive plan which might have gone in to preparation of this pogrom.

A section of media, Sandesh, Gujarat Samachar and their different clones added fuel to the fire by spreading rumours and by carrying these tragedies as sensational headlines. It was to supplement many a poisonous leaflets distributed by different wings of Sangh Parivar. The most notorious of this was one distributed by VHP calling for a boycott of Muslim business establishments and of Muslim community as a whole. Many of these called for attacking the Muslims in the name of self-defense, (Reply Bricks with Stones, CC March 2002, 136). The training in firearms, distribution of Trishuls (Tridents), which were basically disguised knives, went on unabated, before and during the pogrom.

Citizens Tribunal Report

Godhra, Gujarat and Akhshardham have been the major blots on our democratic ethos in post Independence India. In the din of the tragedies which gripped Gujarat for over a period of ten months, different versions were floating about "who did it?' The state leadership had one version, while the events themselves were either difficult to decipher on the face value or were indicating the cause of the carnage in some other direction. It is at this point that Concerned Citizens Tribunal was conceived and most outstanding legal brains of the stature of Justices V.K. Krishna Iyer, P.B. Sawant, Hosbet Suresh, Adv. K.G. Kannabiran, and serious sociologists, Prof. Ghanshyam Shah, Prof. Tanika Sarkar and social workers, Aruna Roy formed this tribunal.

The task was mammoth, the need for knowing the truth paramount and that's what prompted the tribunal members not only to examine 2094 oral and written testimonies, (both individual and collective), from the victim-survivor and Human rights groups involved in relief and rehabilitation. It also examined volumes of relevant material and all this is put together in two volumes, Crimes against Humanity, which in a way is a landmark investigation in situations like these, where vested interests not only try to hide the truth but also to distort the same.

The findings of the tribunal at one level are close to what many a leading Human Rights activists and scholars were suspecting. The immaculate method of investigation leaves no doubt about the high merit of the report. Its findings point to the complicity of state leadership in the whole tragedy. The tribunal in all its fairness wanted to hear the version of State Govt., Central Govt. and many an individual ministers, who did not respond, while few of them did meet the tribunal and opened their heart. This two-volume report gives interim findings also recommendations about relief, rehabilitation and punishing the guilt. But the list of those named by the witnesses is so large that it is practically a 'who is who' of Gujarat political and administrative machinery.

The central point of Godhra, which was made the pretext for the riots, the revenge theory and all that, comes out very clearly in the report. The tribunal concludes that Godhara incident does not seem to be pre-planned. Neither is there a proof of 'foreign hand', which was propagated with confidence. Tribunals' tentative conclusion that the fire was lit from inside and not outside will force us to review the whole action-reaction thesis, which in a way was used to give legitimacy to state inaction in the face of one of the most severe riots in independent India.

Why was the state political leadership so eager to jump at make believe conclusions, and what might have been the deeper design behind the whole carnage becomes slightly more clear after going through the twin volumes. The tribunal also makes it public that witnesses deposing before the tribunal informed it about the meeting called by the chief minister in which instructions were given not to take action against the 'Hindu reaction' to Godhra. This speaks volumes about the real mechanics of the whole tragedy of marathon proportions. Most of the significant part is put in the annexure.

7. Role of State and Police in Communal Violence: V.N. Rai in his book *'Combating Communal Conflicts'* based on the study of major riots concludes that, Police are partial in most of the riots. They do not act as a neutral force but act more like 'Hindu force'. The discrimination is obvious in preventive arrests, enforcement of curfew, treatment of detained persons at police stations, reporting of facts and investigations, detection and prosecution of cases registered during riots. Hindus view the policemen as their friends—*Hindu-Police Bhai-Bhai, Beech main Vardi Kahan Se Aayi,* (Police and Hindus are Brothers, the uniform of police does not matter). Muslims by and large consider policemen as their enemies. Generally policemen, predominantly Hindu, don't shed their prejudices at the time of entering police force and this bias is manifested at the time of riots. Police personnel are expected to protect the communal interests of the community. Amrik Singh (Riots and Law enforcement) points out that the partisan behaviour of the police has a lot to do with, 'the composition and social outlook of police. Most of the recruits come from majority community. Therefore as and when minorities come under attack, there was no one to protect them.'

The bias of police force is very well shown in the report of Justice Shri Krishna dealing with Mumbai riots.

8. Fate of Commisions of inquiry : There are serious limitations in these Commissions of inquiry, as under the Commissions of Inquiry Act, 1952, they are just fact-finding bodies. They are not courts of law, the evidence recorded before the Commission has the following objectives:

(a). To identify underlying background which forms the fertile ground for the riots.

(b). To delineate the sequence of events.

(c). To identify the culprits by their acts of commission and omission (the latter applicable more to the political leadership, the bureaucracy and police).

Most of the inquiry Commissions necessarily take a long time to complete their work as there are multiple angles from which the events are to be viewed, number of witnesses to be examined is great in number. Despite that most of the inquiry commissions have done commendable job and have exhaustively produced their reports. Again these reports have some common pattern, though the inquiry commissions have followed their independent course of investigation. The picture, which emerges from these is that the Hindutva organisations, RSS, Jan Sangh, BJP, VHP intensify their communalisation drive in a particular way. This tempo is whipped up and rumours against minorities are spread doubting their patriotism, propagating that they are foreigners, and the like. Provocative slogans are shouted, leaflets are distributed in Muslim majority area. Media picks up from here and fans the fires. The minorities feel threatened and concerned and situations are so created where either they 'cast the first stone' or they are projected to be casting the first stone. The majority communal outfits come down heavily on the minorities. The police is totally partial and either looks the other way around when this is going on or abets these crimes or actively participates in the crimes started by majority communalists. Of all the inquiry commissions, most of them have been shelved. Symbolic punishments are meted to an occasional police official and there the matters rest.

In the case of Sri Krishna Commission (Mumbai Riots 92-93) the culprits came to power when the Commission was in the middle of its work. Some new precedents have been set by the BJP-Shiv Sena govt. First they terminated the commission, then when they were forced to restart they did it with the added mandate of investigating the bomb-blasts also (even when a special court was hearing the cases pertaining to bomb blasts). Later, after the submission of the report the govt. delayed the report on the ground that 'it will reopen the wounds'. Finally when they had to table the report on the grounds that it is a anti Hindu report. The uniqueness of this trajectory is much worse and fraught with dangers of greater intensity than the treatment meted to such reports earlier.

The Commissions of inquiry apart from pinpointing the culprits have given series of recommendations. Some of these are spelt out in a forthright manner, most of these relate to handling of the riots, the duties of bureaucracy and the police. The representation of the minorities in police and bureaucracy is minuscule, which is one of the 'core' problems in the riot situation. It is obligatory that this lop sided mess is rectified. The communalisation of police force, calls for a training and continuing education in social harmony. Only an unbiased attitude can rectify the partisan behaviour of the police. Transparency in behaviour, representative mohalla committees can be another measure which can tilt the balance in saner direction.

Lately one has been hearing that tabling, publication and implementation of the report will 'reopen' the wounds of the riot victims. This 'cleverly' manipulated argument found many buyers also.

Riots cause an unmitigated misery to those who loose their relatives or property. The sense of 'injustice' is the biggest feeling which grips those who undergo this loss or torture of one or the other type. What do these people desire? They want to forget the wounds and events so that they can live happily? It is not so. After coming to grips with the stark reality of the irreparable loss, the survivors' longing is to seek justice, and to achieve that they will go miles, if necessary. To seek justice becomes one of the central goals of their lives. There are infinite examples where father of the slain victim, widow of a person killed in a riot, have made it a goal of their life to seek justice and to do everything possible to achieve that. Be it the father of Engineering student of Kerala who disappeared in mysterious circumstances, be it the massive numbers turning up in the meetings in the wake of Shri Krishna Commission report, it is clear that they suffer more pain if justice is delayed and denied rather than when steps are taken to book the riot culprits. Recently in Mumbai, most of the meeting called to press for the implementation of Shri Krishna Commission report saw the huge turn out of relatives of riot victims. The only measure which is close to giving any succour to those close to the victims of riots is the move to punish the guilty. Though the riot victims can never be adequately compensated, ruthless punishment of the guilty is the only measure which heals the wounds partly. In addititION, this move gives a signal which will ensure future reduction of such blatant violation of Human rights of minorities. Accordingly it is no surprise even decades after the Nazi pogroms the efforts were made to bring the guilty to book.

The pretext of the government that it will reopen the wounds, is a mask to cover their own misdeeds. Its an escape route to avoid being punished for the crimes they have done. Its a ploy to fool a section of society to keep quiet and not to demand the implementation of the report. Further than that, in a way it is a threat that if there is move to undertake proceedings to bring their crimes to surface, they will again unleash a reign of terror which they did in 92-93 riots.

9. Major Communal Riots : This is not an exhaustive description of all the riots which have occurred in the country. We have selected only few major riots, to be able to understand the different mechanisms deployed by the communal forces to execute their goals. We should also note here that Muslims constitute around 12% of Indian population while more than 65% of riot victims are Muslims, and the number of Muslims affected by the riots is number of times more than that of the Hindus.

Ranchi 1967 : Apparently a procession of Hindu boys (August 67) protesting against the imposition of Urdu was stoned by some Muslims and the rioting began. Prior to this United Legislator Front Govt. had come to power on the agenda, one of which was according Urdu the status of second official language. Jan Sangh despite being the part of this front, opposed the move and gave the call for state wide bandh precisely at the time when Urdu fortnight was to be celebrated. During this anti Urdu leaflets were distributed and processions were taken out giving provocative slogans against Urdu and Muslims. Urdu was branded as foreign language and Muslims were declared as anti national. A call was given to the 'manhood' of the Hindu students to oppose the 'imposition' of Urdu. The anti Muslim atmosphere started building up and Muslims started feeling insecure.

Bhiwandi 1970 : Riots erupted when a Shiv Jayanti procession was attacked by a group of Muslims. This was a response to the gradually building tension of the Shiv Jayanti from previous years. Despite the opposition from police, processionists had been insisting on taking the procession through Justice Madon enquiry report on this riot has this to say: there was, 'a section of Hindu elements, particularly RSS and some PSP men who were bent on creating mischief. Their idea in accompanying the procession was not so much to pay respect to the memory of great Shivaji but to establish their rights and if possible to provoke and humiliate Muslims.' The Commission observes that rioting was the result of the irresponsible behaviour of the participants of the procession. By their acts of keeping the police in dark about the timings and the route of the procession, (Rai, 1998:55). Justice Madon's remark on the 1967 Bhiwandi skirmishes speaks a lot on the dynamics of communal violence, "In 1967 municipal elections which took place after the skirmishes of 1967, so far as Hindu councillors were concerned, all those who had taken an active part in this were elected." Shiv Jayanti Procession continued and reached unbearable peak in 1970. During this time Hindu and Muslim communalisms also gained in their strength. Rai in a perceptive tone observes, "very often, the way in which the first stone is thrown or the first hand raised in aggression, suggests an outside agency at work, that wants to create a situation in which the members of the majority community commit an act that invites severe retribution for themselves." (Rai, 1998:56)

Jamshedpur (1979): Similar route of the procession riots have been witnessed in Jamshedpur. The Hindu communalists usually have been forcing their processions through Muslim dominated areas. Ram Navami procession had been taking a particular route for years. In 1977, Jan Sangh became the part of Bihar ministry and taking advantage of this, pressure was brought on the district magistrate to take the procession through Muslim majority area. They wanted to repeat it next year, which was refused by district administration. The issue was thoroughly communalised.

Bhagalpur : 1989 : This was another major riot in the wake of Ramjanmbhoomi campaign. A Commission of inquiry with Justice Rama Nand Prasad, Ramchandra Prasad Sinha and S. Shamsul Hasan was constituted. As per the Commission, thousands lost their lives, fifty thousand were affected due to burning of shops and houses and 250 villages were affected.

References

Ansari I.A., *Communal Riots, State and Law in India*, Institute of Objective Studies, New Delhi 1997.

Khalidi Omar, *Indian Muslims Since Independence*, Vikas, New Delhi, 1996.

Rai V.N., *Combating Communal Conflicts*, Renaissance Publishing House, New Delhi, 1997.

12

Problems of Minorities and the Laws

The issues related to the minorities have been in the air since quite some time. The two minorities which are in the news are Muslims and Christians. Both have different type of problems and legal issues are also very diverse.

A large section of Indian Muslims comes from the untouchables, Shudras, who converted to Islam to escape the tyranny of Brahminical system of Varna, caste. Majority of this section was poor peasants tied to the land. A good chunk was also in petty trade and artisanship. With industrialisation process, section of Muslims shifted to the cities to take up employment there. The advantages of modern education did not benefit this section of poor sufficiently and they remained marginalised from the employment in general and in higher echelons of jobs in particular. The efforts of the likes of Sir Syed were restricted more for the Ashraf section of Muslims. With partition the large section of educated elite Muslims left for Pakistan, increasing the ratio of poor and uneducated Muslims in the community.

The Muslim minority faces the twin problem of violence and poverty. Due to being artisans and weavers, some concentration of theirs' took place in some cities where occupation based on their skills were located, Meerut (locks), Moradabad (brassware) Bhiwandi, and Malegaon (textiles). In cities majority Muslims were concentrated in poor localities, with less civic and other amenities. The trade rivalry was to be the first which took the better of the democratic norms and resulted in the violence, beginning from the Jabalpur one. Here the violence was aided by the rivalry of *bidi* (tobacco rolled in leaves) traders. Later the violence of Meerut, Malyana, Bhivandi, and Malegaon came up to show this sore of Indian society. Every wave of violence left the Muslims in that area poorer and more marginalized.

The occurrence of regular repeated violence against them has been well documented in various Inquiry Commission Reports (Jagmohan, Vyathathil, Madon, and Shrikrishna). In the communal violence which has taken place between 1961 to 1991, those amongst the riot victims, 80% were Muslims (Muslim population around 12%) This violence and post violence trauma has left the community in a sorry state. On one hand, it has aggravated the poverty and on the other it has caused ghettoisation, which is the root cause for domination of Mullahs in that community. The insecurity caused by violence leads them to concentrate in few areas and then in these areas the orthodox sections become powerful and dominant. This also results in obstructing the process of social reform and change of social norms related to women in particular. In Mumbai, Bhendi bazaar, Jogeshwari and Mumbra are the examples of this. Different cities have seen the emergence of these ghettoes which are derogatorily called as mini Pakistan. The rehabilitation process after the riots is not satisfactory. Gujarat showed the worst of it when the Government refused to initiate any steps to rehabilitate them. At the same time their percentage in employment was low and has been consistently declining.

The losses of minority community, after the violence, just in terms of quantum, are phenomenonal. The Ahmedabad city itself witnessed the massive destruction of property, mainly of Muslims. Tata Consultancy Services surmise the loss of gross value output of goods and services to be about 1250 crores, the loss of trading business about 1000 crores, loss of exports 2000 crores. Many a trading families turned destitute due to the lack of proper rehabilitation and compensation after the riots. The recovery is generally not complete and these families take to economically lower level of occupation.

The families which are victims of this violence, many a times have to be displaced and to rebuild their lives from scratch. The State apathy in their rehabilitation was worst exhibited in the Gujarat violence, which is extreme but in no way the only example of its kind. In most of the riots the rehabilitation process has been half baked, half way and nowhere bringing the victims to their pre-riot economic levels. The compensation which is declared for the victims generally does not reach them. In case of Gujarat the prime minister declared that the victims will be given Rs. 50,000 each. The state government modified it to say that the compensation will be given up *to* Rs. 50,000, and finally the victims got compensation which was abysmally low in amount. This has gone on adding to the process of worsening over a period of time.

The major legal issues pertaining to the Muslim community has been the question of Muslim Personal laws. As per these laws the Muslim men can marry four times and can divorce by proclaiming talaq three times. Shah Bano case was the turning point in many ways. The Supreme Court ruling was overturned by the Government to appease the fundamentalist sections of Muslim leadership. As such there is a strong section of Muslim women who want the reforms to take place. Due to the intimidation process of the violence against the minorities the fear complex has set in and the reform process is not easy to get going. An intimidated community becomes ghettoized emotionally also and in such situations reforms are very difficult. One has to recall that the Personal laws in all the religions are different and most of the Personal laws are against the interests of women of those religions. All the communities need more and more reform to give gender justice. In case of minorities the problems are always more difficult and in India it is worse off because of the intimidation which they have to face due to spread of communal violence, communal thinking and demonisation of minorities. It needs to be recalled here that in Muslim countries where the process of intimidation is not there, these personal laws have been changed in favor of more secular and just laws.

The second aspect of the laws related to Muslim minorities is related to reservations for Muslims in the professional colleges and jobs. The basis of reservation has been social disability which results in a handicap for the progress of the community. Such provisions were given to the dalits and it had a marginal impact in improving their condition. Communal forces are generally against the affirmative action for weaker sections of society. In case of Muslims the opposition is very vehement. The Muslim community does require an affirmative action to ensure that there is some progress in the community but barring few Indian states which are an exception this is not coming through.

The Christian minorities have been facing different type of problems. From 1996 the section of Christian population living in the far off places and Missionaries, in particular has been attacked. The Christians have been charged with the accusation that they are converting the poor gullible Adivasis by force and fraud. On this pretext many a churches have been attacked, Bibles burnt and Missionaries attacked. Pastor Graham Stains working amongst the Leprosy patients was burnt alive by Dara Singh, who was working with Bajrang Dal and other Hindutva organisations. In the face of these accusations, the Christian community is feeling intimidated and insecure. As such it is interesting to note that while it is being said that Christians are converting, the population of Christians is on the decline, 1971-2.60%, 1981-2.44%, and 1991-2.32% and in 2001-2.30%. Even in the Keonjhar area where Pastor Stains was working there was no significant rise in the Christian population. This marginal decline in the percentage of Christians is due to the better educational and social status of the Christian population.

To legitimise the acts of the attacks on Christians, various state Governments brought in the legislation to prevent the conversions. It is another matter that there is nothing illegal about choosing one's religion. The case of Jayalalitha, Tamil Nadu is very interesting and shows that anti Christian tirade is just a political move. When BJP led NDA was in power, she brought in a legislation which required that prior permission should be taken before the conversion. When BJP led NDA lost in the general elections and Jayalalitha had to bite the dust in the Lok Sabha elections she promptly withdrew this legislation.

Indian Constitution grants the right to all of its citizens to practice and propagate one's faith. The sudden coming up of the issue of conversion and 'threat to Hinduism' is a propaganda for the agenda of Hindu right which wants to do away with democracy and bring in a religion based nation. The rise in the anti minority violence from the decade of 1980s is related to the political processes and does not reflect the clash between relgions or religious communities. In the atmosphere of propaganda against the minorities it has become difficult to protect their constitutional rights and affirmative action for weaker sections is becoming a distant dream.

13

Khaki Prejudice

The episode of (9th April, 2000) police force barging in to the hostel of Jamia Milia Islamia on the pretext of looking for two offenders, and then going on rampage is not only highly disturbing, but is one more reminder of the communalisation of State apparatus, in general and of the police Force in particular. Earlier there was a fracas in which two of the students were involved and were to be apprehended. The police contingent of close to a thousand broke open the gate of the hostel, beat up the warden and then mercilessly beat all around while hurling highly communal abuses, calling the students Pakistani agents, ISI agents and also made other derogatory remarks. It is worth recalling that Jamia Milia Islamia is one of the products of the struggle for independence and has been the flag bearer of Indian nationalism, secularism and democracy.

The list of biased behaviour of police can be infinitesimally long. Not very long ago in post demolition Mumbai riots most of the victims of police action were Muslims. In the first phase of riots when police was using the bullets with gay abandon, the victims who during this phase happened to be mostly Muslims suffered bullet wounds. While in the second phase the victims suffered stab wounds mainly due to the action instigated by the Shiv Sena.

A police officer, Vibhuti Narayan Rai, conducted a study into the behaviour of police in the communal riots (Record of Police Neutrality in Communal Riots, *Indian Journal of Secularism*, Dec. 1997). The finding of this study is very disturbing. The study is based on the interviews with the community leaders, feedback from serving and the retired police personnel, record of the police academy, and study of the reports of different communal riots. While we know that 65% of the victims of communal riots have been Muslims, the arrest and casualty figures are very revealing.

In Bhiwandi riots 1970, out of those arrested in cognisable offences, 21 were Hindus while 901 were Muslims; casualties-wise, 17 were Hindus and 59 were Muslims. In Meerut riots of 1982, the pattern is no different. A total of 124 Hindus were arrested, as against 231 Muslims, while 2 Hindus and 8 Muslims were the victims of casualty. As in Mumbai, here also police bullets selectively hit the body of Muslims and soul of secular values. In Bhiwandi (1970), Firozabad (1972), Aligarh (1978), Meerut (1982) there was not a single Hindu victim of police bullets while the number of Muslims dying of police bullets respectively was 9, 6, 7, and 6.

Let us have a look at some of the glaring examples of police partiality. In Meerut riot in 1987, P.A.C. was deployed to control the riots. As the violence continued unabated for some time, PAC following the theory that Muslims are responsible for the riots and should be taught a lesson, picked up more than two dozen Muslims from a locality known as Hashimpura and killed them at two places in Ghaziabad after transporting them in their truck.

One of the worst complicity of the police in communal violence was seen in Bhagalpur riots (1989). Here the police was a mute witness to the murder of 116 Muslims who were buried in a field and cauliflower was grown on it to cover up the episode. Bhagalpur police administration kept denying this till another police party led by a DIG dug out some of these dead bodies. Because of the heavy communalisation of the police force it believes that communal riots are due to Muslims and this is what guides their conduct. Their communalised consciousness is supplemented by brutal savagery, which gets further compounded by their non-professional approach in dealing with these situations. Many Muslim predominant areas are termed as 'mini-Pakistan' and police forces while entering these areas enter with the preparation and the spirit as if they are entering the enemy territory. This also makes them do the riot investigation in apathetic manner and year after year they keep sitting on the available evidence, which goes against their deep-set biases. Two of the comments from inquiry commission reports will give us a good glimpse of the attitude of some of the officers of the police. In the Bhiwandi-Jalgaon riot the Madon commission commented,

"The real reason for the inadequacy of the measures taken by the authorities was the communal bent of mind of some of the officers and incompetence of others. Unfortunately, the SP, Mr. S.T. Raman appears to have possessed a communal bent of mind and perhaps a pro-Jana Sangh (Previous avatar of BJP) he fully realised the seriousness of situation but chose to turn a blind eye".

In more recent Mumbai riots people who were implicated in the riots dubbed Justice Shri Krishna as anti-Hindu. The police also got its 'due share' in the report, "police officers, particularly at the junior level, appeared to have an in built bias against the Muslims which was evident in their treatment of the Muslims and Muslim victims of the riots. The treatment given was harsh and brutal and, on occasions, inhuman, hardly doing any credit to the police. The bias of policemen was seen in active connivance of police constables with the rioting Hindu mobs on occasions, with their adopting the role of passive onlookers on other occasions, and finally, in their lack of enthusiasm in registering offences against Hindus even when the accused were clearly identified (Vol. pp. 25-26). And "Despite clues, miscreants were not pursued, arrested and interrogated, particularly when the suspected accused happened to be Hindus with connections to Shiv Sena or Shiv Sainiks. This general apathy appears to be the outcome of built-in prejudices in the minds of average policeman that every Muslim is prone to crime" (Vol. I, p. 26).

Commissions after commissions of inquiry are full of these and similar type of examples of maltreatment and biased behaviour against Muslims. Police not only behave in a partial manner during riots, in most of the 'regular' situations also these biases govern their attitudes. Mostly the police act more as a 'Hindu force' rather than as an arm of secular state. The discrimination in their behaviour is obvious at all the levels. By now minorities have started looking at them as the hostile force. Lately it is the experience of the second largest minority, the Christians as well.

What is the remedy to this impasse? On the one hand, the communalisation of society is cornering the minorities and on the other, the supposedly protective force has no qualms in conniving and even acting on behalf of the offending communal elements. This is of course due to multiple factors. The recruits to the police force are from the same group, which is on the communal offensive. The training programmes of police academies etc., are not at all geared for secularisation of its trainees. On the contrary, many a top officials themselves are having heavy communal bias. The representation of the minorities in the police force is abysmal and the recruitment policy of the state has remained lop sided resulting in a very low percentage of Muslims in the police force. All these need to be reversed as early as possible. Not only that there should be a conscious effort to improve the percentage of Muslims in the police force but also the training programme needs to be recast with an emphasis not only on the human rights of minorities but also the general communalisation has to be fought against at all the levels.

14

Riot Report: Apportioning the Blame of Communal Riots

During the elections of April-May 2004, many a Muslim leaders, or self proclaimed representatives of the community, like Shahi Imam of Jama Masjid, came out with Fatwas to vote for BJP, to give it a chance. The argument was that during BJP regime only Gujarat riots have taken place while during Congress regimes thousands of riots have taken place.

Riots, communal violence have become a sad reality of India's life. There are many an observations pertaining to the riots. The major one being that after every riot BJP in particular becomes stronger in that area. Also that the majority of the victims of riots in India are Muslims. The data from 1961 to 1992, shows that during these four decades 80 percent of victims of communal violence have been Muslims. During the 1984 Delhi riots, nearly 4000 Sikhs were done to death. In a similar vein another minority; Christians saw the ghastly burning of Pastor Graham Stains along with his two minor sons.

Who is to be blamed for these riots? In case of 1984 anti Sikh riots, the role of Congress was most abominable. In addition to overt role of Congress one has to see the role of RSS also in this tragedy. In one of the articles in a Hindi Monthly, *Pratipaksha,* Nanaji Deshmukh a veteran of RSS wrote around that time that there is a threat to the National unity, due to Sikh extremism, and so Rajiv Gandhi should be supported to the hilt. Needless to say, it was Rajiv Gandhi who blurted during these riots that when a big tree falls the ground shakes. The role of RSS during 1984 riots is anybody's guess. It was around this time that Bajarang Dal, the storm troopers of RSS was formed. The rise of Sikh militancy, rise of Bhindranwale, attack on Golden temple, Operation Blue Star and murder of Indira Gandhi preceded the anti Sikh violence. The anti Sikh tragedy had different dynamics than the two other minorities (Muslims, Christians) who have also been under the chopping block.

The Muslims and Christians have been targeted for slightly different reasons. The anti Christian violence has also not assumed the form of riot as such. While we talk of riot, the major phenomenon which comes to mind is the so-called Hindu Muslim riot. From prepartition times, this name stuck to such skirmishes, which went to assume more and more horrendous proportions over a period of time. There are calls for bandh, calls for direct action or at times an event is given the twist to project as if the community is under the threat of an attack so there is a need to take up arms.

This becomes possible to begin with due to the massive hatred spread against the 'other' community. In prepartition times Muslim League indulged in spreading anti Hindu poison and Hindu Mahasabha and RSS indulged in spreading anti Muslim venom. These sentiments of hatred against the 'other' community are the fertile soil in which particular events can be given a communal twist, or calls for attacks in a veiled language can be given. So many a events can take place in the society but unless the inherent hatred for the other community is there these cannot be translated into violent episodes.

After the partition process, those from amongst the hate spewing machines, Muslim communalism got deflated, Hindu Mahasabha got eclipsed and RSS proliferated as the time passed by. It went on from strength to strength, and from organisation to organisation manned by the Hate embodiments, the RSS Swayamsevaks, whose core ideology is based on the Hate 'other'. By now there are over 150 RSS progenies doing the job at various levels apart from its Swayamsevaks who have infiltrated in media, education and bureaucracy.

Grounded on hate, certain incidents are twisted to give it a provocative interpretation, a call for action to attack the other community. Sociologist Dipanakar Gupta in one of his articles in a popular newspaper outlined the role of ethno-preneures in giving such a twist to the events. These soldiers of communal politics are on the look out for the chance to convert a human tragedy into a ladder for their political enhancement, into enhancement of their communal agenda. In recent past two such ethno-preneures can easily be discerned. The first one amongst these is Mr. Balasaheb Thackeray, who gave an open call to Hindus to 'deal' with the rising attacks on them. The detailed analysis of the events of Mumbai riots shows that the scattered isolated, unrelated events of murder of Mathdi workers and the burning of Bane family was projected as the onslaught by Muslims on Hindus. And so the call that Hindus should become aggressive. The call was duly backed up by regular instructions, and then one sees over 900 dead bodies. One witnesses property worth 10,000 crores going up the smoke. Most of this is well chronicled and investigated in Shri Krishna Commission report. On the dead bodies of the riot victim's Hindu community got its first Soul Emperor (Hindu Hriday Samrat), none other than Balasaheb Thackeray, who was the ethno-preneur.

A train is burnt in Godhra. One is not sure how and why it has happened. It needs to be investigated and the guilty need punished. Here another ethno-preneurs is lurking in the wings. Without wasting time he declares that this is the act of International terrorism, in association with the much hated Pakistani ISI and their natural associates the local Muslims. He instructs all those concerned in controlling the riot, to sit back and relax. Those given these instructions take the cue and duly assist the 'process of revenge of Godhra'. Two thousand lives down the gutters of fire, twenty crores worth property down the drain, another Hindu Soul Emperor emerges.

Prior to this many a riot had taken place. In most of the investigations of the riots, Madon (Bhivandi), Ahmedabad (Jagmohan) Kanyakumari (Vythathil) Bhagalpur, Meerut and others the inquiry commissions did come to the conclusion that the role of ethno- preneure is played by some scattered RSS organisations, especially put together for the purpose but drawing from the existing organisation already being conducted by a Swayamsevak. Congress was ruling. Within Congress and within administration there are elements that have been communalised. Congress does deal with these while looking the other way around. Guilty either gets promoted (Thackeray, Modi) at worst and remains unpunished at best.

To look at riots as to under whose regime they took place is to overlook the bigger reality. The truth of riots involves multiple factors and each of this contributes at a different level. Pastor Stains burning took place under a particular regime, looking at that alone does not give us the full picture. We have to see as to who is spreading the anti Christian venom in villages and Adivasi areas, which is instigating others to join in such inhuman acts. Anti Muslim riots took place aplenty under Congress regime. We have to see who has been spreading hatred against this community, the myths about them which by now have become a social common sense are systematically spread by different progeny of RSS, this is the ground on which the events are taken up by ethno preneuers and converted into the riots, which benefit their political agenda. Shahi imam and others observation that more riots took place under Congress regime is a very superficial and distorted way at looking at things. It does not help us in apportioning the blame of riots properly. We have to delve deep in order to understand the nature of these political formations to come to conclusions, especially which are going to have a far-reaching effect on our political future. In that sense the worst of Congress crimes come nowhere close to the machinations of RSS which operate at multiple layers and which is making the life of minorities miserable in this country. It is this, which is a big obstacle to the efforts to get the justice for the weak sections of society.

The RSS like formations, and their progeny are in a different league altogether. Since they do not hold to the values of democracy, affirmative actions and human rights, they should not be compared with potentially democratic organisations, which under grass root pressure can be made to become better suited for India.

15

Why is the Liberal Muslim Bypassed?

The article by Sagarika Ghose, 'Will the liberal Muslim please stand up?' (HT, Oct 27th 06) is thought provoking and relevant in today's context. Her comments about the condition, status of Muslim community today, gives some clues to the answer of question she has raised. Is it only a subjective factor whether the liberal Muslims are standing up or not? Does any community deliberately want to remain backward? The impression given is that it is on design that liberal voices amongst Muslims are staying in the TV studios, edit pages and avoiding the *maidans*. Taking the question further, why does the large chunk of Muslim community respond more to Olema's obscurantist and their semi-insane views, why does the large mass come out in response to Danish cartoons or the US invasion on Iraq rather than take the Olema head on when they pronounce judgments like the one in Imrana's case? While one will like to go by her opinion that more liberal Muslim voices should come out and confront the Maulanas, one will also like to submit that in the type of social and political atmosphere built up all over the globe and also in India a large section of Muslim community is gripped by the real phobia, fear, insecurity of physical and social survival.

The subjected communities generally tend to become inward looking and tend to respond more to orthodoxies rather than the liberal voices. One must realise that there are good number of liberal voices amongst Muslims even today. Problem is that the community is not able to receive them, to a large extent due to the external situations in which the community has got stranded.

Before one takes up the current scenario, one should have a brief look at the decades past when the Islamic, Muslim communities did make substantial strides towards liberal values. Was it the charisma of Saddam Hussein that Muslim community in Iraq marched towards liberalism, or was it the social security which played a major part in development of liberal values? Same has been the case of Turkey, Egypt, Ethiopia and partly Malaysia and Indonesia. One need to be reminded that in the seventies all over the world many a Muslim rulers were trying to bring in Islamic Socialism. Here in India one could name many liberal Muslims who were heard with respect. Even in India till 1992 the Muslim community was making some journey towards liberal values. Ghose as a journalist should refer to the special issue of *India Today* (The Modern Muslim) of 1992, before the Babri demolition to realize that till that time the fear had not become seriously imbibed by the community, there was a space for liberal voices and also for the talk of process of reform. How the matters changed after the Babri demolition needs to be understood from socio-psychological angle as well.

Around that time while teaching in IIT, Mumbai, despite being confined in the small community, I could see the sea change in attitude of minorities within the campus. In the campus the Shiv Sena followers wanted to check the belongings of Muslim employees/their relatives entering the campus. One of my research scholars, who till that time, was not putting any Muslim identity, started growing Muslim trade mark beard and took special permission from me to visit the mosque in the afternoon which he was never doing earlier. A girl working in the campus started putting the scarf and displaying her Muslim identity. To cap it all, one Christian friend started going to Church on Sundays, which he never did earlier. This friend of mine was a sort of atheist but after the communal violence he said he feels that it's one's community which may help in the times of crisis. At around the same time began the process of intra-city migrations of Muslims to Jogeshwari and Mumbra, 'areas where our own people live'. The process of ghettoisation intensified. Pray, tell me who dominates in the ghettoized community? Can the ghettoized community hear the voice of a liberal Muslim? In Gujarat the Government refused to rehabilitate the riot victims and those displaced due to riots. Muslim charitable trusts came forward to rehabilitate them. In the rehabilitation colonies, away from the city, the mosques are bigger and houses are tiny! Those battered by the communal violence are further driven in the lap of orthodox elements. Can the liberal voice reach there easily?

One understands the custom of burqa was not much prevalent in Kerala before eighties, it has now started picking up, firstly due to a section of Muslims going to Gulf for jobs, turning Wahabis and secondly the overall increase in the threat perceptions of Muslims all over and in equal measure here in India. Those wearing burqa and those imposing burqa may be selectively impervious to liberal voices, I presume!

While one partly concedes that liberal Muslim finds place in the TV studios and edit pages of media, one should note that a section of visual media is sensationalizing the issues and that there is just a miniscule presence of Muslims in the language press and the small newspapers scattered all around.

Coming to liberal Hindus, Ghose is right that a large section of them raised their voices against the Modis and Togadias. But they do have an inherent advantage. The Hindu right wing has not yet come for secularists. Their slogan, *Pahle Kasai, Phir Isai, Uske baad Safai.* (First the Muslims, then Christians and than the Secularists) has given some respite to Hindu liberals. While it is true that the defeat in the last elections has broken the back of BJP, the Hindutva politics is going strong all around. In BJP ruled states it is ruling the roost and in other states it is spreading its poison through various mechanisms right under the nose of the secular government. Hindu name is a good deal of advantage for secular workers, at least for the time being.

There is a vicious circle, violence, intimidation, emotional alienation, emotional ghettoization, physical ghettoisation and the strengthening of the powers of Mullahs and Maulvis. I think there is good number of significant liberal Muslim friends making their valuable intervention all the time. The question is they are either ignored or bypassed at various levels giving the impression that they are not there. In the wake of Godhra train burning, many of them issued the statements condemning the heinous act. Media enamoured by the violence, which had already broken out, did not bother to publish these statements, this in turn was used as an excuse by the communalists that since 'they' did not condemn the violence enough, the violence went on worsening.

One can not pour water of reason on the upturned vessel. The scarred, intimidated, battered Muslim community will naturally fall prey to the fatwas of Maulanas and may have the tendency to ignore the Muslim liberal voices. The vicious circle can be broken, the community can be made more receptive to liberals, by punishing the guilty of riots, by rehabilitating the victims of riots, by ensuring that communal violence is curtailed, by breaking the emotional ghettoisation, by stopping the process of demonisation of minorities. Quite a tall order that!

16

A House for Shabana Azmi

One of the major contributions of Shabana Azmi in the arena of human rights was to work for the housing rights. It was ironical that the actor of such exceptional talents and the social activist with such dedication and commitment was denied the purchase of house, not once but twice in the locality of her choice. Voicing her pain she did comment in a TV show that Indian democracy is being unfair to the Muslims and recounted her experience. (August 2008). Apart from other people, a few from film community swooped on her, criticizing her statement as false, irresponsible, communal and what not! Even the actor of stature of Shatrughan Sinha criticized and admonished her.

One journalist from a prominent newspaper wanted to prove her wrong; he rang up few builders from his plush office and came to the conclusion that there is no discrimination in the selling of houses. One of the film persons stooped to the level of counting Azmi's houses, and said that if Muslims are denied they should be living on the streets! Such 'brilliant' logic in a sensitive socio political issue can only be expected from those who live in the ivory towers unaware of the social realities.

To begin with, it is a not an issue as to how many houses Azmi owns. The point is that she wished to buy a particular house and the broker told her she cannot get it as she is a Muslim. Muslims are not living on streets, but a large section of them have to live in ghettos, is known to all and sundry barring the one's wearing saffron glasses. There are colonies of Parsis and Jains and vegetarians who do not let those not belonging to their ilk to buy the flats in their colonies. This trend can neither be idolized nor be compared to the large social phenomenon of Muslims being denied housing, as these communities (Jains, Parsis) themselves are too tiny, their reasons and their inward looking tendencies are retrograde but having different socio-psychological reasons. The case of Muslims came more to the fore from the decades of nineties, after the communal politics has started threatening the democratic polity in a serious way, resulting in increase in the intensity of communal violence.

The Mumbai violence of 92-93 was followed by the internal migration of the battered minority. Many from minority were displaced or chose to shift to areas, which may be safer for them, Mumbra, Jogeshwari, Bhendi Bazar being the foremost. Incidentally the population of Mumbra before the violence was less than a lakh; today it is more than 7 lakhs! Similarly many a friends from minority community sold their houses in the mixed areas to shift to the Muslim majority areas, increasing the pressure on civic amenities in those areas.

In Gujarat also 'borders', 'Gaza Strips' have come up to supplement the 'mini Pakistans'. As the extent of myths, biases, stereotypes against minorities are going through the roof, the mental partitions are created and these partitions get converted in to the ones of brick and mortar. The communal partitions are the definite aftermath of the communal violence. In Gujarat, the victims of violence were not permitted to return into their own houses, even the written undertakings were demanded from the victims that they will not seek legal justice for whatever happened to them during the violence.

Today, six years after the Gujarat carnage, nearly five lakhs Muslims have to live in isolated ghettoes, and that too in abysmal situations. The extension of civic and other amenities to these areas is conspicuous by its absence. Water, sanitation, health, education, banking and other amenities and facilities are not reaching these areas. These internally displaced people are being helped only by conservative Muslim groups, who are competing with each other in increasing their area of influence amongst them. This is also becoming the zone with poverty, illiteracy, hunger, disease and misery. These conditions are worst in the whole of state. Since the state is shirking from its basic responsibilities of provision of infrastructure for social life, the Muslim fundamentalist groups are providing the same and are also having a field day in these areas. Who is to blame for this, a particular religion or the communal politics which not only resulted in the massive genocide but even now is dictating the state policies by abandoning the responsibilities of the victims of violence and others from minorities who have felt insecure and shifted or were made to shift in these areas!

The message of communal agenda manifested through violence and through creating difficult situation for minorities is now isolating them in most parts of India. So one can see the trajectory of violence as follows, it begins with pre violence biases, stereotypes, then violence, post violence neglect, isolation, ghettoization finally leading to partitioning of the national community at emotional and physical level.

The communal violence always polarizes the communities. In the initial phase till, say the seventies, the ghettoisation was minimal. From the decade of nineties, on one hand the communal violence has gone into higher gear, 'hate other' sentiments have worsened and this 'non sale of housing units to the Muslim minority' started becoming unwritten norm. What can be more ironical than the fact that a housing rights activist herself is denied the house, just because she carries a Muslim name!

The second irony is that the RSS politics, which is based on Brahminical values, codes of Manu in a modern form, the caste system in a subtle form, which disguises it by coining the term 'integral nationalism' is creating new ghettoes. The traditional Varna system created the ghettoes for untouchables. This social thinking, finding place in Brahiminical tones justified the exclusion of dalits from the villages. So separate housing for them. Typically Maharwadas (dalit ghettoes outside villages) in Maharashtra were the norm. Now the same thinking is creating new untouchables, and so barring few exceptions the average and even middle class Muslims have to look for housing in 'special areas'.

Critics of Azmi deliberately overlook the social reality being created due to the politics of communalism. Due to the rise of communal violence, due to the social common thinking which is becoming worse by the day, its worst culmination goes on to equate terrorism with Islam and Muslims.

Most of those involved with social work do come across such cases of discrimination time and again. No builder in majority, mixed area is going to put the hoarding that Muslims are not acceptable, it operates subtly. There have been sting operations also where this fact has been brought to light. Surely going by Azmi's experience, one only feels that now even a person totally seeped in Indianness, upholding human ethos with utmost sincerity, can also be denied house because of her Muslim name! Normally it should be a matter of honor that such an accomplished actor and committed rights activist lives in one's neighbouhood. If she is denied the house the only inference is that the communal partitions are near total.

Where is national integration? During freedom movement, the major task of father of the nation was to cultivate and highlight the national Indian community. That's how people of different religions joined the movement, shoulder to shoulder to build Indian nation, Indian community. What is going on with the rise of communalism is not merely the violence against this or that community; it is an assault on the values of Indian nationhood, on the values emerging from freedom movement. We do need a second freedom movement, freedom from communal mindset, freedom from the divisive politics in the name of religion?

SECTION–IV

AYODHYA, BABRI DEMOLITION AND THE AFTERMATH

17

Revisiting Babri

This 6th December (2007), it will be 15 years when Babri Mosque was demolished by the RSS combine in a well coordinated operation. When Babri was being demolished, it was not just demolition of a mosque and hurting the sentiments of largest minority in the country, it was also a blow to the democratic Indian ethos. It was a complex process and multiple factors were involved. Who is to be blamed for the whole episode needs to be understood in the perspective of the political factors unleashed by sectarian politics. Rahul Gandhi (March 2007) stated that had Gandhi family person been around, meaning especially Rajiv Gandhi; the Masjid could not have been demolished. It is one of the big ifs of history.

That the then Prime Minister Narasimha Rao aided the demolition is beyond any shadow of doubt. Some have gone to the extent of saying that RSS and Rao were in collusion, some have gone to the extent of saying that Rao was wearing Khaki shorts underneath his dhoti, like many other Congressmen, who are ideologically compromised and are in Congress mainly to enjoy the fruits of power. They have nothing whatsoever to do with the values which were the dominant part of Congress, the values which had lions share in leading the struggle for India's independence. While the political phenomena have their own logic, the values held by the leaders matter a lot. And it is here that Rao was aiding the RSS project of deepening the politics of hate in India.

Let us recapitulate the events as they unfolded in the decade of eighties in order to understand the process of demolition. It was mainly a reflection of the rising clout of RSS. Beginning with 1980s one witnessed the discomfort in the sections of middle class Hindus, who saw the 'disturbing' change in the form of dalits coming to the fore, the women coming out from the four walls of the house and making their presence felt in the social sphere. Both these sections of society, living as subordinate and subjugated groups for centuries saw the possibility of striving for equality, as enshrined in Indian constitution. This subtle but sure phenomenon of Indian society was unacceptable to the entrenched affluent middle classes. Their discomfort with this change came up in the form of opposition to reservations for dalits, Gujarat anti Dalit riots 1981 and Gujarat anti OBC/dalit riots of 1986, being just a manifestation of the same.

It is during this period that communal polarisation started coming up and the case of Shah Bano acted as a trigger for consolidation of the RSS supporters. This time Rajiv Gandhi's lack of grooming in the deeper understanding in politics, led him to bypass the court judgment. This in turn was used as a pretext for polarising of Hindu upper middle classes under the leadership of Sangh combine. This act of Rajiv Gandhi was 'successfully' propagated as appeasement of minorities and pseudo secularism. These formulations were lapped up by the dominant middle classes, who started responding more and more to Yatras and other VHP initiated campaigns. After playing this 'Muslim card' the immature Congress leadership decided to play the Hindu card by yielding to the pressure of BJP/VHP and company for getting the locks of Babri opened and later permitting Shilanyas for Ram temple. This pressure of Hindu rightwing was also discernible when Rajiv launched the campaign for 1989 elections on the plank of Ram Rajya. These came in handy to Hindu consolidation, which later got further boost when V.P. Singh, for his own compulsions, decided to implement Mandal. To bypass Mandal, BJP resorted to intensify Yatras, identity based politics. Keeping electoral compulsions in mind, BJP's politics revolved around Ram Temple as its central agenda. Incidentally Ram temple was no where on the agenda of BJP, which was harping on Gandhian socialism, till then. Its discovery that Lord Ram can be of great help in garnering votes led it to put most of its eggs in the basket of the campaign and conspiracy to destroy the Babri Mosque.

Ram temple issue became the symbol of assertion of affluent Hindutva politics in opposition to the democratic values. Identity, especially religious one, came up in a big way and waylaid the real issues of the poor and struggling majority of Hindus as well as other sections of society. As Congress, after Nehru's death, had already been open to heavy compromises on the issue of secularism, a fertile ground was already there starting from Indira Gandhi to undermine the secular values and to merely pay lip service to secularism, to use Muslims only as vote banks. It is under these circumstances that Narasimha Rao could enjoy his siesta when the shovels and trishuls of RSS combine were piercing Indian constitution, when Babri was being mauled by the saffron foot soldiers. These foot soldiers were indoctrinated by the ideology of Hate Muslim, Babar as the invader, the Muslims as destroyers of temples and killers of our mother cow. It was the most clever and wily move by Brahminical politics to use the downtrodden to hoist the saffron flag atop Babri and to herald the political assertion of *Manusmriti's* values in the garb of Hindu glory. While the leadership wanting to impose Hindu Rashtra, ignited and incited, the sections of poor community acted as the foot soldiers behaving as if under trance, under the spell of opium of religious identity.

Coming to the events, National Integration Council concerned with the events took the promise from UP chief minister Kalyan Singh of BJP that he is under constitutional obligation to protect the mosque. The same Kalyan Singh later called it as a matter of honor for him to have supervised the demolition. It is another matter that as a weather cock he kept changing his versions from glory to shame, depending on the political contingencies. He was strategically located as UP chief minister. State Government was responsible for supervising law and order. The RSS combine mobilized crowds, which also included some of those elements that were specially trained for the task of demolition. It is unlikely that the intelligence agencies would have missed it. Rao played the ideal foil to these designs and not only during demolition but also prior to that when the heat was building up, cleverly slept over the build up for demolition. He had the 'ideal' home minister in the form of Shankar Rao Chavan, who had no mean role in aiding the process of demolition.

While one does concede that probably Rao was the worst person to be in the seat of power, one also notes that with the rot in which Congress had been falling at ideological level, how much any body else could have been able to protect the mosque is not clear. Rajiv himself had blundered on various secular issues all through. Anti Sikh pogrom in Delhi, opening the doors of Masjid and Ram Shila Pujan, all these showed that irrespective of his intentions he had no ideological tools to protect the Babri. One may partly grant Rahul Gandhi's point, but one must look at the deeper societal processes and the will of the leadership to stand for values even at the cost of power. While currently there are some encouraging signs from the Congress top leadership on the issue of secularism, that's not only inadequate, it can not hold the nation together on the grounds of national community. Even Rahul Gandhi's own statement betrays the lack of political training amongst the leadership of Congress, in general and all non BJP parties in particular. While BJP has the heavy influx of RSS trained volunteers, the one's trained in the ideology of Hate other, in the ideology of Hindu nation disguised as nationalism.

Have the parties like Congress tried to introspect as to what are the ideas which its cadre is having? With the current ideological frame of its workers it cannot be trusted to uphold the torch of values of Gandhi-Nehru i.e. freedom movement. As such, Rahul Gandhi's statement grasps just a minor part of the problem. For the nation, question is not just of this or that leader but of the values of Indian Constitution. It is not just a matter of Rao versus Rajiv, but of democracy versus Hindu Rashtra. For the nation the issue is of undertaking political steps which should wean us away from identity politics to the issues of people, the issue between democratic nationalism and pseudo i.e. Hindu nationalism. The issue relates to address the concerns related to bread butter, shelter, employment, health and education and bypassing the agenda set by RSS, the agenda of temples and similar emotive campaigns.

18

Post Babri Demolition India

The Ramjanmbhoomi agitation launched during the late 1980s culminated in the demolition of a historic monument. This was immediately followed by massive violence in many a cities, more particularly in Mumbai. This was not just a demolition and violence; it was a major watershed in the politics of the country.

India had begun on the path to democracy and secularism, with a baggage of uncompleted land reforms and the grip of blind religiosity. Nehru, the architect of Modern India, put in his best efforts to steer the path of the country based on the values of Liberty, Equality and Fraternity. The large sections of Indian society started adopting rational thought process. This process was slow. The state machinery was slowly becoming secular, shedding its communal biases. The success of this process is debatable at one level. The media, education and other markers of thought process began to reflect the spirit of the values of freedom movement. The minorities had diverse attitude to the change.

Muslim minority was already in the shell and this shell started to loosen slowly. By 1980, from amongst Muslim minorities, large sections of youth started opting for modern education, professions and jobs despite their being discriminated against in Government and private jobs. The other minority, Christians on the whole were feeling safe.

The decade of 1980s threw up the challenges which started attacking these very processes. This was the beginning of agitations in the name of Ram Temple. Still the society maintained its secular stance for quite sometime. The opposition to secular values was muted and religion based nationalism was in the backyards of the society. Even with the beginning of this communal onslaught in the name of the Ram temple agitation, the threats were there but they could not affect the social fabric, as its foundations were very strong, the foundations lay down during freedom movement. The democratic-secular values of our society emerged from the biggest ever mass movement in the world, India's freedom movement. These were integral part of society and not a superficial graft.

Babri demolition changed it all. The very concept of secularism, Indian nationalism started being challenged. The communal forces, the Sangh Parivar, the organisations which are political children of RSS, BJP etc., started becoming more powerful and assertive. It paved the way for the ideas, sectarian one's, which were coming in the form of hatred for minorities. These perceptions started becoming more entrenched in the popular psyche. A section of media gradually turned sympathetic to Sangh Parivar ideas. It started becoming openly partisan to the values of religion based nationalism. The state machinery also gradually started becoming more biased against the minorities.

This demolition of the masjid was not only the destruction of the historic monument, a national asset, it was also an attack on Indian Constitution, attack on the plural heritage of India, the attack on India's diverse cultural expressions. The attack came as a cover for bringing forward the political values which had their origin from the feudal sections of the society, the values of birth based hierarchy of caste and gender. Since these retrograde values were laced in the language of religion, they gained some respectability in the sections of society. It encouraged blind religiosity which helped the status quo, which stood opposed to the slow but sure process of caste and gender equality, which was an accompaniment of freedom movement and which got a boost after India became Independent.

The dominant discourse in the society easily started accepting that religion is the primary and main marker of the rule of the kings and it is the main point of differentiation in the communities today. This also asserted that Muslims and Christians are foreigners, and have no right to live here in this country. The main social thinking started accepting that religion rather than poverty and illiteracy are the cause of population rise; the other myths about minorities also became part of the 'popular perceptions' at larger scale.

The state policies became much more biased against the minorities, due to the pressure from right wing. Along with this began the process of suppression of dalit rights, either by directly attacking them or by co-opting them through cultural and social mechanisms. The Adivasis were wooed in the form of Ghar Vapasi, their struggle for land rights were blunted by the cultural and religious manipulation like Shabri Kumbh and the work of Swamis of the ilk of Laxmandnand or Aseemanand or Asaram Bapu.

The attitude of social authorities towards minorities gradually started becoming like treating them as step citizens, paving the way for relegating them to second class citizens. No part of state machinery remained free from this change in the gear of state policies. Gradually two sets of norms and attitudes started becoming rooted, one for the affluent and powerful of the majority community and the other for the minorities. The goal of communal forces to relegate minorities to 'second class citizenship' started being actualized.

Even section of judiciary spelt that Hindu religious books should be treated like Indian national books. The parties which should have been secular got tilted subtly in the communal direction. The parties like left did not pay any attention to the need for affirmative action for weaker sections of society, while the main party, Congress, kept adopting opportunist stance more often than before.

The plight of minorities started worsening by the day. Economically, while the Muslim minorities as a whole were never 'well to do', majority of them being artisans, poor peasants and the like, now their situation started worsening fast. Their percentage in jobs, which was already very low, started dipping low further. Their political representation started declining massively. Due to insecurity and lack of equity they felt threatened and resorted more to the minority identity. The hold of conservative elements started increasing due to these circumstances. The ghettoes of minorities started going up and the emotional barriers between the communities started taking the shape of walls of brick and mortar.

There is a wide spectrum in this divisive politics also. While on one side the situation in states like Gujarat is to the extreme in other states there are different shades of divisiveness. The demolition has affected each and every aspect of our political, social and economic life.

The biggest damage inflicted by this demolition has been to the plural, syncretic, mixed traditions of India. We had a thick interaction of Hindus and Muslims in all fields of culture, music, literature, architecture, food habits and religious traditions. The medieval period was most instrumental in bringing together the two communities at all the levels. The society at large and different communities preserved their rich interaction through ages. Now that's something which is being openly attacked by conservative elements from both the sides. Muslim followers of Bhakti tradition are being discouraged and a section of Hindus is shunning the rich heritage which they were living all this time.

The current expression of social and political arena is so different from the decade of 1950s to 1970s in particular. It is high time that those respecting the culture and traditions of India, during the medieval period or during the period of freedom movement need to wake up try to restore the democratic, plural values in all spheres, from the political, legal, bureaucratic and social-religious level. With Liberhan Commission Report, the original understanding as to who demolished the Masjid and who wants to attack Indian Constitution, time and over again stands reconfirmed. We do need to reconstruct the damaged edifice of polity and culture.

19

Bridging the Divides : Setback to Amity Initiatives in Ayodhya

In the otherwise dismal scenario of communal amity one good initiative by Sant Gyandas of Hanuman Gardhi, the biggest temple of Ayodhya, had come as a whip of fresh air. Few years ago he invited the local Muslims for Roza iftar in the temple premises. He repeated it the next year as well. Meanwhile to match these sentiments one Babu Bhai from Muslim community took the initiative of Hanuman Chalisa recital on Id Milan. One Madhuban Das, not to be left behind, went on to distribute Ram Rahim Chadars to people. The Muslim community which earlier in the wake of the proposed Kar Seva was planning to abandon Ayodhya out of fear felt reassured and stayed on. Under the influence of VHP a section of Hanuman Garhi mahants filed a case in the court that such Roza Iftar is against the by laws of the temple, and court ruled in their favour. Also, many a VHP activists sat on a Dharna in front of Hanuman Garhi to oppose the Muslims entry into the temple premises for the Roza Iftar party.

What is the worth of efforts of the likes of Mahant Gyan Das or various other groups who are trying to bring different religious communities together through such festive occasions, through mutual respect for each other's sentiments?

A thriving democracy, needs the principles of Liberty, Equality and Fraternity (community) as the base of its existence. In India we have seen mauling of these values under the impact of a politics, which derives its legitimacy from the religious identity of the people. With rising pitch of communal violence, the physical and emotional polarization of communities along religious lines has been taking place. In places like Mumbai, post 92-93 the Muslim dominated areas have come to be called a 'Mini Pakistan', in Ahmedabad the Muslim majority area is called, 'border' and one hears that Muslim localities are also being called as Gaza Strip. Post 92-93 Mumbai violence, a huge chunk of Muslim population living in mixed localities shifted to places like Mumbra and Jogeshwari, which are becoming exclusive Muslim areas. Similarly the builders in previously mixed areas are refusing to sell the housing units to minorities. In places like Gujarat the economic boycott of Muslim community persists in substantial chunk of places.

One was aghast to know about the conversation of two Hindu women, in Anand; Gujarat, when one said that she lives in a good and clean locality, the other one went on to say that she lives probably in a better area as there are no Muslims at all in her area. It is common place to hear such things like 'Oh one is good despite being a Muslim', in Gujarat.

On Navaratri festival one was pained to hear that in Indore, the local VHP put a ban on the entry of Muslim youth in the Garba dance festival, on the grounds that Muslim youth will lure away Hindu girls, 'our girls'. Those using religion on the chessboard of politics are working overtime at a deep societal level to create a wedge between the communities. At the same time the propaganda is promoted to the effect that we the Hindus go even to the Sufi Dargahs but the Muslims do not come to our temples. This has been a frequent question fielded in the National integration workshops conducted by many of us. The polarisation along religious lines strengthens the communal forces; the ghettoisation of minorities strengthens the fanatics of that community and gives a free run to the Mullahs to dish out their fatwa's on the community. And the vicious circle begins.

The democratic nation state can only be based on the values of Liberty, Equality and Fraternity (community). The national community is the basic pillar of the democracy. The country fragmented on the lines of religion or caste can not stay together, cannot progress. As such also most of the times the pluralism and diversity are a matter of celebration till the vested political designs step in. India's rich syncretic traditions have seen the boundaries between religions as the point of meeting of the people and not as the point of separation. The interaction seeps into all aspects of social life, religion being one major component of that. It is keeping this in mind that Dara Shikoh, who was a scholar of

Persian and Sanskrit, went on to write in his book *Majma ul Baharain* that India is a great ocean, the meeting point of two seas, Hinduism and Islam. The same is manifested in our religious traditions (Bhakti and Sufi), in our food, dress, architecture, music, dance, literature and what have you. This is what was envisaged by founding fathers of our nation as the ground on which India was to stand. This was the base of our national movement. This was in contrast to the ideas of communal stream, Muslim League (Urdu, Muslim, Pakistan) and Hindu Mahasabha-RSS (Hindi, Hindu Hindustan). The latter tendencies were rejected by the freedom movement, by the people of India.

With ascendance of Hindu right, the exclusivist politics based on dominant culture is being asserted and brought to the fore. The present trend of polarisation, ghettoization is seriously undermining the National integration. It will breed in to divisive trends in sections of society. We need to choose as to in which direction we have to go, direction of the efforts like that of Mahant Gyandas which can bring the communities together, or in the direction of VHP associates who under one or the other pretext want to exercise the exclusionist politics. The Mahant, rather than getting discouraged by the court ruling has decided to take out Ram-Rahim Yatra, which surely is the best way to continue his earlier initiative at Hanuman Garhi. One can just compliment the efforts of Mahant Gyandas, Babu Bhai and their likes and hope that their tribe increases.

20

Ram and Allah as Good Neighbours

The leak and tabling of Liberhan Commission Report created a big turmoil in the country. While most of the sides have been shouting hoarse about their own position on the issue, not much has been talked about the future solution of this vexed problem.

We recall that the mosque built by Mir Baqui around five centuries ago has been deliberately dragged into the controversy. At the time of Independence it was a mosque, no political party had claimed anything to the contrary. As per the understanding in the Constitution, the status of 1947 was to be maintained in cases of places of worship. The installation of Ram Lalla idols by deceit in midnight of 22nd Jan 1949 sowed the seeds of controversy. Later in 1975 the dispute between two local groups was taken up by Vishwa Hindu Parishad and in 1989, BJP decided to make a political issue out of it. The tragic demolition and the making of makeshift Ram temple there have added new dimensions to the issue.

It is around this issue that Hindu and Muslim communalists raised the emotional pitch and the tragedies which followed, the demolition, the post demolition communal violence and communalization, polarization of society along religious lines are too well known by now. The court case regarding the same is dragging from last several years without any outcome so far.

Where do we go from here? Do we let this sore to continue on the body politic of the nation? This may act as the trouble spot for the future. It is time that we look at all the aspects of the issue and try to bring a peaceful solution to the issue.

The first step in the issue is to realize that the communal forces from both communities have claimed that they represent the community and so they will decide on behalf of Hindus or Muslims respectively. The fact of the matter and, this has been confirmed by Liberhan Commission report, is that these communal groups neither represent the community nor reflect the opinion of the communities as a whole. It is imperative that we look forward to the liberal sections, leadership from these communities to come forward and talk in the language of reconciliation. The liberal sections are those who have so far been ignored, but they are the one's who have talked of peace and accommodation. The election results have also shown that those claiming to represent the aspirations of a particular community have been routed in popular elections. The elected representatives of the area have a major role to play in bringing the consensus. We cannot undo the past but we can definitely chart a peaceful path for future. The peaceful talks between these sections along with the local people of Ayodhya are the central core for solution.

The people of Ayodhya have been the major victims of the demolition and other offshoots of the dispute. What they think should be done at the site has to be taken seriously. They have to be taken on board along with the liberal leadership of the communities. The most amicable solution has to veer around respecting Ram and Allah both. Both temple and mosque can be accommodated in the area, with equal importance and respect.

Along with temple and mosque in the same spot we need to bring up a small museum dedicated to the great tradition of Ayodhya. Ayodhya has not only been popular for Lord Ram, but it had also been a place for Buddhists and also people of other faiths as well. It has been a sort of 'No War zone' (A- no, Yudhya- War, Ayodhya-A no war zone), and that spirit has to be cultivated all around. The emotive and divisive appeals need to be rejected by the nation as a whole. In that light the museum-memorial includes material related to syncretic traditions, of saints who were followed by Muslims and Hindus both, of Sufis who again were respected by Hindus and Muslims both? While the history has been made to degenerate into hoarse shouting, a cool reasoned archeological based understanding should help us to go further. The negotiations between the communities have to be encouraged to the last.

The second line of action has to relate to the court verdict. The court verdict should be final for all of us. The formulation that faith will decide the birth place of the Lord has no place in a society governed by law and reason. The community leaders must give undertaking to respect the court verdict and act accordingly. Those not having faith in the courts cannot be part of the process of reconciliation as reconciliation has to be done in the framework of Indian Constitution. We have invested too much in this issue and it is time that not only this but even other such issues are not given any importance to ensure that the country, nation, can focus on the issues related to bread, butter, shelter, employment and health.

21

Liberhan Commission Report: Better Late than Never

The leakage and subsequent tabling of Liberhan Commission report on Babri demolition has brought forward lot of known things, lots of guesses have been confirmed and the truth behind those have been ratified and well documented. It's true that nothing startlingly new has come out, nevertheless Liberhan has been able to put together with meticulous care, evidence for the demolition with exactitude. This is a contribution as we know that when demolition was going on the Kar Sevaks had targeted the journalists, the photographers and destroyed most of the evidence on the spot. One is very critical of the inexcusable delay, the 48 extensions and the exonerating of Narasimha Rao in the whole episode. Another weak spot of the report is the part on recommendations, with so many observations and conclusions one could have given recommendations to ensure that the law of the land is applied properly and the guilty are given suitable punishment. That notwithstanding, the conclusions of the Commission are a lesson for the whole nation.

A short background of the dispute needs to be recapitulated. Babri mosque is nearly a five century old structure, built by Babar's General Mir Baqui. The history of this got mired in controversy over a period of time. The seeds of controversy were sown by British in pursuance of their policy of 'divide and rule', and their introduction of Communal Historiography. The British Official Mrs. A.F. Beeveridge translated *Babarnama*, and when the reference to the Ayodhya Mosque came, she put a baseless foot note that there might have been a temple there, before the mosque was built. This became the seed which later blew up into a major controversy. The concoction about its being the place of birth of Ram came up from the communal thinking. In pursuance of that, Ram Lalla idols were installed, in the mosque by deceit on the night of 22nd January 1949. Till that time Namaz (prayer by Muslims) was regularly performed. After this the Jan Sangh supporter, District Magistrate, K.K. Nayyar got the mosque locked and namaz was stopped, after that. Sensing trouble Pandit Nehru wrote to the UP Chief Minister G.B. Pant to get the idols evacuated. Somehow that was not done. K.K. Nayyar after his retirement from Government service contested elections on Jana Sangh, BJP predecessor, ticket for Lok Sabha.

The matter remained frozen as a court dispute between the Akhara of Mahant Ramchandra Das and the Wakf board. After 1975 Vishwa Hindu Parishad took up the matter of 'Liberation of Ram Janmbhoomi, Temple'. In response the Muslim groups formed All India Babri Masjid Action Committee. From the decade of 1980 due to various social changes, a section of middle class in particular, started veering round VHP and the programmes led by VHP for Ram Temple started getting more response. Due to rising social pressure, Rajiv Gandhi got the locks of masjid opened and Shilanyas was performed. From 1989 Lal Krishna Advani of BJP took up the issue as the main agenda of BJP. Declaration of Mandal Commission for OBCs was met with the response of intensification of Ram Temple agitation. Advani's Rath Yatras started getting more aggressive after this point of time.

The Kar Seva which was to take place on the 6th December 1992 was promised to be a symbolic one. Atal Bihari Vajpayee promised so in the meeting of National Integration Council (NIC). Kalyan Singh promised to NIC, and gave affidavits to Supreme Court that Masjid will be protected. But he also deceived and ensured that the police and other paramilitary forces don't act, the roads to Ayodhya were blocked. Once the masjid started falling Kalyan Singh sought the advice of Advani, about resigning. Advani advised him to hold on till the whole masjid is demolished.

About demolition, whatever reports came out showed that the rehearsal of demolition was performed one day in advance. In this rehearsal all the big instruments for breaking the mosque, the ropes, shovels and other implements were there in place. On the day of demolition only trained workers were allowed to go in, this was manned by certain people. These trained kar sevaks were wearing saffron bandana. They not only demolished the mosque with military precision but also removed Ram Lalla idols and cash box before the demolition process began. Later they also built the make shift temple. Many of these things were vaguely reported as a section of Kar Sevaks was given instructions by the central coordinator to beat up the journalists and destroy all photographic-video evidence.

It is in this light that we need to look at the Commission report. Its first conclusion is that it was a well coordinated and planned action, 'Joint common enterprise' as characterised by Liberhan. It was done with military precision. This is contrary to the propaganda that it was an outburst of spontaneous anger of people, who were denied their logical claim for the temple at the place of birth of their lord. Commission points out that the whole exercise was not a mass supported one; those mobilised and behind the demolition were the Sangh Parivar supporters, mobilised from all over by well planned exercise. In this dastardly act, BJP, VHP, Bajrang Dal, Rashtra Sevika Samiti and other progeny of RSS was involved. RSS played the role of coordinating their attack. So far we do know that most of the top level leadership of these organizations comes from the RSS trained swayamsevaks, barring the top leadership of Rashtra Sevika Samiti, as women are not allowed to be part of RSS. All this stands confirmed with this report. RSS top brass was doing the central coordination as per the report. This report also confirms the analysis of scholars/ activists about the relationship between RSS and its progeny.

So apparently, there were three lakh followers of RSS in Ayodhya but the core job was done by a select group, well trained for the purpose. It also tells us the secretive and opaque nature of RSS, which may be capable of doing sinister things, but its role does not become apparent as investigations don't go to that level and the marginal organisations, which any way are front organisations implementing RSS agenda, are blamed and the real organisation remains insulated from the blame of the act well planned by it.

Liberhan Commission concludes, "I conclude that the RSS, BJP, VHP, Shiv Sena and their office bearers as named in this report, in connivance with Kalyan Singh, the then Chief Minister of U.P., entered into a Joint Common Enterprise for the purpose of demolition of the disputed structure and the construction of the temple in its place. They practiced intermingling of religion with politics as a well thought out act to subvert democracy."

Lot of shock is being expressed about the Commission blaming

Vajpayee also. It is generally presumed that he was above such issues and machinations. It seems such an image was also deliberately cultivated to woo the liberal sections of society. As such Vajpayee did speak in the meeting in Kanpur on 5th December, which gives inkling that he knew the whole game. He stated that he does not know what will happen the next day. He also said that the land where Babri Mosque is located will have to be flattened. He was playing his assigned role, and was waiting in Lucknow to join the Kar Seva the next day. Later he said that he has been asked to return to Delhi. VHP has gone on record to say that Vajpayee was part of the Ayodhya issue.

Clearly he was to take care of the national scene and protect the criminals of demolition by holding fort in Delhi. Later he did protest when action was taken against Advani and Co., who were present at the site of demolition. After demolition Vajpayee was the one who began by saying that we are sorry to the nation but later on took an aggressive stance to justify the demolition by saying, 'this is what happens when the sentiments of people are not respected'. One knows that the so called sentiments are the sentiments of RSS followers who by that time had smelt that the path to power is paved by the communalisation of social space by misusing the Hindu traditions. What an irony, the whole game of power was played in the name of Lord Ram, the one who renounced power to respect the promise given by his father to one of his wives!

The Commission does well by pointing out the so called movement for Ram Temple was not a movement of average people as it was restricted to the followers of Sangh Parivar only. Ordinary people had no role in the same. Even the role of Muslim leadership has been correctly criticized when Liberhan says that Muslim leadership failed those whom it is supposed to work for.

The demolition and aftermath led to severe communalisation of society. RSS is the central player in the game of communalisation of society. Similarly the so called Muslim leadership has been shown to be out of sync with sentiments and needs of average Muslims.

There is enough to criticize the delay, exonerating of Narasimha Rao etc., of the Commission, but we don't have to throw the precious baby with the bath tub, if the water around is murky.

SECTION–V

GUJARAT: MUSLIMS AS SECOND CLASS CITIZENS

22

Godhra's Truth

Manufacturing Explanations for Communal Agenda

Half an hour after the burning of Sabaramti Express's S-6 coach on 27th Feb. 2002, Gujarat Chief Minister Narendra Modi made a definitive statement that the burning of the coach has been the handiwork of local Muslims in collaboration with the Pakistan's ISI and the International terrorism. This was followed by a prompted 'reaction' to the 'action' (Every action has equal and opposite reaction, Newton quoted by Modi), the massive Gujarat carnage in which apart from the loss of property two thousand Muslims lost their lives. Around two and a half years after the tragic incident, Justice U.C. Bannerjee came out with the truth of Godhra. According to the interim report of this Commission this tragedy was a mere accident and was not a preplanned one as claimed by Narendra Modi and the RSS and its progeny.

Immediately after the release of this report BJP spokesperson Arun Jaitley stated that this report is meant to cover up the criminals behind this crime, it is to appease the Muslim community. As such one can expect such a reaction from Hindus. How else they cover up their own acts of commission. It is nothing new to come out with such distractions from the content and analysis of the reports of riots. One knows that most of the inquiry commission reports have indicted RSS progeny for being the main players in these riots, it is not for nothing that a close cousin of this progeny Shiv Sena, which as per the meticulously investigated Shri Krishna report, was the major player in the anti Muslim pogrom in Mumbai riots in 92-93, came out with a defense by saying that this report is 'Anti Hindu'. There is no analysis and no rebutting of the charges. Just a rhetorical diversion from the crux of the matter. Jaitley operating on the same wavelength, rather then analyzing the weakness of the report comes out with a subtle self defense of his party.

Immediately after the train burning, Jayanti Ravi, the collector of Godhra, who knew better, said that there is no evidence of the pre-planned conspiracy, but was overruled by Modi, who calculated in a shrewd way how to use this incident as a pretext to unleash anti Muslim carnage to consolidate his hold on the levers of power, to march towards 'Hindu nation in one state-Gujarat.' All the norms which were needed to be followed were thrown overboard and here the NDA ally of BJP played as per the script of RSS. As per the Railways Act all major accidents have to be investigated. Sidetracking this norm the question of investigating the accident was totally ignored, the evidences contrary to 'Modi Expalnation' were put under the carpet.

Haren Pandya, the then Home minister of Gujarat, for reasons best known to him spilled the beans by telling the Citizens Tribunal that Modi in a meeting of top officials of the State on the same day told all involved with controlling law and order that the revenge of Godhra will be taken by Hindus and we should sit back and let the things take their own course, democratic laws can be put in the deep freeze. What followed was beyond the worst fears, loss of lives; violation of women; loss of property and to cap it all the semi-permanent divide between the Hindu and Muslim communities, the intensification of the process of Ghettoisation of minorities.

Modi was thoroughly backed up and defended through and through by other Swayamsevaks who were supposed to ensure that states behave as per the Indian Constitution. The union home minister Advani certified that Modi's handling of the riots is exemplary and the Prime Minister Vajpayee, while shedding crocodile tears went on to say 'but who lit the fire?' Citizen's tribunal did come to the conclusion that there was no preplanned conspiracy. no definitive evidence of involvement of Muslims, Muslim organizations, of ISI and International terrorirism could be produced by Modi. He took just half and hour to come to the conclusion, but despite the lag of years he has not been able to produce any evidence. He hid behind the opaqueness of POTA and imprisoned over two hundered Muslim, without any evidence.

The aggressive propaganda of RSS progeny made a large section of civil society to believe what was being dished out by them was the truth. A large section of social workers doubted this but in the din of hysteria produced they remained a marginal voice. Since Modi had adorned the cloak of national security, those put behind the bars were left unattended with total violation of their democratic rights and civic rights. How does one go about in the society in such situations? The garb of national security is a convenient ploy to suppress the voice of reason. BJP used the bogey terrorism to the hilt, it showed the burnt coach of Sabarmati express while fishing for votes in the rivers of blood to come back to power with a huge majority due to the polarization created by the violence and the way propaganda was dished out by the section of media.

The argument that the report is just for electoral purposes will not wash. No doubt a politician like Lalu may try to get benefit out of this, but the real point is the defense of truth, the suffering of those who have been jailed under POTA, those who have lost their lives in the Gujarat carnage! How long will the society give sanction to the imprisonment of the innocents one's who were supposed to have burnt the coach, will they be released immediately? Will they be compensated for the false implication which they have suffered in the past? That's the real question for the large number of citizens of India?

23

Saviour or Devourer: BJP Ruled Gujarat State's Naked 'Glory'

In the worst ever communal flare up Gujarat has lost over 2000 of its citizen's, over 3000 crores worth of social wealth, most of it belonging to Muslims, and has witnessed the decimation of religious places, Dargah's and Masjids. It is not for the first time that we have seen state not playing partisan role but here the matters are qualitatively different. The demand that state administration should be transparent has been fulfilled in the wrong direction, the participation, compliance and encouragement of state personnel in supporting the rioters was transparent and no alibis were used for breaking the laws, in twisting the meanings of the clauses. The state apparatus was a mighty tool in the hands of the pogrom conductors coming from the stable of Sangh Parivar.

To begin with one of the civil servants, Harsh Mander was so aghast with the role of his peers and colleagues from the administrative services that he could not overcome his disgust and resigned from the administrative service. Then 'Super Cop' Julio Reibero was equally shamed but his colleagues in the Khakis who were supposed to be manning the 'riot control' were behaving in a way that it was difficult to distinguish the rioters from the one's who are supposed to control the riots. One also recalls many a ministers operating from the police control rooms and directing the anti-minority operations. Most of the human rights reports like Human Rights watch report stated that State officials of Gujarat, India were directly involved in the killings of hundreds of Muslims since February 27 and are now engineering a massive cover-up of the state's role in the violence. When approached many of the police officials told the approaching victims that we have no orders to protect you. (http://hrw.org/reports/2002/

india). One of the researchers from South Asia Watch pointed out that what happened in Gujarat was not a spontaneous uprising; it was a carefully orchestrated attack against Muslims. And that the attacks were planned in advance and organised with extensive participation of the police and state government officials.

The seventy-five-page report from the Human Rights watch documents some of the attacks against the Muslims and concludes that the police were directly implicated in nearly all the attacks against Muslims. The standard response was 'We Have No Orders to Save You': While in some cases they were passive observers in other instances the police officials led the charge of murderous mobs, aiming and firing at Muslims who got in the way. At times, on the pretext of offering assistance, some police officers led the victims directly into the hands of their killers. And the phone calls made to the police and other support agencies did not bring in the dutiful responses.

The acme of the degeneration of the duties of the state has been reached. When Hitler was on rampage against the Jews, other weaker sections of society, and against those who were opposed to his policies, it was State, which implemented the programme of annihilation of the Jews and others. Probably the hairs breadth difference still lies between what we witnessed in Gujarat and what happened in Hitler's Germany. Here though the Sangh Parivar is controlling the state apparatus it itself is not the state apparatus.

The trajectory of communal violence has come a long way since they first began in the last decade of 19th Century. These riots provoked by the communal politics (Muslim and Hindu both) came up in response as a reaction against the rise of Secular Indian National Congress (INC). British had a two-pronged strategy as far as the communal politics was concerned. At the political level they did promote the communal outfits of Muslims and Hindus both to pursue their policy of Divide and Rule. At the level of communal violence they were fairly neutral. After independence before seeing the role of state in Communal violence as such we must remember that due to the Partition tragedy most of the Muslim communal elements had left for Pakistan and Muslim League's impact became very weak. Right since the beginning the Hindu Communalists, in addition to having their own outfits

(Hindu Mahasabha and RSS) had also infiltrated in the INC. Also the trained Swayamsevaks of RSS started entering all the wings of state machinery right from the beginning. One notable example is that of district magistrate of Ayodhya, K.K. Nayyar in late forties, who came forward in helping RSS in laying the foundation of a dispute of Babri Mosque. Such characters were there in all the walks of administrative machinery, media and the armed forces.

In most of the riots, which have pained us since the first Jabalpur riot of 1962 one sees a common pattern. While the bureaucracy soft peddles the offence of wings of RSS, police plays the partisan role. While the administrative machine is 'sympathetic, to the 'Hindu sentiments' (read Hindu Communal politics), the communalization of police has been blatant. There are instances (Meerut-Malyan, 1987) where the Provincial Armed Constabulary lined up around 300 Muslims besides the canal and shot them so that the bodies get disposed off in the canal. There are instances (Bhagalpur 1989) where the police along with the rioters killed 180 Muslims, buried them in a paddy field on which cauliflower was grown. Most of the inquiry commission reports have shown the partisan role of police in the riots. The Shri Krishna Commission also indicted the police especially its Addl. Commissioner R.D. Tyagi for his shooting of the innocents in the Suleman Bakery.

One also recalls the communal virus seeping in the various state sponsored institutions, right under the nose of the Government which is supposed to be protector of secular values as per the Constitution. After the demolition of Babri Mosque, Lal Bahadur Shastri Academy students, the future administrators etc., celebrated the event with unusual gusto.

So the rot is set all around. And its qualitative transformation in the Gujarat is a dangerous portent to the values, which emerged from the Indian Freedom struggle and got enshrined in the India Constitution. Where did the things go wrong? Why the infiltration of RSS Swayamsevaks in state machinery could not be checked? Why did the Nation adopt a complacent attitude towards the proliferation of communal virus in the police stations and other offices? Did most of us think this 'outdated' ideology will die its natural death and does not deserve to be fought in a proactive way? We need to answer all these if we want to restore the democratic ethos and secular values in our political and social life. What needs to be done to stem the rot, the polity is seriously ill. A serious effort and careful nurturing of values is more than called for to promote the plural democracy which celebrates differences. What matters at political level is not one's religion but one's citizenship, which is supreme and non-negotiable.

24

Erosion of Democratic Norms: A Case of Modi

Current Gujarat elections, irrespective of their results, will remain etched in the memory of the nation for wrong reasons. Gujarat witnessed the burning of Sabarmati express at Godhra in Feb 2002. The carnage which followed this train accident claimed the lives of thousands of innocents and simultaneously polarised Gujarat along religious lines. The process of ghettoisation of Muslims and the fear of minorities constructed in the minds of majority community are staring in our face. At the same time the threads of democratic nationalism, national integration are breaking rapidly. While various citizens' inquiry reports did point out the pre-planned nature of the pogrom and the role of RSS combine led by Modi in the carnage, we could all see the same for ourselves thanks to the Tehelka Sting Operation expose. The consequent polarization led to the victory of the leader of the carnage back to power in the elections which took place a bit later. In the elections of 2002, the main opposition party, Congress did not gather strength to take on Modi with full vigour. One of the reasons was that Modi deflected the criticism directed against him and against RSS combine as the insult to 5 crore Gujaratis, and his assertion was well received in a section of society.

The Tehelka sting showed some of the perpetrators boasting about their crimes in front of the camera, and this made most of the people realize once again the gravity of the crime. Now most of the society got a direct feel of what had happened, who did it. Society also registered that the reports of citizens groups were on the dot in pinpointing the malaise of Gujarat society. It was in this background that Sonia Gandhi in her election campaign called the Modi led BJP as the merchants of death. Modi realised that the truth is being said after all, and tried to raise the communal and criminal sentiments by justifying the extra judicial killing of Soharabuddin, who was killed in a fake encounter by the police.

The ploy was that since a section of society has been communalized enough, the illegal act of killing someone will get him sympathy votes. He took 'credit' for this 'bravery' of killing of Soharabuddin and his wife. Human rights workers raised the issue of Modi communalizing and criminalizing the people's mindset. And as is his won't, he presented the criticism against him as the insult of people of Gujarat, of Gujarat itself!

Usual damage control exercises unrolled, he has been quoted out of context, he does not justify the extra judicial killings etc. But the damage was done and election commission took a serous note of it. The frail nature of legal mechanism, as to how a democratically elected chief minister, takes oath in the name of constitution, then openly incites the public and tries to bask in the 'glory' of this illegal act done by state machinery, is there for all to see.

The larger issue of democratic norms, morality and polity are put at the backburner, with the leaders doing their electoral arithmetic of what will help them more in getting the power. Now the issue can be discussed at the level of legalities and also at the level of electoral arithmetic. All these do have their importance but one also needs to be concerned about the deeper and broader issues related to our constitution, as to what is happening to the values of democracy enshrined in our constitution?

In Gujarat the legal norms have been put aside in matters of rehabilitation and in the post violence justice. In 'regular' life patterns, now a section of Muslims are willing to bend on their knees to survive, willing to 'forgive' unilaterally, while no body is caring to ask for their forgiveness. The 'charisma' of Modi is on the rise. He was keeping the communal card, under wraps till the word Merchants of death was hurled upon him. And then he unraveled his communal face with full force just before the polling. All this sounds so unusual but we are becoming used to the prevalence of these things. Does it ring familiar to something which happened in history? While there are lot of differences from what happened in Germany some similarities are too glaring.

The targeting of minorities, the total abolition of democratic space, the social common sense directed against the minorities and secularists, and consensus built around the fascist state are very similar. 'Kill them, kill them' is what Modi could easily extract from the section of crowd for Soharabuddin. What distinguishes Gujarat from the Germany's state of affairs in 30s and 40s of last century is that here the process is taking place at a slower pace and the same process is on with different intensities in different states of the country. So can we use the term Chronic Fascism in Gujarat in contrast to acute fascism of Germany. Whole of Germany was totally gripped by this politics, while in India Gujarat is worst but all the same in other states also this fascism is strangulating democratic space, though with different degrees of intensity. The biggest similarity is the 'successes' of a fascist party, which in Germany took the pretext of race and here it is wearing the garb of religion. Interestingly earlier and even now the fascist parties are using the democratic space to come to power, to precisely abolish the same in due course.

During last two and a half decades the rise of right wing politics has taken place on the pretext of Hinduism, while it has nothing to do with the humane streams of Hinduism. It claims to be for Hindus, while majority of Hindus have become victim of this intimidating politics. It reflects the state of erosion of our democratic norms and gradual strengthening of the forces which do talk about democracy but are deeply wedded to the RSS, the organisation which is opposed to democracy and wants to bring in a Hindu nation. That the concept of Hindu nation is for Hindus, is just a pretext. It essentially aims to abolish the values of liberty equality and fraternity and strengthens the hold of section of Hindus, the elite, males, on the whole society. The trick is the agenda of a small dominant section of society has been propagated as being for all Hindus.

Coming to Gujarat, one can clearly make out that there is a slow but dangerous march towards a fascist state. The classical fascism which one witnessed in Germany and Italy in the early decades of last century was marked by the targeting of minorities, of social rights groups/parties and at the same time doing away with all democratic norms. It created a terrorizing atmosphere, where the handful ruled the roost with the charisma of leader like Hitler, who swayed the people, worked and he got the anti democratic things accepted by people in the initial part of the rule, till Germany itself collapsed under the weight of the fascist boots. Such politics does discover and project a single charismatic leader, in Germany it was Hitler, in Gujarat it is Modi. Incidentally RSS nationalism also took lot of inspiration from Hitler's Nationalism, "German national pride has now become the topic of the day. To keep up the purity of nation and its culture, Germany shocked the world by her purging the country of Semitic races-The Jews. National pride at its highest has been manifested here. Germany has also shown how neigh impossible it is for races and cultures, having differences going to the root, to be assimilated into one united whole, a good lesson for us in Hindustan to learn and profit by." (We or Our nationhood Defined, 1938)

The politics of RSS combine has cleverly adopted itself to the Indian situation and has gone on to create a fear of the miniscule minority. It is quite similar to Hitler creating a phobia against Jews, holding them responsible for the plight of Germany, and using that as the center of his policies terrorizing the whole nation into submission to the agenda of fascism, abolition of the concept of rights, something which is the life and breath of democracy, something which is a shield for the average people to survive. While a large section of Gujarat, Minorities, dalits, adivasis and women are suffering, the middle and affluent classes are able to get their way through the agenda of vibrant Gujarat!

The analogy does not end here. The terrorizing atmosphere created in Gujarat does remind us of the status of minorities. Now the large sections of minorities feel that they have been relegated to the second class citizenship status. Their insecurity is the index of our democratic ethos. It is correctly pointed out that if you want to see the state of health of democracy, have a look at the status of its minorities!

SECTION–VI

MUSLIM WOMEN: DOUBLE VICTIMS

25

Communal Ideology and Violence Against Women

In many a third world countries in the name of religion, communal politics is having a field day. One of the major components of communal politics is the perpetuation of patriarchal values. By patriarchal norms we mean a value system in which men have control over the lives of women. With secularisation process, which began the world over from 18th Century onwards, a ground has been laid whereby the patriarchy can be questioned and challenged. In many a third world countries reaction to secularisation process (which stands for the values of Liberty, Equality and Fraternity) has occurred in the form of rise of communal and fundamentalist movements. These movements, which initially found their support base amongst the declining Feudal elements of society, are lately being spearheaded by the affluent middle classes and the section of society which thrives on the percolation of retrograde norms, in the name of religion. The Fundamentalist ideologies are based on the norms selectively culled from religious practices, norms that can sustain the domination of the elite males of the society in the name of religion. Communal politics has a large overlap with this fundamentalism; it is based on the hatred of 'others religion' and is inherently oppressive to the weaker sections of society, including the women. This ideology is upholder of patriarchal norms and thereby is oppressive to the women in a subtle manner.

This ideology inflicts both covert and overt violence against the women. Patriarchy as such builds the identity of community through the bodies of women and through that route the hatred of those belonging to others' religions gets compounded by the idea that women are the property of men. It is this which makes women's life a living hell in the highly communalised atmosphere.

The worst of this violence is seen in the manifest form in the communal riots, where women are the victims in the multiple ways. Violence against women of 'other community' in these cataclysms becomes a part of the pogroms against the minorities. There are ghastly stories at the time of partition where women from both sides of the divide were subjected to humiliation of the worst kind and on the top of it, many of them were subjected to being tattooed on different parts of there bodies as an act of 'achievement' and some of the culprits even went on to tattoo their names on the hands of victims. It must be recalled here that in the rehabilitation process, the women who were left behind in both the countries were not easily accepted by their relatives on the grounds that by now they must have become 'impure' in the hands of the 'enemies'.

It is interesting that many a communal violence have been sparked off by spreading the rumors that women of 'our' community' have been 'defiled' by the men of 'other' community. The recent rumors (! truth) about the rape of Muslim women in Surat riots, in the aftermath of Babri demolition were a big eye opener as to what this communal ideology can do to pervert the minds of those indulging in these barbarian crimes. As such, communal ideology justifies these acts on the weird ground that these are the best preventive measures to protect 'our' women. One of the ideologues of communal ideology while commenting on Shivajis's noble act of 'letting go' the daughter-in-law of Nawab of Bassien went on to opine as follows (from Dhananjay Keer "Veer Savarkar", Popular Prakshan,1966, p539) "...had expressed his opinion that the liberal policy adopted by Shivaji in case of Muslim women was wrong as this cultured and human treatment could not evoke in those fanatics the same feelings about Hindu women. They should have been given tit for tat, he observed frankly, so they might have realised the horrors of brutality." This spine chilling prescription of dealing with "others' women" can come only from the ideology of hate which generalises the communities, projects a uniform enemy image of them and then also goes on to underline that women are essentially a property of men, so protecting one's property and defiling 'others' propery are two sides of the same coin.

The attitude of communal ideology vis a vis the women becomes painfully obvious by different incidents which we will like to narrate in brief. Recently the 'Self Respect' killings are in news from the media. In areas of Pakistan those women who face Talaq and abandonment by their husbands have been killed or being encouraged to commit suicide, by fundamentalist sections of society on the plea that it is better to die with respect rather then live the life after being divorced. Similarly we can also remember, many years ago Roopkanwar was burnt on the funeral pyre of her husband. This came under intense criticism from the progressive sections of society. Surprisingly one top functionary of a Communal party not only defended the act but she also went on to arrange a demonstration in front of parliament, the slogan of the demonstration was 'It is not only the honour but also the right of Indian women to commit Sati (Being burnt on the funeral pyre of husband). Lately in the intense anti-Christian atmosphere, few nuns were raped in Jhabua in M.P. As condemnations poured in, similarly in came the appreciation from one MP of a communal party. He went on to call this rape as an act of Patriotism!

Coming to the communal holocausts which our society has been witnessing; it has been an elementary observation that women of minority community are victims of 'double' attack. On one hand, the violence coming from Majority community shatters their bodies and souls and leaves many of them without the breadwinner in the family. On the other, the communal elements of their own community later blame them for not sticking to the religious tenets (as interpreted by these elements) because of which these acts are taking place. Also these incidents give them more ground to restrict their lives further for the fear of the majority community. Also as communal ideology is founded on the selectively picked up precepts and practices which give more power to the men, this ideology justifies the 'low intensity covert violence' against the women. There are leaders of so called Women's movement affiliated to communal politics who justify wife beating, dowry etc. (Mridula Sinha: Telegraph Interview; 1993) She went on to say that domestic violence is meant to bring the women on the proper track for the smooth running of the family, she also conceded having given dowry for her daughter and having received the same for her son's marriage!

As the primary relationship in this ideology is that of 'ownership' of the women, the inter-religious marriages are seen through the angle of 'loss' of 'our' property (woman), i.e. the appropriation of 'our women' by the 'others'. It this mindset which resulted in the terrorisation of some Muslims in Gujarat villages where few adivasi girls got married to some Muslim boys, and the punishment of this crime was meted out to the villagers belonging to the minority community. The starting point of communal ideology is the subordinate position of women, and having accepted that the women's wings of these organisations operate within the defined limits of the male organisations, which prescribe the overall framework in which these organisations have to operate. This politics claims to be respectful to the women but this 'respect' is proffered only when the women live within the prescribed limits imposed on them. And this is the ground on which both covert and overt violence is unleashed against the women of their 'own' community and women of "enemy's" community.

It is puzzling as to how many a women can be 'taken in' by communal ideologies despite the fact that these ideologies are against their interests. Here one has to appreciate that communal politics operates in the name of religion. As Ayesha Imam (Making the links-Anti Racism and Feminism; Paper presented at CRIAW-Toronto-1991), "....Religious beliefs are not simply imposed but generated and developed in the process of appropriation and reconstruction of social and personal experience........ Fundamentalist groups can provide security in having a total way of life set out, giving a focus for identity and relief or empowerment therein as a welcome value placed on much of women's unrecognised labour in the domestic realm."

While most of the religions can also be interpreted in a way where the status of women and men is on par (Shramanic traditions from Hindu religion and the basic tenets of Islam as interpreted by many liberal Islamic scholars) the practices which go on in the name of religion are highly discriminatory against the women. These are worst compounded in multi-religious societies where the prevalent political situation and power play, elite of the society resort to communal politics and use (! misuse) the name of religion to perpetuate their hold on the social affairs and in the resulting inter-community clashes the violence which takes place against women is the most ghastly and condemnable.

26

Ayesha and the Scarf

While walking down the pavement a few days after the 25th August (2003) blasts in Mumbai, I got a bit of a shock when I saw Ayesha covering her head with scarf, duppata. I have known her from her childhood and her father happened to be well acquainted to me. She is the only child of her beard-sporting father. She grew up as a bright young child in the English medium school. One could never see any typical Muslim identity from her dress. So in a way I was taken aback with her taking duppatta on her head. Since this has been a comparatively recent phenomenon, one presumes this way of putting the duppata has been a post Gujarat carnage effect for her.

While seeing her like that some more incidents flashed instantly. It was during the Mumbai riots of 92-93 that my doctoral student Salim, who earlier was indistinguishable from any other student, started sporting a typical Muslim beard and walked into my office one of the days telling me that if we have to die like this why should we not kill few before dying. It was a very traumatic experience for me to be unable to convince my student that violence is no answer to the ongoing anti Muslim pogrom. It was during that period only that one of my friend born in a Christian family, who was an atheist, told me to my utter surprise that in the aftermath of the Mumbai riots he has started going to the Church regularly, essentially searching for his community association, which may be the only savior in such situations.

One more incident at personal level is worth recalling here. One of the activists of Muslim women's rights group confessed that their movement got a serious setback in the wake of Mumbai riots. This movement of Muslim women had primarily been demanding abolition of triple talaq, end of polygamy and opposition to burqa. This had started picking up slowly in mid eighties, had a setback post Mumbai riots, came up a bit later and again was pushed back seriously in the wake of Gujarat riots!

Of course, Mumbai riots were a severe jolt to me as well. But initially it was difficult for me to comprehend as to why Salim has to grow beard, why he has to go to the level of insanity in talking the language of an eye for an eye, knowing fully well that in this case it is the whole body and not just the eye which is at stake, knowing fully well that this is not going to compensate for the lives of co-religionists who have lost their lives. It gradually dawned upon me that a life lost in violence sets in chain of socio-cultural thought process and makes the holes in the feeling of security of the community and that of the person.

In the times when Osama bin Laden and Kashmir centered terrorism is stalking the globe and the country, one can only feel the heat through the expressions of communities and people in their lifestyles. Narendra Modi demonstrated the limit of this when without naming the local Muslim community he could give a clear message that Muslims are terrorists and so need to be given a punishment. How could Modi give this message? How could the average common sense accept that the neighboring Muslim deserves the same treatment, which should be meted out to the criminal terrorists? In a way the process of demonisation of Muslim community, which has been, going on at social level found its culmination in the Gujarat carnage. Now when one talks of terrorist it is not even necessary to use the prefix Muslim, as terrorist has become a synonym of Muslims. One wonders as to what must have been the plight of an average Sikh during the Khalistani movement.

What must be the image of an average Tamil in Srilanka where LTTE has been indulging in the acts of terror at mega scale. What impact Dhanu's acting as a live bomb to kill Rajiv Gandhi, must have had on the image of Srilankan Tamils in India. It is fortunate that these acts of terror have not crossed the critical level where the whole community continues to be branded in that stereotype.

Coming back to Muslims, Islam and Ayesha, one is struck by the critical levels having been crossed many times over. Multiple factors have contributed to stereotypes about Muslims. To begin with the continuation of Pre' Indepencedence communal politics of Muslims surfaced in the decades of 80s to play the retrograde role in the Shah Bano case in particular. The more assertive Hindu communalism kept going up and up all through again getting its critical mass in the decade of 80s when it used the Meenakshipuram conversions of Dalits to Islam, the Shah Bano case, and the rising Dalit presence in the social space, to launch the Ram Temple campaign. This campaign took the anti Muslim propaganda, spread through RSS Shakhas in a consistent manner from decades, to the higher levels. And from this time on every incident has served to increase the heat of communalism. The riots, which accompanied this politics, saw that the number of victims from Muslim community is proportionately much larger in numbers. Also it was successfully propagated that Muslims start the riots and than Hindus just retaliate. This has no grain of truth in it whatsoever, but in a polarising society this formulation found an easy acceptance. This was further compounded by the problem of adverse Indo Pak relations on the issue of Kashmir and alienation of Kashmiri youth.

The phenomenon of "Islamic terrorism" emerges from three major components. The first and major being the formation of Israel, the plight of Palestinian refugees. This is closely associated with the US lust for control over oil resources, its intervention in Afghanistan through Jihadi Muslims to evacuate the Communist occupation, its alliance with the despotic rulers and curbing of democracy in this region with an overall view that it is easier to manipulate the Sheikhs and dictators than the democracies. The unresolved Indo-Pak relations getting manifested in the Kashmir imbroglio is another major factor contributing to the triad of reasons contributing to 'Islamic terrorism'. One has to slightly introspect as to what is primary. Terrorism or US imperialist polices of control over oil resources? What is primary, Palestinian militants or the Israeli highhandedness in controlling vast lands or Palestine? The terrorism of Kashmiri militants or the alienation of Kashmiris? The Gujarat Muslim revange group or the Gujarat carnage? Modi and his ilk want us to belive that Godhra, an act of Muslim terrorism in Godhra led to Gujarat, but this popularised version has too many holes in it to believe that. In a nutshell, whether terrorism is a disease by itself or whether it is a manifestation of the deeper diseases needs to be understood.

The Gujarat carnage has many a lessons to learn from. Two of these stick out in prominence. When an affluent and socially prominent Ahsan Jaffery is killed after being mutilated what message it sends to millions of less privileged Muslims? When the Muslim women is being violated, what signal it sends to millions of women of that community? And to top it all who then gives the shelter to these hapless survivors of the violation of their democratic rights? As witnessed in Gujarat, it was the mosque or the Muslim run charity, which gave shelter to the survivors. What message it sends for the whole community except increasing the hold of obscurantist mullahs and orthodox elements in the community.

My atheist friend born in a Christian family starts going to Church when he witnesses the violence against another minority community. My research scholar Salim grows the beard to show his Muslim identity in the face of the Mumbai riots, can Ayesha be far behind in succumbing to the pressures of the same elements to start putting the duppatta on her head? Will Salim's progeny take to terrorism or will they come to take the path, which their father had taken before the 92-93 riots in Mumbai? Will Ayesha graduate into a burqa clad women in due course or will she revert to the earlier carefree self of pre-pogrom phase is a question which has no clear answers today. If we can provide a situation where Ayesha is not intimidated by the violations outside, then the internal pressures will get diluted. Its time we struggle against the deeper disease which gives rise to the symptom of terrorism rather than letting a particular religious community be demonised by the vested elements globally and locally.

27

Lifting the Veil

The statement of Nicholas Sarcozy that Burqa is not welcome in France, that it is a symbol of oppression and not of religion has raised serious debate all over. It is France again where five years ago the display of religious markers, head scarf, Sikh turban, and Jewish skull cap in schools was banned. Public servants cannot use the same in place of work.

France as a secular state has adopted a particular version of this policy. France has been setting example for some of the countries in this imposing type of secularism, like Turkey. It has another dimension and that is large number of poor Muslims coming here are from its old colonies who live in very abysmal conditions. One recalls a large section of these immigrant Muslim population lives in suburbs, poor localities in economic deprivation. A couple of years ago right here some Muslim youth began a series of violent acts out of frustration due to unemployment and poverty. The cultural economic differences between these sections are very wide and urban affluent ones' are very gross.

How is secularism to be implemented? One way is that social situations are transformed and the hold of feudal elements is done away with and state encourages the society to adopt the norms of social and gender equality. And with this, the symbols of gender inequalities start receding in the face of changing social situation. There is no uniform pattern in this. Even after the democratic regimes come to being formally, many old norms take time to vanish. Surely there are some of these which have to be done away by strong legislation. In India during freedom movement forcible prevention of Sati, burning of wife after husbands' death, had to be resorted through legislation.

Burqa has not been the mandatory part of Koranic teachings.

Here the emphasis is on dressing modestly. In earlier societies and other societies also, different dress codes have imposed on and also adopted by women, some as honour and more of them to impose controls on them. Dr. Zeenat Shaukat Ali, a noted Islamic scholar points out that long before the advent of Islam, veiling and seclusion appear to have existed in Hellinitic-Byzantine era, and also amongst Sassanians of Persia. In ancient Mesopotamia veil of women was regarded as sign of respectability and status.

During feudal times, the patriarchal norms were operated in the society through the institution of religion. With persistence of patriarchy the women were made to wear the identity markers in different cultures and societies. Stronger the patriarchal norms, stronger the social presence of clergy, stronger is the imposition of identity markers. These may be *Ghunghat*, (India head scarf) in different cultures and *burqa* amongst Muslims. From the beginning of twentieth century, the status of women started improving slightly and women started coming to social space. By 1980s in many a Muslim majority countries also women came to their own and prevalence of burqa came down, and at places totally done away with. The situation started worsening with the Global War on terror at world level and with communal violence in India intensifying.

With so called 'war on terror' the intimidation of Muslim communities' world over started worsening. With this orthodox and conservative sects in Islam came to the fore. Fundamentalist tendencies like Taliban propped up at places and worsened the situation by giving senseless *fatwa's* and dictates. Taliban imposed the norms in most inhuman way. The sense of insecurity in the wake of war, invasion of Afghanistan and then Iraq increased the sense of insecurity and the consequent hold of conservative sections, who generally impose such restrictive norms on women increased. Still in many a countries, where the women enjoyed a safe and secure social condition, the use of burqa came down. If we have a look at global scene we will find great amount of diversity in this matter. Broadly one can say, more the insecurity, more the hold of orthodoxy, more the burqa.

In India one can see a great diversity in the use of the same. In Kerala it was not much in use and in Kashmir it was practically absent. In Kerala its use started going up with the rising communal violence of the decade of 1980s and with the rising influence of Wahabi Islam through those taking up jobs in Gulf region. In Kashmir the rise of militancy after 1990, the communalization of the Kashmir issue, led to rise of conservative sections who wanted to impose the veil, but Kashmiri women held there ground and resisted the same.

Also many a misconceptions have been constructed around Islam, burqa and local traditions. Recently India's President, Mrs. Pratibha Patil stated that the Ghunghat in Rajasthan has been introduced due to the fear of Muslim kings, to protect women from their atrocities. One can ask those arguing on these lines, how did Sati come into being? Can hiding the face protect women or make them more vulnerable to atrocities? Sati, Ghunghat etc., have been more a mark of patriarchal values than due to the impact of Muslim Kings. Even today Ghunghat persists not because of the fear of Muslims but the strong hold of patriarchal values. The occasional cases of Sati also fall in that category. Bal Thackeray of Shiv Sena came for a strong praise of Sarcozy for his stand on Burqa. The same Shiv Sena has been intimidating girls on Valentine day off and on and giving the *fatwa* that girls' should not wear jeans. What a case of crass double standards!

The social and political situation leads to the social psychology and individual psychology of women is shaped around that. Men have held the sway in dictating such norms, and social situation is created where women internalize these norms. The Sufi tradition of Islam was not for the use of burqa. There are two essential points which the rulers have to keep in mind. One is that the very basis of democracy is freedom and liberal space. The countries like Saudi Arabia impose burqa. The countries like France want to do away with the same through a dictat. What is the difference? Secondly the point today is to see that globally and within the nation states, the minorities are given the feeling of security, they are provided with situations leading to equity. These will ensure that the identity issues will take the back seat. Today the communities where security is the issue, equity is eluding the community, identity becomes the major rallying point. Just the statement about identity markers, without changing the social situation leading to such phenomenon is a hollow move.

SECTION–VII

GLOBAL TERROR

28

Terrorism: Facts Versus Myths

The current times are full of insane acts of terror. All over the globe and also in India acts of violence by political groups seeking justice or revenge are dime a dozen. Not a month passes when one does not hear about the death of innocents in one more such act in one or the other corner of the globe. Many a times one can make the correlations, which tell us the cause of terror, the underlying group involved. The Mumbai blasts of 11th July 2006 took place in the first class compartment of the Western railways. Prior to this the blasts in Mumbai took place in 2002, immediately in the aftermath of Gujarat violence, and the earlier one's taking place in 1993 were in the aftermath of Mumbai carnage. On 8th August 2006, two blasts took place outside a Masjid in Malegaon, Maharashtra killing over 40 people.

The attack on Afghanistan and then on Iraq later was followed by acts of terror in Spain, Madrid and in London. All these countries incidentally were the one's who had been allies of US in its invasion of Iraq. In India various such acts have been sometimes been related to Kashmir issue, sometimes with the overall attacks and intimidation of minorities. On 11th July when Mumbai was rocked by the blasts, the same day saw the blasts in Kashmir and the next day one heard of blasts in Sri Lanka, forcing South Africa to withdraw from the trilateral series. One keeps hearing of the acts of violence in North East on regular basis where the ethnic issues have not yet been resolved. Irish Republican Army just a couple of months ago went on to declare that it will no longer indulge in acts of terror.

It's not that these are only terrorist groups which are wreaking havoc. There are several States that are adding up to the problem by getting some such acts stage-managed to defame the terror outfits. Many a suspicions have been raised about, Chittisingpura massacres of Sikhs during Clintons visit to India, about the Ansal

Plaza act, about the attack on parliament and even about UK claim that they have unearthed the link planned explosions in the flights taking off to US.

The picture could not have been worse at any point of time. The impact of this has been all around on the lives of people affecting their social life to a great extent. The Worldwide security has been tightened on airports. Huge forces have been deployed at airports to check and cross check the people traveling. People have become used to being frisked, searched during the travels. Muslims have borne the biggest brunt of these searches. Just being Muslim is enough of cause for someone to be thoroughly probed and searched. In the wake of Mumbai blasts wholesale arrest of Muslim youths has been the norm with the police. The ground is that they must be harboring terrorists, they must be having sympathies with the terrorists since they are Muslims. The social life is getting affected in an adverse manner. The liberal values are coming under the chopping block of security. The orthodoxy and right wing religio-political streams are coming to the fore in very aggressive and assertive manner. To cap it all some messages have been filtered down the social conduits, the one's related to Muslims and Islam, as propagating that they are the fountainhead of violence and terror. Along with this the sense of insecurity amongst average people is going up and some political elements are harping on this to increase their political clout. The atmosphere is full of suspicion. To worsen the matters there is a section of global and local media playing on this sentiment to widen the divide between different religious communities. There are sectarian groups, wearing different garbs who are having a field day, in reaping the harvest of hate.

There are different spots in the world which are more prone and have come to the limelight due to the acts of terror. West Asia, Iraq, Afghanistan and Lebanon seem to be the high voltage area, with death stalking the streets and the gods of death having picnic on regular basis. The source of information on these issues is also very vague. The information coming from the state machineries is the major one. Such acts cannot be ratified by independent civic sources. International citizens initiatives cannot go to the extent of investigating it for different reasons and citizens tribunals, which have investigated on the war crimes against Iraq and Afghanistan are practically unheard of while the US propaganda machine rolls out its dossiers in full strength on regular basis. In India a large section of media follows the lead of Western media and also a large section is influenced by the communal propaganda of RSS combine. The odd brave journalists and human rights activists, who do try to give the alternate vision and interpretation of what seems to be the obvious, do it at great risk. Also there are few retired personnel who have been giving out the sources which give us a peep into the happening in the highest echelons. There is no dearth of books on the topic but few are the one's which do not toe the line of big Sam or the authorities at places.

Defining terrorism is not very simple, various interpretations and definitions have come up. The states have focused on talking of terrorist acts, violence; death of innocents in this process. As such in popular parlance, in some regions, in some circles these acts of terror are legitimized as an act of political campaign. LTTE, ULFA, IRA, Kashmiri militants, who are labeled as terrorists are looked up as freedom fighters amongst a section. The case of Sardar Bhagat Singh is equally interesting. While he was dubbed as a terrorist by British, he is looked up as one of the greatest revolutionaries, as a freedom fighter. As such it can be understood "as an act of violence against unarmed civilians as a means of bargaining politically over specific demands or making a general statement." (Hensman, Terrorism, Imperialism and War, p. 29) Further Hensman adds very aptly, "It should be irrelevant whether the perpetrators are state parties or non state parties, and other characteristics (like skin colour, ethnicity, gender, religion, nationality, sexual orientation, disability, social origin or anything else) of the perpetrators or the victims should likewise be irrelevant. (Terrorism, Imperialism and War, p. 156)

While such groups have wreaked havoc, even the elected governments have also resorted to this violence. "Statists definitions (*of terrorism*) portray terrorism to cover sedition, conspiracy, killing, murder, arson, explosions and public disorder to undermine the state..., twist due process of and evidentiary norms against the individual and prescribe heavy punishment...political terrorism abjures the state's definition and seeks to define terrorism as political freedom struggle to support the claims of justice and self determination with no holds barred."(Dhavan, Times of India, August 23) Accordingly state governments formulate harsh laws and try to go overboard in their response to the extent of punishing the innocents in the process and so the "War on Terror", POTA, armed forces acts. Dhavan further adds, "A people's definition of terrorism draws from the experience of civilian populations. Post World War II, terrorism against the people acquired a new dimension when America bombed Hiroshima and Nagasaki in 1945 and later carpet bombed Vietnam with Napalm". The experience of Afghanistan and Iraq is no different, neither the one of Israel's attack on Lebanon.

Compared to the decades of sixties to eighties the air is thick with fear and intimidation. Values of humanism are being forced to take the backseat while the powers that be are keener to increase their powers by projecting the fear of terrorism. The global and local war on terror is a construct, which is contradictory in itself. Terrorist outfits are not a legal entity, so how can one talk of such a war defies all logic and imagination.

There is a heavy propaganda that all Muslims are not Terrorists, but all Terrorists are Muslims. This has been widely circulated in via SMS and also by word of mouth. Since the 11th Sept. 2001 WTC attack, this started being popularized and by now it has become part of social common sense. In India, the Kashmir militancy indulged in by a section of youth is again cited as example of Muslim terrorists. To add to this the incidents of Akshardham temple, Ansal Plaza, high jacking of Indian Airlines plane to Kandhar, attack on parliament are blown up as, in all these either Muslims were involved or in some cases it was projected that they were. Some of these reports had serious holes in the story presented by the authorities, but since there can be no ratification by citizens committees, it is difficult to doubt or believe in some of these. All said and done, there is enough number of cases where Muslims are involved and organizations like Al Qaeda, Lashkar-e-Tayyba, Hamas have become household names. But interestingly there are many other organizations using violence which are not much taken note of.

One of such major organizations is Liberation Tiger of Tamil Elam (LTTE), the majority of the members of this are Hindus.

One member of this group, Dhanu strapped a bomb and killed Rajiv Gandhi. Similarly Khalistani movement was the major force resorting to terror just few years ago. Those belonging to Christian and Hindu militants are active in North East India. Worldwide, the Irish Republican Army militants belong to Christianity, the one who bombed a Hotel in Cairo in 1942 was a Jew, and the Oklahoma bomber was a Christian, Timothy McWeigh. Wherever dissatisfaction goes beyond a particular level some of the people do resort to violence to achieve their supposed goal. It is not related to any one religion in particular. National Democratic Front: Bodoland, All Tripura Tiger Force, Japanese Red Army, Lords Salvation Army, ETA, Spain are some more examples of organizations which are scattered in different parts of the world, using terror tactics for their political goals and have nothing to do with Islam.

During last decade and a half, Islam has been projected to be violent. The media and many a state apparatus have on purpose 'sold' this image of Islam. Muslims are no uniform community. The basic assumption which comes from this formulation is that religion is the cause of terrorism. On the contrary, terrorism is a phenomenon, which comes into being due to social, political and economic circumstances. Religion is used as a cover for the terrorist activities. The identity of terrorists is not always derived from and is not always around religion. Khalistanis derived their identity from Sikhism. The alleged Muslim terrorists had multiple identities; the ones in Palestine, from where terrorism began had Palestinian identity, in Kashmir it began as Kashmiriat. The Islamic identity with this sort of terrorism came more particularly with Al Qaeda, which was set up by the CIA, the US through ISI of Pakistan to fight against the USSR armies in Afghanistan.

There is also a misconception that while terrorists coming from other religions have ethnic or other identity, those who are Muslims have Islamic identity. As a matter of fact, the identity assumed by terrorists changes from place to place. It is true that some of the terrorists are showing the Islamic identity but that's not true all through. Khalistanis also operated on Sikh identity. Even with this large spectrum of Islamic identity, the ones trained by CIA wore this identity prominently on their sleeves and they tried to present as if they are doing Jihad, they are killing the

Kafirs. As such they were indoctrinated in the madrasas especially set up for this purpose by CIA. These Madrasas were set up under the Kissinger doctrine of 'Asians should be made to fight Asians'. It was formulated in the madrasas as that the Communists are *kafirs* since they don't believe in Allah, killing them is a Jihad and those dying in this Jihad will straight go to *jannat*, where 72 virgins are waiting for them. This concoction of US set up madrasas had strong impact on the Muslim youth who came in to get training in these with the readiness to lay down their lives for the US goal of occupying Afghanistan in the long run.

As such, what is called as Islamic identity of terrorists, only those trained in madrasas set up by CIA-ISI nexus, that Islamic identity, Jehad and Kafir are used in the main. The one's who began from injustices heaped by Israel had Palestinian identity, the one's in Kashmir had the flag of Azadi to begin with. Even here religion has been the cloak only for few.

Here there is a clever manipulation of the words like Jihad and Kafir in particular. As we know the historical meaning of these with the origin of Islam were much different. Also there are many an interpretation of these words. During the last decade and a half Islam has been projected to be violent. The media and many a state apparatus have on purpose 'sold' this image of Islam as being associated with terrorism. Muslims are no uniform community. And there are different interpretations of Islam. The media highlights any sensational violent act and ignores the pacifist ones'. Comments of fanatics are projected prominently as the Islamic voice. The sober and moderate statements are either ignored or find their place in some small corner of the media.

The misuse of the word Jihad by fanatics adds to the problem. Any act of Muslim terrorists is supposed to be a Jihad, as some of them project it in the same manner. As such, Holy war, Crusade, Dharma Yuddha is not an uncommon usage in different religions as kings have launched their campaign for expansion of their territories in the name of their religions, times and over again, and Islam is no exception. It is believed that Allah wants to spread Islam by the sword. Dr. Asghar Ali Engineer one of the liberal interpreters of Islam states, "It is Jihad, which is one of the pillars of Islam precisely because it does not necessarily mean war. Jihad...means utmost effort, not violence and it is obligatory on

Muslims to make utmost efforts (in wisely manner) to spread the message of Allah so as to create a just and compassionate society. This is what is obligatory, not waging a war at all. Prophet himself has exemplified it on many occasions especially at the time of Sih-I-Hudabiya (i.e. peace of Hudaibiyah and Fath-I-Mecca). (Engineer, Institute of Islamic Studies. Oct. 98)

As for these radical Islamist groups, Jihad is being used as a cynical ruse to whip up religious fervour for their cause. "Historically, Jihad was used rhetorically by the imperialist powers to justify their worldly expansionist designs. In its original sense, Jihad was more of an inner moral cleansing for the community. This was called jehad-e-Akbar (The Great Jihad). But now, the whole notion of jihad is being used as an instrument for legitimising militaristic, monarchic and dictatorial regimes. (Mushirul Hasan, Interview, Tehelka.com)

Arundhati Roy in her essay "The Algebra of Infinte Justice" points out that in 1979 after the Soviet invasion of Afghanistan, the CIA and Pakistan ISI (Inter Service Intelligence) launched the largest covert operation in the history of CIA.Their purpose was to harness the energy of Afghan residence to the Soviets and expand it into a holy war, an Islamic Jihad, which would turn the Muslim countries within the Soviet zone of influence, against the communist regime and to eventually destabilise it. When it began it was meant to be Soviet Union's Vietnam. It turned out to be much larger than that. Over the years, CIA funded and recruited 1,00,000 radical Mujahidin from 40 Islamic countries as soldiers for American proxy war. (*In Afghanistan*)

The saying that the terrorist violence is due to Religions, especially due to Islam is a myth. It is true that some fanatical Muslims found on the fringe, use certain medieval interpretation and usage as eternally binding and believe that kafirs should be slayed. Also those hostile to Islam use this term to show the intolerance of Islam.

Most of the ideologies develop their positive and negative terminology. Christianity for example has derogatory terms like pagan, non-believer, Hinduism has *maleccha, yavan,* etc. Islam coined the negative terms like *kufr* (disbelief), *nifaq* (hypocrisy), *rafz* (rejection or deviation). These terms are many a times or rather most of the times used against the different sects in the same religion? They are a tool in the hands of vested interests for their material gains and for the increase of social power. Many a Muslim rulers used the word Kafir while fighting against non-Muslim kings, the same one's then struck compromises also with different kings. We are aware that the Muslim kings were in alliance with Hindu Kings and also had Hindu subjects in large numbers, whose religious and other needs were considered by them (e.g. Babar's will to Humayun) These worldly affairs most of the times have been given religious veneer for the benefit of the ruling groups. Which if interpreted narrowly can attribute tolerance and intolerance to particular religion.

Some theologians have spread the myth about Ummah, a homogenous world Muslim community. The truth is that there is no single goal or unified vision in the Muslim world. Different sects of Islam have serious differences with each other. Talibans are for example condemned by a large section of Muslims. Ummah is one of the progressive ideas as enunciated in Quran. In its original form, it struck at the roots of parochialism and nationalism. It was an effort to create a Muslim personality that would not bear the lineage of race, language, colour and other parochial denominations. But in reality in later centuries this was designed as an exclusive notion.

The concepts of Dar-ul-Islam (the land of the pure) and Dar-ul-Harb (the land of the enemy) are again used to project the lack of patriotism of Muslims in countries where they are in minority. In Quran, there is a distinction between "the land of the peace" and "the land of the enemy". But this distinction made sense at a time when the Muslim communities were trying to evolve a code vis-à-vis the rest of the world. Today in the plural diverse world we have seen different Muslim countries battling against each other for material gains. Also in South Asia, Bangladesh split from its co-religionist Pakistan in 1971 due to cultural and material reasons.

The terrorist attacks on world trade center and the consequent US aggression on Afghanistan has revived the misconception that this is an indication of the truth behind the "Clash of Civilisation" theses of Samuel Huntington. "It is my hypothesis that the fundamental source of conflict in this new world will not be primarily ideological or primarily economic. The great divisions among humankind and the dominating source of conflict will be cultural. Nation states will remain the most powerful actors in world affairs, but the principal conflicts of global politics will occur between nations and groups of different civilisations. The clash of civilisations will dominate global politics. The fault lines between civilisations will be the battle lines of the future." These gems are from Samuel Huntington the new philosopher of this era representing the age in the world when America's economic and political domination is close to complete. It is an era where America along with its minions is calling the shots. It is an era when the Non-Aligned movement of yesteryears has been well forgotten and the possibility of World Democratic order seems a Utopia. The injustices done to a large section of Muslims in the Gulf region and Africa have been showing its repercussions. The militant opposition of Palestinians to the repression by Israel initially got expressed in P.L.O. led by Yasser Arafat. The other acts of commission by US and other hegemonic powers have left a sense of injustice amongst a large section of Muslim masses. Also one is aware that the chances of International grievance settlement channels practically do not exist with UN being reduced to the desk in the state Dept. of the US and its Secretary General helplessly watching the might of imperialist powers attacking Iraq, and soliciting UN sanctions for its terrorism. The same man watching from the sidelines, America's aggression on Afghanistan and the aggressor this time not even bothering to get it ratified by the World body, the facade, which it kept so far. And this person now is being rewarded with Nobel Prize for peace, for keeping quiet when the US is on rampage in country after country. In this phase what is the way for the people of the World, which is feeling that injustice has been done? How should they protest? Which doors should they knock for grievance rectification?

This is aggressive terror aimed to dominate and control the World. This is the terrorism of the mighty out to enslave the weak. This state terrorism kills the innocent non-combatants, like the ones in Hiroshima and Nagasaki, like the one's dying in the US aggression on Iraq in 1991, like the one's dying in the streets of Kabul currently.

The other terrorism is of the one's who have been victims of the unjust policies of Nations and World, those whose ethnic aspirations have been suppressed, those who have been deprived of their home and hearth due to the greed of the World powers.

Today the ideological cover of 'defending Freedom in the World' is no more adequate for its expansionist goals. The resistance of the weak has to be dubbed in a more scathing manner to justify the terror of the mighty, and so the 'Clash of Civilizations' thesis. Ideology of the imperialism in the times of oil hunger, ideology of the hegemonic powers is to crush the resistance in places where they want direct and indirect control over the resources of the World. So the 'backward Islamic civilization' is clashing with the Modern West, say the new ideologues of imperialists. Here in the clever maneuver, for those having oil wells, religious identity is imposed and those who aspire to satisfy their oil hunger by buying it for peanuts, the geographical category are used. The Muslims today, a two billion strong, are reduced to a stereotype, clones of Osama bin-Laden or members of Taliban. The diversity recognition amongst the target group is dangerous for the oppressors. So even in India we see the Muslims being projected as a uniform community. It is easy for the dominant group to deal with the monolithic image of minority. More backward the projection of the image, the better it is. It helps in all the ways including during the times when violence and other suppressions have to be unleashed in pursuance with their politics.

So the Muslims in Iraq, Iran, Saudi, Indonesia, and Bangladesh all become cast in a single mould. And now the next step becomes easy, since Muslims as a community can be projected to be opposed to modernity. They are terrorists so there must be something in Islam, which promotes violence and terrorism. And so when the pogroms are unleashed against them in the form of communal violence or aggression is launched against innocent Iraqis or Afghans, consent gets easily manufactured for the aggressive acts of the super powers. The political ratings of the one saying 'you are either on our side or on their' (terrorists) soar to maddening heights and those bequeathed with social common sense clap with each missile hitting the home for the old or shelter for the people or the hospital. Some applaud the 'beauty ', the precision with which the missiles do their job; others rejoice that 'they' (the Muslims) deserve this lesson. So on overt level Uncle Sam retreats back after endorsing the 'clash of civilisations' and to appear politically correct, the boss reverts to 'Infinite Justice' as the ideological cover for bombing the hospitals and children and the old people's homes.

'White Man's burden' thesis came up with the colonization, Defending freedom came up while suppressing the rising nationalisms and now the clash of civilisation is being put forward when US is trying to control the taps of oil resources. There are many an Islamic countries in and around these resources, who had to be rubbed the wrong way, in order to maintain and extend the flow of oil towards fuel tanks of the powerful countries of the West. Keeping in mind this projection, which exploiters have generally kept for their own interests, some ideological cover has to be maintained. If Colonial masters are usurping the resources of colonies, it is White man's burden to civilize the people of the colonies. If Imperialism is crushing the Nationalist sentiments to be able to continue its hegemony on the World; it is fight for freedom of the World. Here both these have been used as a cover for the proactive deeds of Imperialism. Now the 'Clash' theory is there to explain the 'reaction to the injustices' done to the section of Arab world. One knows that most of the Muslim Nations are with the US in its efforts to control the Afghan territory through the new puppet, which will be pro-US. One also knows that the Muslim dominated countries like Indonesia, Malaysia and many significant one's are with the US for its 'sacrifices to save the freedom' in the World.

Will the US led 'War on Terror' rid the world of the problem of terrorism as claimed by US ideologues? 'War on Terror' is a euphemism, for the US aims to take political and military control of different areas of the world, either for acquisition of oil wealth or for military goals. The acts of terror by the groups scattered here and there are no uniform entity, which can be subject to aggression and eliminated. Since they are scattered and are faceless, it is difficult to identify them and restrain them. In the process what happens is that US and its allies have been picking one after the other areas and bombing them into deserts. The civilian population, the non combatants are the biggest victims of the same. Operation Iraqi freedom was launched after the pretexts of Weapons of Mass destruction failed miserably. UN observer recommendations were bypassed and a war was launched, which has met massive resistance from the people of Iraq? It is a war against Iraqi people and incidents like Abu Garib prison, where the prisoners were stripped naked and asked to make human pyramid, and butchering on the Iraqi streets has been made the norm by the US army. This army by now is desperate and all the attempts by US to outsource the war and to rope in the soldiers of poorer nations has not met with any success, as the US aim of making the sacrificial goats out of the poor countries people has failed. Even the US army is comprised mainly of the underprivileged sections of US population.

List of Countries that America has been at war with and bombed-since World War II

China 1945-46, 1950-53	Korea (1950-53)
Guatemala (1954, 1967-69)	Indonesia (1958)
Cuba (1959-60)	The Belgian Congo (1964)
Peru (1965)	Laos (1964-73)
Vietnam (1961-73)	Cambodia (1969-70)
Grenada (1983)	Libya (1986)
El Salvador (1980s)	Nicaragua (1980s)
Panama (1989)	Iraq (1991-99)
Bosnia (1995)	Sudan (1998)
Yugoslavia(1999)	Afghanistan (2001)
Iraq (2003)	Iran (on the list)

US as a matter of fact has been the major terrorist state in the recent times, killing the innocent civilians to achieve its political and economic goals. The multinational corporations who are at the back of the policies have the greed of profit and the lives of human beings, especially from other races, and other regions do not matter for them. The recent events of West Asia clearly exemplify the goals of imperialism in the region. To begin with Saddam Hussein was lured to attack Kuwait, which was pumping out the oil at massive speed. This would have affected the Iraqi oil reserves also. Due to the intense economic pressures, Iraq planned to attack Kuwait. It informed the US administration, which subtly provoked this attack. Once Kuwait was taken over by Iraq as 24th State of Iraq, US immediately planned to attack

Iraq to protect the sovereignty of Sheikh of Kuwait. Saddam's offer of withdrawal were rejected and Bush senior went for a decisive victory. Iraq has to be bombed to pre-industrial age. The retreating Iraqi armies were trapped and massacred. Baghdad and Basra were bombed relentlessly. Thousands of civilians were killed. Around 1,50, 000 Iraqis died during this invasion. Electrical Sewage treatment system and water treatment plants were ravaged with the result that water borne diseases spread. Severe economic sanctions were put which further resulted in the loss of lives of Iraqis. Madeleine Albright when asked by a reporter that in the sanctions imposed by US on Iraq over half a million children have died due to that, whether it was worth it. To this she replied in affirmative saying that 'we think the price is worth it.'

After 11th September 2001 WTC attack, Osama bin Laden thanked Allah for the same. He spelt his motivation on 7th Oct 2001, "What America is tasting now is something insignificant compared to what we have tasted for scores of years. Our nation (the Islamic World) has been tasting this humiliation and degradation for more than 80 years, its sons are killed, its blood shed, its sanctuaries are attacked and no one hears and no one heeds. Millions of children are being killed as I speak. They are being killed in Iraq without committing any sins...To America; I say only a few words to it and to its people. I swear to God, who has elevated the skies without pillars, neither America nor the people who live in it here in Palestine and not before all the infidel armies leave the land of Muhammad, peace be upon him."

On the pretext of catching hold of culprit of 9/11, without producing any evidence against Osama, War on terror was launched by attacking Afghanistan. In this war close to a million lives were lost. While Osama is safe and sound thousands of innocent Afghans were butchers. In due course US puppet Govt. has been installed there and US multinationals are swooping there to make their killing.

The lack of any credible reason for attacking Afghanistan led many an observer to comment that, "...the war against Afghans was very much in line with the US's historical role in Afghanistan. In 1970s, the US hired seven different parties of fundamentalists called Mujahidin. These were extremists hired by the CIA during the cold war 'to draw the Soviets in to Afghan trap" as later revealed by former National Security Advisor, Zbignew Brezinsky. The CIA gave arms and ammunition to mujahidin...Using these weapons and sophisticated training in the art of terror, these men successfully drove out the Soviets, but also waged terrible war on their own people killing at least 45000 people in Kabul alone. (Ninan Koshy, WOT, pp. 62-63)

As the invasion of Afghanistan began just within few weeks, the US claim that they did preparation for this in three weeks is to be taken with a pinch of salt. "Credible reports have appeared that the US was planning to take military action against Afghanistan to oust Taliban months before September 11."(Koshy, p. 63) To train Al Qaeda, US had spent over 80,000 million dollars and also provided 7000 tons of armaments, including the Stinger missiles. It is for this that Kissinger doctrine of "Asians should be made to fight Asians" that the Muslim youth were indoctrinated in the Madrasas, that communists who have invaded our Afghanistan, don't believe in Allah, so they are kafirs and waging a war against them will be Jihad, those getting killed in this will go to jannat, where all the pleasures of the jannat, including 72 virgins will be available for them. Most of the current myths about jihad, kafir, and terrorists being bred in madrasas start from this massive operation launched by US. It is this effort which took the shape of Al Qaeda.

The US propaganda machine, keeps dishing out different slogans to serve its foreign policy. In cold war era it was defense of freedom, now it is war on terror. The US media and other media world over following the trails of US, toe the same line.

Do teachings of Islam lead to violence as being propagated. This again is a concoction built carefully in various stages. While on one hand, the US propaganda machinery picked up Islam as the "New threat", after the collapse of Communist states, especially after the US stooge, Raza Shah Pehlavi was uprooted in a revolution which came to be highjacked by Ayatollah Khomeini. Since US was claiming to take control of the oil zone, which it had been planning since it implanted the state of Israel in the middle of Arab states, near the oil rich zone. Now with a vengeance, US propaganda machine started projecting every political happening in the region in the colour of religion. As such Islam stands for peace and it is the message of peace which

Prophet brought to the warring Arab tribes. Its scriptural meaning has many a time been distorted by the Muslim rulers at times to use it for their political purposes, and lately by the US propaganda machine for promoting the demonisation of Islam to give it the pretext to attack country after country in the oil zone. In the past also Kings belonging to all religions have resorted to violence for their political goals. Crusade, Jihad and Dharmayuddh were the cover for the expansions of kingdoms, involved lot of violence and were sanctioned by clergy. The people, the downtrodden were on the path of peace and harmony despite being exploited by the landlords and kings. It is they who were more with the message of peace of saints of all religions. Today violence is again related to power. Just as Kings used the language of religion for appropriating power, now a section of powerful countries, especially the imperialists are using the garb of religion for their political goals.

Another myth prevalent in social space is that Islam and Democracy are not compatible. Most of the religions emerged during the phase of Human society when there was prevalence either of Tribal cults, or Feudal relations. With the industrialisation process the process of secularisation (weakening of the grip of clergy on social affairs and development of relations of Liberty, Equality and Fraternity) started coming up. The Nation states, which formed during this phase, had Christianity as the main religion and the secularization process had to confront the church and bring in the new relations of society.

The countries where Islam was the major religion were mostly colonies. And here the freedom struggle did introduce the process of secularization. Unfortunately these countries were also the one's where the oil was discovered. Second WW was for the division of markets amongst the imperialist countries. With the discovery of oil in the Middle East, with the emergence of America as the super power and the leading industrial Nation, the dynamics of the freedom movements changed. US began to thwart the democratization process in different colonies and opposed the freedom movements of many a countries in the name of 'Defense of Freedom'. In many countries it had to loose face. In Vietnam, where despite facing heavy odds the Vietnam people held out and US had to retreat from its mission of "Saving Freedom", but in some of them it could achieve the installation of puppet, feudal or the dictatorial regimes. In Chile, the democratically elected Salvador Allende regime was overthrown and Pinochet, a military dictator was installed. In both these countries the leader of the Govt. or revolution was Marxists. It is interesting to note here that in some of the colonies the freedom movement and industrialization process could not be undertaken by the Industrialist class and so the collective bureaucracy assumed the functions of the industrialist class.

Second WW also saw the formation of Israel in the heart of the Islamic nations, surrounding the oil resources. Here the democratisation process was quelled or counter-revolutions managed to push back the secularisation and democratisation process.

1. In Iran the Govt. of Mossadegh was overthrown and Raza Shah Pehalavi was installed as the ruler in 1953 under the watchful eye of CIA. Mossadegh was considering the nationalisation of Oil industry. Shah acted as a puppet and permitted the plunder of his oil resources, brought in the symbols of modernisation, while suppressing the social transformation. The result was the widening gulf between the rich and poor. Also he stifled the democratic institutions. The anger, frustration and helplessness of the people gave rise to the massive uprising against the Shah and installation of the clerical regime of Ayatollah Khomeini. Khomeini called America as the great Satan. Iraq and Iran had a long stretching war following this. In the war America supported Iraq and pumped in funds and ammunition to get the war going.
2. The story of Afghanistan, currently facing the death from the bombing is very peculiar. In 1978 People's Democratic Party came to power and went in for democratic reforms on secular lines. Following year, this Govt. was overthrown by conservative elements. Soviet Russia sent its army to bring back the rule, which could go in for social reforms and modernization. America decided to promote the most fundamentalist sections of rebels like Osama bin-Laden

and the fundamentalist outfit called Taliban, and helped them through and through to overthrow the Russian army. And that brought in the rule of Taliban, which was nurtured by US through the conduit of Pakistan. Meanwhile US did practically everything to violate the unwritten and written rules of the International behaviour.

3. In Iraq on the pretext of restoring the freedom of Sheikh of Kuwait, which had been merged into Iraq as its 23rd state, US launched a massive attack on Iraq with aim and purpose of restoring the 'Freedom of Sheikh'. Sheikh of Kuwait is a puppet to the US through which US is able to control the oil taps of Kuwait. In the ensuing aggression of US, nearly 2 lakh people died and later 5 lakh died due to the sanctions imposed on Iraq due to which its supply of medicines and necessary items were stopped by the US.
4. Pakistan was the product of British policy of Divide and rule. It quickly came under the grip of Military Mullah Complex. US backed up Pakistan in all its internal repression of democracy and its offensive role in Kashmir. Bangladesh broke away from Pakistan in 1971. It has been trying to restore democracy in some way, though slowly.
5. In Malaysia and Indonesia, which are predominantly Islamic Nations, there is a good effort to nurture democracy, despite limitations.

In a nutshell, in the countries with Muslim majority population there have been efforts to bring in democracy. The imperialists have crushed most of these efforts in order to control the oil wealth of the region. Most of the Islamic nations are post-colonial states caught up with the limitations and are unable to march comfortably towards democracy. Despite these limitations the ones away from the oil zone have been more successful in planting the seeds of democracy in their countries. Wherever the colonial hold and restrictions are there, the feudal relations and pre-democratic systems are promoted and sustained by the imperialist countries. The Imperialist countries promote the Fundamentalist elements in the society. So the "Free World", the imperialist countries first ensure that democratic transformation should not take place in these countries as it goes against their material interests and in the second step they blame that these countries do not have a democratic set up due to Islam. It serves the double purpose for them. They can launch the general anti-Islam tirade to sustain their control in these regions.

As such, fundamentalism can come using any religion, depending on socio-political circumstances. It is necessary to define the term fundamentalism first. It is used in two senses. The orthodox believers of religions or ideologies use it in the sense of going back to the fundamentals of a particular religion or the doctrine. Here the emphasis is on the original scripture of that particular ideology or religion. The second meaning pertains to the use of religion for political goals of dominant sections of society. In this sense the selectively culled out parts of the scriptures or practices, which are against the human rights and equality of weaker sections, are implemented to suppress the libertarian aspirations of these sections. We are using the term in its second sense (political misuse of religion).

Fundamentalism comes up in different situations. Mostly it is a response of declining sections (Feudal elements) backed by clergy to put brakes to the process of social transformations towards Liberty, Equality and Fraternity. First this phenomenon came up in the Protestant sect of Christianity in America in the face of the Industrialization process in the late Nineteenth Century and early Twentieth century. Ten small booklets were published, which emphasized the basic values of Christianity. Most of these were against the vassal's and women's legal equality. This phenomenon withered away with further industrialization. From the late twentieth century one is witnessing this phenomenon, particularly in the Islamic countries for reasons, which are a bit different. Ayatollah Khomeini's regime was a Fundamentalist one. It was the only available channel of rebellion as Raza Shah Pehlvi of Iran stifled the democratic mechanisms. In many a Middle East countries similar value systems, mostly targeting at the liberation of women came up, by suppressing the rights of women and other weaker sections of society. Similarly many an Arab countries also were already resorting to this ideology. In most of the Islamic countries around the oil zone, US encouraged the rule of Sheikhs and Mullah backed regimes as these were easy prays for satisfying the oil lust of US.

The status of clergy in Fundamentalist regimes is very exalted. In our own neighbouring Pakistan, these trends were there from the beginning as the Feudal lords and Mullahs dominated it. With Zia ul Haq's regime it got institutionalised. At different times different religions have been used as a cover for the political goals of sections of society. Islam based fundamentalism is just one of them. In that sense, Islam is no different as far as its political misuse is concerned. Lately new terms have come in to offing. These convey the fundamental politics while retaining the religious root of the term like-Hindutva, Islamism. These are not religions but since their names have the components of religion to mislead the gullible into supporting this politics. These terms help in mobilising the broad sections of society, who get the impression that it is part of their religious striving.

"Islamism began in 1920s. The 1980s saw a third generation come of age. Because of their militancy they are mostly referred to as Jehadists, and they state in all clarity that for them jihad is not a matter of moral rearmament (as many Muslims wish jihad to be understood), but armed struggle, their favorite form of self purification being 'martyrdom' (Khalid Durran, The Globalisation of Terrorism, In Review, Fall 2000). The concept of Jihad as armed struggle began from 1927 with a book on Jihad, *Al-jihad fil-Islam*; parts of this were translated into English on Muslim self statements in India and Pakistan (Wiesbaden, Harassowitz, 1970). Just to reiterate as per Quran, Jihad means striving, expending power and effort, to spread the word of Allah to create a just and compassionate society.

The other definition of Islamism is spelt in Political Islam in the Indian Subcontinent (F. Grare, Manohar, 2001). This one goes on to state, "Islamism can, indeed, not be reduced to religious fervor or to extreme moral rigorism characteristic of the Taliban or be reduced to the recourse to violence. It is defined essentially, in its relationship to politics and hence to the state, by its efforts towards realisation of a truly Muslim society." in Islamism the conquest of political power is justified by the will to impose the Sharia, the sole juridical basis of social relationships before which no other non-Islamic law can exist. "It is an assumption which makes Islamism totalitarian."(Ibid) And that conforms to any political system deriving its legitimacy from religion or race. Asghar Ali Engineer a noted Islamic scholar, who has interpreted Islam in a liberal manner, points out, "The concept of Jihad in Islam has been grossly misunderstood by Muslims and non-Muslims. It is thought that Islam encourages violence and force and that Allah wants to spread Islam with sword or at the point of gun. The acts of some Muslim extremists and terrorists provide proof for this violent image of Islam. Truth is quite otherwise" (Islam and Modern Age, Vol. I, 1998, Mumbai). Engineer further points out, 'there is no question of force or violence in spreading Islam. This was popularized by the West after the crusades, which again had nothing to do with spread of religion. It was, in fact the wars of territorial conquest. As far as the spread of religion is concerned Quran rules out violence completely through number of pronouncements. It very forcefully states, *la ikrah fi'al-din* (there is no compulsion in religion (2:256). Also it makes it plain that one can invite to the path of Allah through wisdom and godly manner (16:125). It is no less important that Quran accepted the truth brought by Prophets before Muhammad." (Ibid)

The Khalistani movement was also fundamentalist in nature. It remained only a movement of rebellion and did not achieve power to exercise its control on the weaker sections. Hindutva had come up in response to the rising secular movement of Indian National Congress. It did not grow to threaten democracy in India. But during the last two decades it has assumed menacing proportions due to the rise in the number of middle classes, (Rich peasants, rich professionals, petty industrialists, etc.) It also derives its legitimacy from a particular version of Hinduism (Brahminical) and is repressive to women and Dalits. The Islamic terrorists harbor the same values i.e. being repressive towards weaker section.

This use of Religion for retrograde politics, which is against the Human rights of weaker sections of society, cuts across different religions. It is true that currently the major fundamentalist stream derives its legitimacy from Islam but that is more because of peculiar circumstances and the role of Imperialism and not because of any peculiarity of Islam as a religion.

References

Asghar Ali. Engineer, *Islam and Modern Age*, Vol. I, 1998, Mumbai.

Asghar Ali Engineer, *Islam and the Concept of Jihad*, Institute of Islamic Studies, Vol. 1, Oct. 1998.

Asghar Ali Engineer, *Concept of Islamic State*, Aman, April-May 99.

Dhavan, Rajeev, Get the Guilty, *Times of India*, August 23.

Grare, F. Manohar, New Delhi, 2001.

Hasan, Mushirul, (Interview, www.tehelka.com)

Hensman, Rohini, *Terrorism, Imperialism and War*, Build Mumbai 2002, p.29.

Imam Raghib Asfahani, *Mufradat al-Qur'an*, pp. 916-17, Lahore, 1971.

Khalid Durram, *The Globalisation of Terrorism*, In Review, Fall 2000.

Puniyani, Ram, Communal Politics, Sage Delhi 2002.

Puniyani, Ram, *Terrorism, Imperialism and War*, Build Mumbai 2002.

Suri, Sanjay. The Great Britain Bust, *Outlook* 28th August 2006.

29

Islam Today

Religion has always been one of the most complex phenomenons to grapple with. The range of its facets, interpretations and applications is very wide. While on one side it has aided in the development of moral values, on the other, religion's identity has been used or abused for political goals in the society. Different religions have come up in different parts of the world, in different contexts, and at different times of evolutionary scale. So their concerns and expression of the concepts have been very different. Because of the vast facets, which have been put in the kitty of religion it has also been more vulnerable to abuse by vested interests. It is precisely because of this in contemporary times, one religion has particularly been the topic of criticism by some political formations. The negative image of Islam and Muslims has become part of popular perceptions. Since the time US media coined and propagated the word Islamic terrorism after 9/11 2001, this religion, Islam came to be snubbed by diverse elements.

While globally the criticism came up more so after 9/11, in India this has been projected by a section of political stream since colonial times. After the war of 1857, British introduced the policy of divide and rule and brought in communal historiography. People were fed with the communal view of History, the events of past assumed sectarian color. Hindu communalists spread the distorted view that Muslim kings destroyed Hindu temples and thereby insulted Hindu religion, Islam was spread by sword, Jazia was imposed on Hindus so that in order to escape being taxed they will become Muslims and that Muslim kings did atrocities on Hindu women. Most of this is a a lopsided and selective presentation of events but all the same it created the base for 'Hate Other' and Hindu-Muslim relations worsened due to the political motive of British colonial powers' on one side and local feudal elements on the other. These feudal elements were joined in by some middle classes and intellectuals articulating religion based nationalism, which came up on the margins of national movement. While during freedom movement these streams, Muslim nationalism and Hindu nationalism competed with each other, after the independence Muslim communalism got deflated in India and Hindu nationalism held sway.

The 'Hate other' ideology has been the mainstay of this nationalism. Accordingly Hindu nationalism's propaganda spread myths and stereotypes due to which Muslims as such came to be projected negatively. While theoretically hate Christian was also a part of this politics, in practice it surfaced only after 1990. The communal ideology was not getting much response till the decade of 1980. From this decade due to changed global equations of power, rise of unipolar world and at home the rise of sections of society feeling threatened due the social changes, rise of dalits and women in society in particular, the communal ideology got bigger social acceptance from a section of society. Interestingly the global rise of unipolar world, the rise of US Empire couched its global agenda in the language of religion. Its main goal was to control the oil wells; it made its polices on the ground that oil is too precious a commodity to be left in the control of Arabs, to the nation states of West Asia.

Accordingly a thesis of clash of civilizations came up. It argued that with the collapse of Soviet block the clash is not between classes but amongst the 'civilisations'. The argument went that the advanced Western civilisation is facing a threat from the backward Islamic civilisation. This went on to create the pretext of its future attacks on West Asia.

If Islamic civilisation is a threat, the logical target of US attack should have been Indonesia, but the areas attacked were the one's where oil is in abundance. And this can be regarded as the biggest crime of US in the contemporary times. It put the cloak of religion on the lust for oil resources. It created an atmosphere globally where the Muslim community started being looked down upon, and Islam which came as a religion of peace was made to look synonymous with violence. The perceptions got distorted and social harmony became on premium. No other crime of imperial powers may come close to this ideological propagation.

While indoctrinating the recruits of Al Qaeda in the Madrassas in Pakistan, the syllabus which was devised in Washington distorted the meaning of words Kafir and Jihad. Half truth were employed to indoctrinate the Muslim youth in Madrassas set up with US help. Any non believer in Islam was presented as an enemy deserving being killed and Jihad was made to stand for war against kafirs. Both these are far away from the meaning these words have in Koran. Islam as a whole came under the scrutiny of global media. Whatever could be cooked up against Islam was done aggressively. And this became part of social common sense. And this is how a sort of consent for attack on Afghanistan and Iraq was manufactured.

It is during this period that Hindu right wing propaganda in India was picked up in media in an aggressive way. And its own distorted versions of History and way of looking at other religions came in handy to demonize Islam and Muslims. The prevalent myths against Muslims were brushed up to add new one's, stereotypes were constructed and popularized through word of mouth and the section of media. The increasing violence worsened the matters and led to ghettoisation of the Muslim minorities. Which created more stereotypes and the vicious circle of creating the hate peaked with each massive act of violence.

There is a deeper connection between the global decline of Soviet states, rise of uni-polar world, rise of conservatism, severe attack on social movements, the theory of clash of civilizations and the rise of Hindu right wing in India. The current times have seen this process worsening with the rise of terror attacks. At deeper level, terrorism is due to the US planting Al Qaeda for its imperial goals. Other factors worsening the phenomenon of terrorism are ethno-national problems and rising injustices against the weaker sections of society. What appeared at surface was some Muslim youth associated with the phenomenon overlooking the deeper reasons. Even here, there has been a selective projection. While the largest terrorist organization has been Liberation Tiger of Tamil Elam, while there have enough acts of terror by United Liberation Front of Assam, Khalistani movement and others, what came to be targeted due to clever machinations of right wing and the media was that all terrorists are Muslims. The result was further demonization of Islam and Muslims.

All in all, Islam came under heavy demonization all over and more so in India. It is in this background that Mr. Gnaniah's comprehensive work is a welcome contribution to the significant books dealing with the subject. The unique feature of this work in particular is the insightful comprehensive treatment of the subject, backed by meticulous research and a popular and simple presentation. Gnaniah presents the complex arguments in a simple form without loosing the rigor and logic of the argument.

One hopes that contributions like this will contribute to the social peace and amity by dispelling the deliberate lies and propaganda prevalent widely.

30

Al Qaeda or Al Fayda: Roots of Global Terror

"These gentlemen are the moral equivalents of America's founding fathers." (Ronald Regan while introducing the Mujahideen leaders to media on the White House lawns. (1985) "Americans are asking: why do they hate us? They hate our freedoms-our freedom of religion, our freedom of speech, our freedom to vote and assemble and disagree with each other." George W. Bush, in his speech in US Congress in the aftermath of 9/11. (2001) These two statements reflect the so-called transition of freedom fighters of which US administration was proud to the same one's being called enemies of US. When Tony Blair in the aftermath of 7/7 uttered his feelings that our resolve to uphold our values is stronger than their resolve to break it, he was referring to the people with same ideology and politics whom Regan praised to the sky and about whom G.W. Bush had the totally contrary view.

What has changed during last one and a half decade, have 'they' changed? Or is it that US needs have undergone a rapid transition during this decade? The reference to the ghastly acts of terrorism of 9/11 and 7/7 does send the shivers down one's spine. Not only the killings of innocents, non combatants in 9/11 and 7/7 is extremely heinous and cowardly, but also the aftermath of such actions is something one needs to mull over. The ongoing terrorism and 'war on terror' both are affecting the societies in a painful manner. While on one hand killings of innocents is a matter of deep anguish, the post terror polarisation of communities on religious ground and the demonisation of Islam are the consequences, which have deeper impact on the lives of people world over.

To begin with, the question is, who did it? Surprisingly after 9/11 the investigation has not been very definitive. It was presumed, Osama bin Laden, Al Qaeda are the ones' behind the tragic event. Afghanistan was invaded on the pretext of catching hold of Osama, nearly sixty thousand people were killed by the US attack, but could not be caught hold of. Incidentally it was Bin Osama who was projected to be the primary culprit against whom the war is being waged. US did 'succeed' in installing its puppet Govt. in Afghanistan and also in taking control of the huge oil reserves around Afghanistan.

On the ground that Iraq is a threat to US security, and also that it is harbouring Al Qaeda, it was invaded, thousands of Iraqis have since than perished and hundreds of US armed personnel have been killed. The sexual torture of Abu Gharib prison might have been just a tip of the iceberg hiding more, which we will never come to know. There are also doubts about the real culprit of 9/11 so to say, as conclusive evidence has not been produced by the US. Tony Blair did not loose even minutes to hint that 'same' culprits are involved. Some reports pointed out that it is the act of Secret Organization Group of Al Qaeda, which in its temporarily put up web site, claimed". We continue to warn the Governments of Denmark and Italy and all Crusader Governments, that they will be punished in the same way if they do not withdraw their troops from Iraq and Afghanistan."

Even in the aftermath of 9/11 there were serious doubts raised about the perpetrator of the event, whether it was Al Qaeda or was it some other agency. Any way, a pretext to attack Afghanistan could be cooked up with ease. Even now doubts are being raised that since there is a pressure on the UK Govt. to withdraw the troops from Iraq and Afghanistan and this incident will ensure that troops continue to be in Iraq. On the one hand, we have Al Qaeda and the like, who in the name of Jihad are committing havoc. These actions in the name of Jihad, are the worst enemies of Muslims as a community. These create hatred against this community and the demonization process against Muslims and Islam gets a boost after every such event. The targeting of average Muslims as terrorists and criminals gets biggest justification from such acts. These actions are the ones', which have laid the foundation of the ideology guiding many western powers and also other countries.

The other factor is the policy of Western powers, which so far has been steadfastly supporting Israel's violation of the rights of Palestinian people and its blatant vandalism in the neighboring region. The Jihadi terrorism as such was consciously brought up and promoted not by any Muslim country. It was the handiwork of US, CIA in its goal to contain the influence of Communism during the era of cold war. During that period many a countries strived for nationalism to get rid of the clutches of colonial powers. Most such endeavours were opposed by Western powers with US in the lead. With the success of communists coming to power in Afghanistan, US administration started promoting the opponents of communist regime. Communists tried to bring in land reforms, curtail the opium cultivation, and this hurt the interests of the feudal and orthodox elements.

These opponents to communist regime, the elite, were right wing Islamists. It was from this Muslim right wing that Al Qaeda was formed with the direct patronage of U.S. Billions of dollars of aid and armaments, including stinger missiles were given to Al Qaeda by U.S. Al Qaeda grouped together with the help of Pakistan and Saudi Arabia. With the defeat of communist forces US became more assertive and started interfering in the region with vehemence, the attack on Iraq in 1993 was the first manifestation of the same. The Right Wing Islamists felt the threat of US presence and the rest is too fresh in our memories to be recounted. Anti Islamism now came to substitute Anti Communism as the 'other' of imperialist powers. Lured by the oil wealth of the region US-UK axis has violated every possible international law and have removed all roadblocks to its pursuits for profit (Fayda). This axis also attacked Afghanistan and Iraq telling the world that this is the only way to make their countries safer for themselves.

Can such blatant violation of human and international norms make the world safer? And pray tell me, which is the bigger curse of the World today: Al Qaeda or Al Fayda?

Making of a Terrorist

Defining terrorism and a terrorist will remain as difficult as ever. The one non controversial part of the definition will be killing of the innocents, to intimidate the political powers and society at a particular point of time. Was killing of Indira Gandhi by her body guards, who happened to be Sikhs, an act of terrorism? She was involved in ordering the operation Blue star, the entry of army into the holiest of holy Sikh shrines, the Golden temple. General Vaidya who was Chief of army at that time was also assassinated, terrorism? When Rajiv Gandhi was murdered by the 'suicide bomb', Dhanu, what type of act was that? Rajiv Gandhi had sent the Indian Peace Keeping Force (IPKF), which the LTTE regarded as a big obstacle to their politics. Did this tantamount to terrorism?

Bhagat Singh, the hero of millions, the all time idol of the youths and revolutionaries, was part of the group which killed Saunders. Bhagat Singh himself threw a bomb in Assembly, in which no one was killed. He was labeled as terrorist by the British. While on a lecture tour in Tamil Nadu one happened to give the example of LTTE as the biggest terrorist organisation in the World today to be confronted by the section of audience, which felt that the LTTE is the organisation for freedom of Tamils in Sri Lanka. It is not too far back in the time that Irish Republican Army decided to renounce the use of terror as a tactics to gain its goal. Timothy McVeigh, the bomber who dropped a bomb in Oklahoma to kill over 300 innocent people is still fresh in many a memories. While these acts have there own place in the history of terror, the acts of terrorism to stick to one's mind are the ones by 'Muslim', terrorist groups, here and there, all around. Last decade or so has been witness to many an act of insanity which have been indulged by Muslim individuals and Muslim groups.

The trajectory came to stark focus with the 9/11 attack on World Trade Center, the London rail bombing, and of course the scattered acts going on in Kashmir off and on. The recent act of terror (October 2005) in Delhi sounded another tragic one in the same series, adding on the stereotype that'All terrorists are Muslims'. Needless to say that after each such act the search against all and sundry Muslims goes up. Their demonisation, that the Muslims are violent beings following a religion, which teaches violence, Jihad is ongoing process. And they are the one's out to harass the innocent citizen's of the world, becomes stronger by the day. The Delhi attack has been the tragedy of a serious order. So many innocents being maimed and butchered. The loss of innocent lives and demonization of Islam and Muslims keep running in parallel. Some times one feels that with these terrorists claiming to be Muslims and indulging in such acts, Muslims do not need any other enemies. These elements are doing their 'best' possible to get the whole community stereotyped in an adverse way. Nobody can do a better job in demonizing Islam than the acts of these insane elements.

Why somebody takes up such an insane path? Is it the teaching of religion, the parents of these terrorists, or are there some other mechanisms which create these terrorists. There are multiple routes by which one takes up the path of terror, killing of the innocents. When anti Muslim pogrom was stalking the streets in Mumbai, one did meet many a reasonable sounding Muslim youth who expressed their explicit desire to take to the path of revenge through retaliatory violence. After Gujarat anti Muslim pogrom, many a social scientists prophesied that this pogrom will surely give rise to terrorists. In a vast community surely there are going to be more than the critical mass of Muslims to take recourse to 'revenge' through insane methods, terrorism being one amongst them. This is the anger, hurt and the feeling that guilty will not be punished which later gets channelised through conduits which dish out terror. The Kashmir violence has belonged to another genre of violence. It was the breach of agreement about the autonomy of Kashmir, under the pressure from communal elements, that Government of India started tightening the noose around the autonomy clauses inbuilt in the treaty of accession. Nehru did advocate for winning over the hearts of Kashmiris rather than the political means to reduce the autonomy. The arrest of Sheikh Abdullah, when he complained against breach of treaty clauses related to autonomy, and putting him to jail was the triggering point of dissatisfaction amongst the Kashmiri youth which in due course led to the thorny path of terrorism, of course duly assisted by the designs of Pakistan. Just to recapitulate, it was Sheikh Abdullah who was instrumental in getting Kashmir acceded to India and it was same Sheikh Abdullah who was called a traitor by many who mattered including the Right wingers. The dissatisfaction of Kashmiris in watching their elected Prime Minister (yes he was Prime Minister of Kashmir) might have snapped many a links which help in keeping the cool and sanity.

These disgruntled elements were soon to be joined helped by the trouble making designs of Pakistani Rulers.

It is just a bit later that US started its agenda to fight the Soviet occupation of Afghanistan by the well trained Al Qaeda outfit. The money and arms for this dreaded outfit were routed through Pakistan, and the training to cultivate 'Jehadis', a concocted misnomer for terrorists, was also outsourced to Pakistan. An interpretation of Islam was manufactured to project that killing of communists is Jihad as communists don't believe in Allah. Islamic teachings were mauled by the trainers to project that killing of innocents is also part of the game in Jihad. As such, Islam, meaning submission to the will of god, does not permit killing of the innocents. But the well designed training schools of Pakistan and middle east which were playing in the hands of U.S.'s CIA did not bother as to what the teachings of Koran, Islam mean. Violence was dished out in the name of Islam and allurement of Jannat (Heaven) shown to the young recruits in the path of Islam. This was the group consciously trained to unleash terror, the bait being Islam and the reward of going to Jannat. Many a Muslim youth were recruited and trained by Maulanas in 'Islam as violence' and by CIA-ISI combine in to use of weapons and other tactics.

By this time the world started going in the path of identity politics, the era of progressive radicalism, humane struggles for rights of people started being replaced by religion in the name of politics. Religious identity became the core of politics and terror here, there and everywhere became the major phenomenon. This replaced the struggles for Human rights of the decades of sixties and seventies, the decades of progressive values. US President after President kept resorting to the promotion of terrorism in the Middle East. George Bush the current world emperor is most blatant in expressing the US designs and in this direction he seems to have direct communication with the almighty God himself. His communication system has reached right up to the Lord almighty, who is designing the calendar of invading one after the other country. One was not much surprised to hear his claim that it was on the instructions from the God himself that he invaded Iraq, and now of course God is preparing to give him the order to invade Iran and Syria in due course! One shudders to think of the times to come. The global phenomenon to give boost to the US designs for controlling the middle-east oil resources is overtly visible. Once the identity of terrorism with Islam got established, courtesy the CIA run training camps in Pakistan, now the job is comparatively easy for the world emperor. Any where, the dispute can take the shape of terror; the politics has already put on the veneer of religious identity. The real issues of the world related to environment, poverty, hunger, disease and misery can be shelved to the margins with ease and 'social common sense' can take resort to the understanding that it is due to Muslims that the present sorrows and miseries are happening. As Atal Bihari Vajpayee said, wherever there are Muslims, there are problems. Where do we go from here? How can we ensure that some youth do not take the path of terror? The underlying causes, at multiple layers, need to be addressed if we want a terror free World-India.

31

How not to Investigate and Punish a Crime: Case of Afzal Guru

The death penalty given by Supreme Court, to hang Mohammad Afzal Guru on 20th October 2006, has been deferred by the President. There are two sets of petitions lying on Presidents table, one demanding his immediate hanging and the other asking for clemency and reducing his punishment to life sentence. Guru was one of the accused in the case of assault on the Parliament on 13 December 2001, in which, eight security personnel and one gardener were killed. Guru was not found to be part of any terrorist outfit, nor did he play any direct role in the same. In the trial which took place the provisions of International Covenant on Civil and Political Rights had not been respected. Supreme Court noted that there is no direct evidence of his involvement. The evidence was mainly circumstantial. All three courts including Supreme Court have acquitted him of the charges under POTA of belonging to either a terrorist organisation or a terrorist gang. Court also noted that the evidence was fabricated. Most importantly he was not given any worthwhile legal assistance to defend him during interrogation.

When Ram Jethmalani offered to be lawyer for Geelani, the Hindutva goons attacked his office. One also recalls here that the lawyers offering to hold the brief of accused in 11 July 2006 Mumbai blasts were also threatened by Hindutva outfit, a real case of cowardly display of pseudo patriotism. At best Guru was facilitator in the crime and not a part of directly perpetrating the crime, and the evidence against him is mere circumstantial and that the police lied about the time and place of arrest, fabricated evidence including arrest memos and extracted false confessions. Court noted that he was not a member of any banned organisation, "The conviction under section 3 (2) of POTA is set aside. The conviction under section 3 (5) of POTA is also set aside because there is no evidence that he is a member of a terrorist organisation, once the confessional statement is excluded. Incidentally, we may mention that even going by confessional statement, it is doubtful whether the membership of a terrorist gang or organisation is established." Further that since "The incident, which resulted in heavy casualties, had shaken the entire nation and the collective conscience of the society will only be satisfied if capital punishment is awarded to the offender." So does it mean that the punishment is being given to assuage the collective national conscience? One must add what is presented as this conscience is the consciousness of the section of dominant middle classes.

Many a Human rights activist of repute sat on a *dharana* demanding the commutation of the death sentence, to life imprisonment. They issued appeals to the same effect and also have floated the petitions for clemency. Not to be left behind, another section of activists have floated counter petitions demanding nothing short of death penalty for this terrorist. In various talk shows the angry audience is hooting down those talking of the facts of the case and asking for leniency in the light of the holes in the story built by the police authorities. There are two major questions involved in the case. One, that death penalty should be given in the rarest of rare cases and two, when world over the brutal capital punishment is being done away with, should we stick to it? The other peripheral issues which are trying to undermine the basic issues are the hysterical nationalism of Hindu right and sections of society who cannot think that the crime of those accused of acts of terror also needs to be proved before they are punished, and that the punishment has to be commensurate with the crime. For them once Supreme Court has ruled, the doors for clemency are closed.

The base on which Supreme Court has given the judgment has been built by the police with methods which are questionable, which have also been reprimanded by the court in this case. The argument on the other side is that if Guru is not hanged it will be an insult to those who have laid their lives for defending the Parliament. And that other terrorist acts a la Kandhar may be undertaken to bargain for his release. The other question, which has got mixed up with this, is the fate of peace process, which is going on in Kashmir and South Asia as a whole. In the visual media debates, one can see the hysterical nationalism oozing from every pore of Hindu right wing and some others. Some Muslim spokespersons of this or the other party are finding this as the best opportunity to wear their patriotism on their sleeves by taking blinded firm positions against any consideration of clemency. This became most obvious when Mukhtar Abbas Naqvi of BJP went to the extent of denying that Bhagat Singhs kin can ever make a clemency petition in this case, to the loud applause of the studio audience. As a matter of fact, Bhagat Singhs kin Prof Jagmohan Singh and Anand Patwardhan, the noted documentary film maker and rights activist, had issued the appeal carried by the media. It is unlikely that the BJP spokesperson would have missed it; any way some times even feigned ignorance is bliss to pursue ones political assertions! The response of letter writers in the newspaper columns is no different. Most of them demanding the blood of this 'terrorist'! Nothing else can reflect the state of social common sense in the society. By now communal violence has become passé in the society. It is justified to the extent that those involved in this are neither punished nor even looked down upon. On the other hand, any body remotely linked to acts of terror can be hanged without any pangs of conscience, communal patriotism at is worst is on display.

While Supreme Court deserves all the respect, one has to see that the primary investigation done by the police, whatever its flaws forms the base of the judgment. When that investigation has holes, should it be accepted as it is presented? When the primary culprits are either dead or some of them absconding, can 'the whole truth be out'? Or is it that somebody has anyway to be punished to quench the thirst for revenge, and who better than the one who has a Muslim name and happens to be from Kashmir. The whole trial of Afzal needs to be looked at again; the flaws of the investigation, the weakness of and deliberate violation of norms by police authorities and the absence of competent legal assistance to Afzal should alert us to the fact that something is seriously amiss in the whole story. The worst fallout of hanging of Afzal will be that the real truth will remain buried in the shoddy investigation and the real culprits may not be apprehended at all, who so ever they are.

Merely being guided by Islamophobia is no guarantee for the

correctness of the story of prosecution. Afzals letters and the appeal of his wife have a lot to tell which has been ignored. Even the role of media in reaching Afzal to hangman's noose should be looked at carefully; we need to question that 'trail by media' should not become the base of our legal system. The quality of the judgments is the backbone of the strength of democracy. State is all powerful to hang someone on the shoddy ground but at the same time it will be hanging the very concept of a just legal system. Lets have a look at the vulnerability of Afzal Guru, a Kashmiri, a poor man and an ex-militant not being able to afford the legal cover, is that not ground enough to re-look at the case? Even the latest verdict of Apex court, that Presidential pardon is subject to review by the same system which has given punishment, nullifies the very basic of the provision of Presidential pardon. It needs to be debated whether the President will have this power or from now on there will be no appeal once the apex court has given its verdict even if that be based on the investigation full of gaping holes.

Kashmir has been reduced to 'our' real estate, where we are posting lakhs of our soldiers to deal with couple of thousand of militants! Surely if there is one Indian soldier for every seventh Kashmiri, no wonder Kashmiris will see it as an occupation army. After having said that, the punishment being meted out to Guru is not commensurate with the crime done by him, one will also endorse that the very notion of capital punishment is nothing but barbarism, and it does not become dignified if it is given to a suspected terrorist. Many of those otherwise swearing by non-violence are so communalized at the core that they are at the forefront of some or other moves demanding the hanging of Guru.

One can understand that for RSS and its affiliates this is the golden opportunity to display their patriotism, partly also to wash the sin of accompanying the terrorists to Kandhar by one of their ministers. One can also understand the success of RSS in communalizing the social thinking to the extent that now truth and humane values have ceased to matter in the face of communal thinking. Justice is being converted into revenge and punishment is meant to further communalize the society rather than a means of reform, rather than being an occasion to introspect as to why such crimes are going on. Surely no one is born a terrorist and no one likes to resort to these means by choice. What are the deeper circumstances due to which these acts of violence are taking place needs to be given a thought. One understands that terrorism is a mere symptom of the underlying disease, which has roots in injustices somewhere. One understands the terrorism cannot be finished by killing the terrorists. For that the underlying causes have to be addressed.

The double standards of our society and legal system are becoming glaringly apparent. The perpetrators of communal violence not only get away with their crimes but also some times they get promotions, as in the case of Ramdeo Tyagi of Maharashtra, the one who led the attack on Suleiman Bakery in Mumbai during 92-93 riots. Hundreds of police officials who have been named in the inquiry commission reports are enjoying the 'fruits' of their crimes of omission and commission. Thackeray and Modi, who have been the main architects of Mumbai and Gujarat riots respectively, could not even be touched by the long arm of law. On the contrary they landed up increasing their political clout after presiding over these genocides. While the perpetrators of Mumbai riots are having a gala time, the culprits of subsequent bomb blasts are being meted out the punishments due to them. The general impression is gaining ground in the society that by now there are two legal systems in the society. One for the followers of Hindu communalism, where killer of Pastor Stains, Dara Singh, is spared the noose and is hailed as *Hindu Dharma Rakshak* (protector of Hindu faith), the perpetrators of communal violence who get away with ease. The other one is for those who belong to minorities. In their case even the remotest association with the terror attacks is ground enough for hanging or the severest possible punishment.

In Kashmir, Indian army is seen as the occupation army, thousands of innocents have been tortured by this army, and Chittisingpura is just a tip of iceberg. The hanging of Maqbool Butt in 1984 did give a feeling of alienation and later a boost to militancy. Who do we blame for that? Those calling for a hangman for Guru surely are bent upon repeating the process. Nation can watch the hanging of those who have not committed the crime of such a severe proportion, but while hanging them what processes will be unleashed need to be seen overcoming the communal myopia. We must distinguish between the hysterical nationalism of the likes of those demanding the hanging and the humane nationalism wanting to call for reconsideration of the punishment meted out, to quench the feverish pitch of communalised sections of society. This hanging will surely reinforce the perception of two sets of legal norms which are prevalent in the country.

32

Islam, Fatwas and Contemporary Society

Lot is being heard about the Fatwas on every possible issue, more so pertaining to women's lives, their dress code, their marital alliance, etc. The Fatwas, which made headlines for days pertained to the case of Gudiya, whose missing husband Arif, who was captured by Pakistani army and was presumed to be a martyr in the battle, appeared on the scene. By that time Gudiya was already pregnant from her second marriage. The local Panchayat, without asking her opinion ruled that she has to return to her first husband and after the child is born, she should hand it over to the second husband. In case of Imrana, whose father in law allegedly raped her, she was dictated to live with the rapist father in law and to abandon her husband. Her opinion was not sought. In another of such shameful fatwas, an Arab was permitted to marry both the sisters in a single go, again under the umbrella of a fatwa. Marriages of girls under the age of 18 have also been solemnized under the patronage of Mullas some of whom have been opposing the Child Marriage Act in the name of Sharia.

Undoubtedly the fatwas have come to prominence and fore in last two decades in India more than before. While these claim to be the opinion of Islam, the fatwas (opinion) are different according to different schools of Islam, Shia and Sunni and their sub sects. The fatwa given on an issue in some part of India will be different from another part and surely it will be different in different countries. Theologically, fatwa is just an opinion not binding in any legal or social terms. The most notorious one was against Salman Rushdie for his literary work, which was regarded as derogatory to Prophet Mohammad. In countries like Turkey and many other Muslim countries, the fatwas were dumped in the backyard and secular rules have been brought to the fore.

Fatwas have generally been delivered by the Maulanas, residing in this or that Islamic seminary, cut off from the social milieu of the community. Most of the fatwas are very derogatory to the women. According to most liberal Islamic opinions fatwas are not having any validity as it is made out to be. Surely the very diversity of fatwas on the same issue reflects that.

The real issue is that when a community feels threatened and intimidated it falls more and more in the grip of these conservative elements, which have their own vested interests to grind. In India one can clearly see that with the rise of anti-Muslim violence, the retrograde fatwas are given more prominence. The same fatwas are used by the dominant communal elements to further demonize the Islam and Muslims. The healthy trend is that a large section of liberal Muslims who was earlier keeping quiet in the face of fatwas, is now taking a strong and clear cut stand against the self proclaimed custodians of Islam, the Maulvis and Maulanas. More than that a section of Muslim women themselves are standing firm to oppose these fatwas. Large section of Muslim community in the grip of poverty and those who live with the fear of social insecurity does fall trap to these fatwas. The battle for gender justice, humane values requires internal reforms combined with provision of social security for the community to reduce the vice like grip of fatwa delivering Maulanas.

33

Manufacturing Islamophobia

A friend's son Murali, a bright engineer, was studying in US. Murali is amongst the commonest of names amongst Hindus. This word Murali stands for flute, the musical instrument of Lord Krishna, which acted as a big lure for *Gopikas* (daughters of milkman) to fall in love with the Lord. But my friend's son Murali had a different fate. The US security agencies thought this is a name in disguise for a Muslim called Moor Ali, and the rest was the usual harassment meted out to the Muslim youth, resulting in Murali, returning to his home town, swearing at the US security agencies and all else concerned notwithstanding.

Post 9/11, the demonization of Muslims has gone several notches up. As such the demonisation of Islam, Islam being presented as the new threat coincided; on one hand with the decline of Soviet states, and on the other, with the coming to power of Ayatollah Khomeini, who succeeded in coming to power on the crest of the revolution which threw away the US stooge, Raza Shah Pehlavi. US was making merry with the Shah, who in turn was installed after the overthrow of democratically elected Mossadeq. Incidentally Mosaddeq to the great annoyance of US interests, nationalised Iran oil, and so was overthrown by a coup engineered by US agencies. The phenomenon overlapped in time to pave the way for US media and other propaganda mechanisms to project 'Islam as the new threat', the earlier threat as per the US was Communism. This propaganda picked up by and by and today, God forbid, if you have a Muslim sounding name or face or any other characteristic, the 'security' hounds will get for themselves enough work to show their prowess. The average person on the street will think twice before shaking hands with you, the lurking fear being that you may be carrying some bomb hidden on your body somewhere.

Immediately after 9/11/2001, a Sikh was murdered in US, as

the killer took him to be a Muslim. In many a European countries, the Muslims have faced intense intimidation, which is going up lately. The situation has gone to the extent that even the state governments have to wake up now if they want harmonious sailing of their affairs. Starting from innocuous looking jokes against Muslims, the matters have gone to the extent that a full fledged attempt is on to project Islam as the religion preaching hate and violence and Muslims as the intolerant fanatics. Every other person will tell you as to how Islam preaches to kill the Kafirs, How Jihad is an integral part of Islamic teaching and as to how Jihadis are mere Islamic soldiers. Here in India there is a long list of charges against Muslims, starting from the misconceptions about Muslim Kings breaking temples to humiliate Hindu religion, to every Muslim having four wives, twenty children to every terrorist being a Muslim. As such of course, whatever be the underlying cause of these misconceptions, currently there had been enough number of incidents in which Muslims have been involved in such acts, to give a pretext to the political forces benefiting from this, to give bad name to the whole Muslim community.

To add to the problem, here in India, this Islamophobia, and fear of Muslims has come on the top of ongoing RSS project of spreading Hate against Muslims which has been in operation since last more than seven decades. The interesting point is that a numerical majority has been indoctrinated to believe that this minority is a threat to them. The US propaganda and RSS designs match to a great extent. This outfit has been spreading hate against Muslims using the distorted view of history and lopsided presentation of their current social life. This propaganda succeeds as an average person will not exercise her critical faculties at every juncture when seeing the content of what is beamed on the tube of idiot box or what one keeps reading in print over and over again. As such Gobbles did grasp this mechanism to the hilt and could create the phobia against Jews, as a prelude to the genocide launched by his mentor, Adolf Hitler. Even today one is not interested in the historical content of the use of word Jihad or Kafir, or one has nothing to do with the fact that no religious community can be uniform. But this phobia against the minorities has a serious political role to play. It forms the ground on which violence stands. Which in turn ghettoises the community, intimidates its large chunk and its political rights are taken away despite the formal operation of democracies.

Culture as a disguise for religion; is shown to be at odds with the culture of others. Power stalks in the apparel of religion or culture. While this phobia plays it role in legitimising the aggression against some countries or the carnage launched against them, it in turn also creates a society with deep fractures along the religious lines. The phobia directed outside also turns inside, to create scare amongst the more powerful sections within the community itself. Most of the retrograde processes are bidirectional. Hate outside creates intimidation inside. Creation of phobia against the outsider and the increase in insecurity within.

Even if we grant that the communities targeted will become used to a new rhythm of survival under stress and fear, the bigger question is; can democracy survive in such states/ communities? While the political goals and purposes of imperialist powers, on one hand and social elite, on the other are well served in such an atmosphere, surely the progress of society is the victim on the altar of atmosphere of phobia against others. In this political scenario it is no coincidence that the sectarian understanding of communities thrives. One such sectarian nationalism was propounded by RSS chief, Golwalkar (We, or our Nation hood defined), where he asserts that Indians are basically Hindus, so others have not to be given equal citizenship. This proposition put forward in 1938, has made a strong social and political impact during last two decades. On similar lines, one does not know if there is an inspirational connection, the current US ideologue Samuel Huntington, in 'Who are we?' argues that US is essentially Anglo Saxon and others are a threat to the American ethos. While Golwalkar is the local sectarian ideologue, Huntington is currently playing the similar divisive tunes at global level. The similarity between these two ideologues is striking and the coincidence of the latter coming precisely in the decades of nineties with Hindutva, Golwalkars ideology, picking up nineties, is not just coincidental.

The matters have gone too far. The targeted hate against the Muslims, the construction of phobia against Islam has crossed the threshold. While it served the US to attack many a countries for the sake of oil wealth, it has helped the Hindus to appropriate the social privileges. At the same time it has played and more so now than anytime before; a counterproductive role to those states/ societies and communities themselves. The schism between communities is acting on the nerves of democracies and weakening them as the process of societal development is getting retarded. It surely will have the impact on weaker sections of society and also will affect the economies worldwide. Human values have taken a back seat during this period. This era of dark sectarianism needs to be overcome as soon as possible. The rise of right wing, religious right at various places is a warning to the democracies and the progressive liberal elements all over the world that if this Islamophobia is not checked, the acts of terrorism will continue. The reality in the world is standing on the head many a time; though it seems currently as if terrorism is due to violence inherent in Islam and Muslims, the fact is that it is the political lust of vested interests that Islam is demonised.

We need to work on intercommunity relations, on spreading the words of harmony and peace, to look at religions as a set of moral values and not just a set of rituals or identities. We need to have the humane spirit prevail over the machinations of the interests of those out to grab the global and local resources for their own selves.

SECTION–VIII

PERCEPTIONS AND REALITY

34

Manufacturing Consent: Communalism-Terrorism and Perceptions about Minorities

Noam Chomsky is one of the foremost rights activists, apart from being an outstanding linguist. While analysing the US foreign policies, especially its war against weaker countries, Chomsky theorised that US administration creates consent of the broad layers of population for its acts of aggression. The perceptions which were drilled into popular psyche related to the dangers of communism, while attacking the emergent nation state of Vietnam in yesteryears or weapons of mass destruction (WMD) in Iraq, in recent times. This is achieved in a systematic way when the act is to be undertaken. It is another matter that as the voices of opposition start emerging gradually, the original propaganda starts getting questioned, but the mainstream US propaganda is generally too huge to be countered by the skeptics and its opponents. This is achieved through various mechanisms, the major of that being the media of course, print and visual both. And by the time holes in the state version start appearing in popular mind, the 'goal' of the state is achieved. So even if the critics prove that there were no WMDs, the goal of controlling the oil wells is over. Even if some sections question the veracity of the version of 9/11, Afghanistan is in its pocket.

This thesis can be extended with some modification to other ruling governments also. Another dimension to this comes when the powerful political formations, in power or out of power, achieve the same, through molecular permeation, infiltration in media, through a section of political leadership and other parts of state apparatus. In Indian context the perceptions about minorities can be traced to the role and sustained propaganda programs of 'supra-political', formation which aims to have a particular type of nation and particular type of social relations of caste and gender.

One is referring to today's popular perceptions about Muslims and Christians in India. Currently 'All terrorists are Muslims' is the perception, deep rooted, hardly affected by the reports of citizens fact finding committees or the academic and popular contributions by activists/scholars. The initial propaganda gradually became part of broad ranging perceptions and the policies of the administration, police and other investigating agencies make it the base of their actions. So we see that Batla house encounter in the Jamia Nagar has lot of holes in the story dished out by the vacillating police authorities and the human rights activists have pointed the flaws in the same demanding a deeper probe. The acceptance of such a simple demand is shelved in order to go along with popular sentiments and to 'preserve the morale' of police force! The voice of these activists questioning the version dished out by the authorities hardly reaches at popular level as the media already ensures that police version is part of popular perception. Truth, the desirable guiding principle of the social policies can wait. In different acts of terror, in front of mosques or in other crowded places, always the Muslims are involved and the job of investigating authorities is fairly well cut out. The tragedy with a section of media is that, contrary to ethical norm of doubting the official/ police versions, they are not only meekly accepted; at times they are accepted in highly exaggerated form as well.

Few Muslim youths are caught, tortured, they are made to confess their role in the acts of terror, the mystery is supposed to be solved, criminals unearthed as they have confessed to their crime, and the authorities get a pat on the back. All terrorists are Muslims is the guiding credo of social thinking and state's thinking as well, and now the authorities can rest in peace that they have unearthed the criminal nexus. Here the word "Islamic terrorism', initially popularised US media after 9/11, is generously used while no body has heard of Hindu terrorism when Dhanu of LTTE killed Rajiv Gandhi or Sikh terrorism, when Khalistanis were doing such actions or Christian terrorism when Irish Republican Army was indulging in acts of terror.

The other points elaborated by Chomsky relate to 'Thinkable

thought' and 'Unthinkable thought', these are the out come of the propaganda, indoctrination, which is the culmination of the same process. So by now the thinkable thought is that all Muslims are terrorists and unthinkable thought is that any one else can be also be a terrorist. By now all the acts of terror where Bajrang Dal is involved are either, suppressed' under-projected or forgotten with ease by the social thinking process. So the Bajrang Dal activists getting killed while making bombs in Nanded or Kanpur soon lapse out from popular memory, the blasts where Hindu Jagran Samiti is involved is not taken due note of and in due course they are let off to continue with their 'job'. Now it is unthinkable thought that 'Hindus' indoctrinated in the Hate ideology can indulge in such activities.

The consistent propagation that Christian Missionaries convert by force and fraud and with the help of sack-full of money sent by foreign powers is the thinkable thought, good enough of a pretext to kill and maim them, burn the Churches while the state Government claiming to be secular is unable to apprehend the criminals. Good governance! So arguments are generated in the natural course to let the criminals do there job for good enough time. There are reports by the human rights groups to the contrary, but that is not the story bought by the mainstream, media and others, who so ever constitutes that. Such voices of human rights groups remain marginal, hardly taken serious note of by the majority.

While a section can claim that they are objective, the pattern of reporting of large section of media on anti-Christian violence is hidden in the small columns in the back pages while the acts of terror hog the front page banner headlines. Channels keep screaming about a Muslim terrorist, while the killers of Christian minority and rapists of the nuns, those burning churches, are somewhere buried under the weight of the news of 'Jehadi terrorist', and of those doing aggressive conversions! What Chomsky needs to add to his magnum opus is that it is not only the state which can manufacture consent; it can be a political grouping which can keep doing its sustained propaganda and influence the state to do its work. By now in India even when the communal party is not in power, the job of demonisation of minorities can go on as the millions of trainees from the Sangh

Shakhas are doing their job, as a large section of media, the dominant one, is doing the job for the cultural nationalists, wanting to demolish democracy, democratic nationalism and create a Hindu nation on the grave of the concept of equal rights for minorities.

So today, even when the role of state in the carnage of Gujarat, and Modi's role in leading the carnage in Gujarat is well known, for section of media he is the hero, for whom he is the hope for India. So today when it is a well known secret that VHP and Bajrang Dal are behind the Orissa violence, they can dare the state to ban them and see the consequences! So it is thinkable (and doable too) that SIMI should be banned, it is unthinkable that Bajrang Dal can be banned for its role in Orissa violence. The difference between terrain described by Chomsky and ours relates to the fact that the consent manufactured against minorities in India, is part of the politics to demolish the very values of India's syncretic traditions, which created the India community, it is a subtle attack on the values of our freedom movement which upheld pluralism and fraternity.

35

Madrassas Versus RSS Run Schools

Since 9/11 2001, it started being propagated that Madrassas are the training dens for terrorists. This went on becoming part of social psyche to the extent that even the West Bengal Chief Minister Buddhadeb Bhattacharya came to state some thing on similar lines. It is being repeated ad infinitum at various forums by many a people. This added to the prevalent communal propaganda against Muslims. Recently in a (October 2009) meeting of EKAL school teachers, Mohan Bhagawat, the RSS Sarsanghchalak, came out with one such formulation again. While speaking to the teachers of EKAL schools (single teacher schools set up by RSS affiliates, mainly in Adivasi areas), he said that Madrassas are the breeding ground for terrorism. He also contrasted Madrassas with the work of EKAL schools. As per him EKAL schools are contributing to the cause of nation building, teaching humanity, by inculcating moral values.

This is not only a sweeping statement but is far from truth. One can say the statement about Madrassas is based on half truth while the one about EKAL schools has nothing to do with truth at all.

One concedes that some Madrassas were set up in Pakistan by US through CIA, to indoctrinate a section of Muslim youth into terrorism. These Madrassas were funded by US and the syllabus used in these was created in Washington. This syllabus was aimed to indoctrinate the youth to take up arms against the Russian army occupying Afghanistan in the late 1970s. This syllabus was so designed that the core words of Koran were distorted and hate was manufactured against non Muslims, to begin with against Russian communists. The meaning of the word Jihad, which in Koran stands for striving, to struggle to cover one's own evils and struggle against the evils in society, was reduced to the word war. The word Kafir, which was used for the non-believers in Islam attacking Muslims, was changed to mean all those not believing in Allah. This was a ploy to 'use' Muslim youth for US war against Russians during the cold war era. From these indoctrinated youth, Taliban, Al Qaeda was organised with Osama bin Laden in the lead, funded heavily to join the anti-Russian forces, to control the oil rich zone, the central goal of US during that era. As matters turned out the, same Al Qaeda, after the Russian army was defeated, turned its guns-bombs against US and others, including India. Currently Pakistan herself is the biggest victim of Al Qaeda terrorism as they cannot tolerate the struggle of democracy to root itself in Pakistan. One such place where the trainees were becoming uncomfortable for the rulers of Pakistan, Lal Masjid was attacked by Pakistan army, a couple of years ago.

Barring these few terror centers, the concept of Madrassa as such is meant for teaching Koran and Fiqh (Jurisprudence), which will be different according to the sect of Islam, in each Madrassa. In India there are many types of Madrassa's. Mostly these are the places where poor Muslim children, who cannot afford the modern education, are sent for some learning. Nearly 4% of Muslim children are studying in these places. They mainly teach Koran, they also train the children to become Maulanas, the tribe most poorly paid for all their labour. There has been no case of terrorists being trained in these places. There are efforts by various social organizations to modernise them so that the children can come up to get modern jobs in the society. Recently, in the state neglected refugee camps of Gujarat, while the Maulanas are insisting on just madrassa education, many a Muslims in rehabilitation colonies have been trying to send their children to modern schools, but as there is a total neglect from the state they have no option but to continue with these schools. The need to introduce modern teaching, science, English, computers and all whatever can give jobs to the children is a crying need of the hour. And this is something not being addressed by the state and society as a whole, depriving a large section of Muslim children from the education which should make them come to the spaces of decent livelihood and employment. It is also needed that the misconceptions about madrassa's deliberately spread by political forces are countered by social auditing of the Madrassas. People form their perceptions on hearsay, while a visit to Madrassa, an observation of what is going on, going through their syllabus should make it clear that these are the neglected places of learning needing our urgent attention, miles away from anything which smacks or training children into terrorism.

About EKAL schools and other RSS run educational institutions the least said the better. Number of scholars and activists have studied their curriculum. Many an objective scholarly studies are available. Reports point out that EKAL schools and other RSS run educational institutions are teaching history and social sciences to suit the agenda of Hindu nation. These include projecting Muslims and Christians as foreigners, glorifying caste system, spreading hate against minorities. In their curriculum the communal historiography as introduced by British, to implement the policy of divide and rule, to demonize the Muslim kings is, the fulcrum around which the curriculum revolves. The battles of Hindu kings against the Muslim kings are presented as the battle between two religions. The power aspect of Kings rule is bypassed e.g. Rana Pratap becomes a Hindu king fighting for Hindu honor, while as a matter of fact the Rana Pratap-Akbar battle was on the issue of designation, Das Hazari (ten thousand) or Panch Hazari (five thousand). Akbar never came to Haldi Ghati where the battle took place, it was his commander-in-chief Raja Mansingh who was fighting against Rana Pratap and Rana Pratap himself was having Hakim Khan Sur as his General in the battle.

EKAL schools are primarily set up in tribal areas. They indoctrinate the children against minorities. Christian Missionaries working in the Adivasi areas are targeted as their work in the area of education and health is empowering Adivasis and that is the cause of concern to the elites-affluent people who form the power base of RSS. The Christian missionary activities may be there for over a century, but the violence in these areas has begun from last two decades in particular. The EKAL schools have been set up precisely a decade or so earlier to the beginning of the violence in these areas. So what is the correlation? Interestingly the terrorists of the ilk of Sadhvi Pragya Singh Thakur, (Malegaon blast) Bajrang Dal workers who got killed in Nanded while making bombs and others involved in bomb blast in Thane-Panvel and Goa etc., all derive their inspiration from the indoctrination module dished out in its shakhas (branch) and schools.

Is it not time we modernize Madrassas and do the auditing of the curriculum of Madrassas and Ekal schools both? Let the values of Constitution be the judge and the guiding factor for evaluating the curricula in all the schools and educational system in the country.

36

Shiv Sena Ire Against Shahrukh Khan

In the past, (January 2010) Shahrukh Khan, the celebrated film star, voiced his opinion that Pakistani Cricket players should not be prevented from playing in IPL cricket League. This sparked a big row of protest from the local Shiv Sena supporters, who criticized Khan and tore the posters of his film, 'My Name is Khan', they also went on to say if Shahrukh's 'Khan' is awakening he should very well go to Pakistan and be there. At the same time Shiv Sena is spearheading a violent campaign, 'Mumbai for Maharashtrians', to which even cricket star Sachin Tendulkar, a Maharashtrian, amongst others voiced their opinion that all parts of India belong to all the Indian citizens.

Mumbai is currently seeing the turmoil around these twin issues, regionalism, and communalism in its worst form. One knows that India-Pakistan relations have been quiet strained right since the beginning. There have been three wars between these two neighbors. The people living across the borders, with relatives on either side have been moaning with pain and anguish due to this strife between the two countries. Many issues have been a bone of contention between the two neighbours, the major lately being terrorism.

Terrorism needs to be understood in its depth if it is to be eliminated. The roots of this terror lie in the politics of oil, creation of Madrassas on the soil of Pakistan to train the Al Qaeda terrorists by US. US wanted to confront the Russian occupation of Afghanistan in the late 1970s. This Al Qaeda was created by indoctrinating the Muslim youth by instilling distorted version of Islam. Osama bin Laden was brought in again by machinations of US, same Osama was given millions of dollars and tons of armaments to join the anti Russian forces.

After the defeat of Russian forces this indoctrinated outfit turned against others in the region. It did create havoc and continues to torment the region. It has been like a Frankenstein's monster, which has misused the identity of Islam for the acts of violence and currently Pakistan is the major victim of this monster.

While terrorism's base might be in Pakistan, it is not the Pakistani state, or Pakistani people or democratic elements that are supporting this poisonous cancer. As such, Pakistan lost her ex-Prime Minster and regularly we see the acts of terror in Pakistan. To eliminate this cancer, the civilian Government in Pakistan is trying its own bit, but the Military-Mullah complex in Pakistan, patronized by US, is the one, which nurtures this phenomenon. While we are fully justified in condemning terrorism, calling upon civilian government to control it, it is also true that gestures of friendship to Pakistan will strengthen civilian government and eliminate terrorism in the long run. So peace with Pakistan has to be strengthened through music, sports, business and educational exchange. A Hate campaign between the neighbours will be harmful to the interests of both the countries.

So while anger against terrorism is natural, we can't ignore the deeper dynamics of the region and shun peace. Peace is the pre-requisite of progress of the region. The insinuations by Shiv Sena against Shahrukh, asking him to go to Pakistan, just because his name is Muslim, is against the values of Indian Constitution and the spirit of the National movement, which built the country. The divisive nature of regional politics is to be condemned through and through. Our concept of citizenship is not based around religion. People of all religions are equal citizens of the country. To doubt the patriotism of any citizen just because of 'one's religion' is the insult of Indian Constitution.

Same way, while appreciating the fact that the metros like Mumbai can't accommodate the population beyond a point, there is also a need to introspect as to why so many people migrate to Mumbai? As such, it is lop sided development of the country which forces people to migrate to such a metropolis. So while demanding a curb on Shiv Sena for its hooliganism and anti national utterances, one also has to focus attention for a pattern of development where people don't have to migrate just to survive. That's where the crux of the matter is.

Shiv Sena has a complex history. It was supported by industrialists and partly nurtured by a section of Congress leadership decades ago. The idea then was to smash the left trade unions, which were struggling for workers rights in an honest way. Later the same Shiv Sena attacked the South Indians, then Gujaratis and finally North Indians for sometime before jumping on the Rath (chariot) of Hinduvta spearhead by BJP's Lal Krishna Advani. Shiv Sena has been the most firm ally of BJP and its communal politics all through. Shiv Sena's supremo Bal Thackeray has also been indicted in the Sri Krishna Commission Report, a report which has been put into cold storage by the Congress government. Interestingly Shiv Sena, SS, presents its role in Mumbai violence as being that of protecting Hindus, a formulation which is from the World of make believe, which presents victim as the culprit, as Shri Krishna Commission makes it very clear.

The methods employed by Shiv Sena earlier and MNS (Maharashtra Nav Nirman Sena) of Raj Thackeray show the parallels with the ones' employed by Hitler's foot soldiers, i.e. to intimidate people through street violence. In this direction on regular basis Shiv Sena in particular, attacked artists, Gulam Ali, a Gazal singer from Pakistan, M.F. Hussain, a Painter, and now Shahrukh Khan. The 'storm trooper' methods of SS had been associated with the parallel ones from RSS stream, Bajrang Dal, etc. The idea is to vandalize and make a glaring attack on liberal values of democracy. While outfits like SS, MNS and Bajrang Dal are fascists, they use democratic space, the lapses of opportunist centralist politics to come up in the social space. Hitler also used the democratic space to come, to abolish the democratic space itself. The analogies of such formations with Hitler, fascists are too glaring to be ignored. They are a product politics of vested interests, taking advantage of centrist formations like Congress and than turning into Frankenstein's monsters.

With Bal Thackeray trying to pass on the mantle of his fascist politics, Uddhav and Raj, son and nephew respectively, claimed the inheritance. Bal Thackeray decided to anoint his son Uddhav as the heir apparent. Peeved by this the more aggressive Raj launched his own outfit, Maharashtra Nav Nirman Sena. In the formative period of MNS, Congress again played a complicit role by sitting pretty when Raj unleashed his aggression against hapless taxi drivers from North India and Bihar. This acted as the tonic for the MNS, and it became bold enough to unleash rampage time and over again. It has come to stay as a political force. The role of Congress has been very compromising as far as formation of Shiv Sena and MNS are concerned.

Shiv Sena-MNS primarily belong to divisive-fascist anti national ideology of communalism and regionalism. Their disregard for the values of Indian Constitution is there for all to see. Their politics also proves that divisive ideologies strengthen each other. Both these outfits, particularly Shiv Sena has been using both these sectarianisms for its political benefit.

Shiv Sena and its offshoot, Maharashtra Nav Nirman Sena, both thrive on the divisive sentiments. The spirit of National integration is being attacked by the actions of these regional forces. We should not target our citizens in the name of religion or region. The encouragement of Hate against Pakistan is shortsighted and is playing to the crude emotions, ignoring the deeper causes of terrorism, for that the finger of accusation should point to the US policies which has been pursing its politics of control in the region and has used Pakistan as the base and ally for its ambitions of appropriating this Black Gold. One must support the rights of all our citizens within the limits of Indian Constitution and restrain the regional and communal forces for the sake of national progress.

37

Lamb Allies with Wolf!: Kerala Christian Group and VHP join Hands Against Illusory Love Jihad

At a point of time there was a slogan by RSS combine, *Pehle Kasai Phir Isai* (First the Muslims then the Christians). And lo and behold that was the pattern of communal violence. First it began against Muslims and in the decade of 1990s Christians were also put on the chopping block. It must be a real ingenuity of RSS combine, popularly called Sangh Parivar to rope in the Kerala Bishops Council to fight against the Love-Jihad, a word coined by their propaganda mill, a word which combines two words and converts them into a tool to torment the lovers, in case the boy happens to be a Muslim and the girl a non Muslim. It is the latest tool to launch attack against Muslim minorities.

The level of communalisation of society and institutions can be gauged from the fact that this 'love-Jihad' was taken to be something real not only by a section of society but also by the High courts. In its ruling, the Karnataka High court, in the case of Sijalraj and Azghar, said that the facts had "national ramifications... concern security, besides the question of unlawful trafficking of women,"! So it ordered the Director-General and Inspector-General of Police to hold a thorough investigation into to 'love jihad'. Pending that, the girl was asked to stay with her parents. Nothing can be more illegal and influenced by the propaganda prevailing in the society. How can the court ask the adult married girl to separate from her husband just because the disapproving parents have complained against the choice of husband made by her, a citizen of the country?

In a similar case earlier the Kerala High Court while hearing the appeal from two parents passed a similar order. Two Hindu girls had eloped and got converted to Islam and planned to get married. The court stated that this marriage of girls to Muslims smacks of a systematic plan, related to trafficking of Hindu women. Kerala court also ordered the Police authorities to investigate this phenomenon. The police investigation showed that there is no such phenomenon as Love Jihad. The Karnataka state PUCL enraged by the decision of the court to send the girl to her parents is planning to knock the doors of Supreme Court.

The propaganda began by organizations like Shri Ram Sene etc. They spread the word that over 4000 Hindu girls have been lured into conversions. The propaganda was that the Muslim youth are receiving money to lure Hindu-Christian girls to convert them to Islam. As per this propaganda the Muslim youth are given a brief to lure the girls for which, they are provided with a lakh of rupees to buy mobile and a two wheeler. They are made to pretend to fall in love, to elope, to convert the girl to marry and to produce four children. This concoction has been aggressively propagated through various mechanisms.

This laughable, figment of imagination spread like wild fire and frightened the parents. Shri Ram Sena associates helped couple of girl's parents to go to court. In one such case the girl was made to stay with her parents by the court order. The trajectory of many of these girls who initially state about their love for the boy and voluntary conversion, changes after they are forced to stay with here parents. Under a sort of emotional blackmail, some girls give in and later say that they were brain washed, shown a Jihadi CD and what not.

We have witnessed such inhuman acts in the form of propaganda in Gujarat in the wake of carnage, that Muslim boys are luring Adivasi girls. Shri Ram Senas Babu Bajarangi, who was also a major participant in carnage, formed a goon-gang. This gang attacked couples and forced them to separate if they belonged to different religions. All this is presented as defense of religion! We have the case of Rijwan Ur Rehman where Priyanka Todi, daughter of an affluent and powerful business magnate also turned around under emotional blackmail from parents and relatives. Later Rijwan Ur Rehman was forced to commit suicide. In all such cases the role of police, state machinery, has been totally against the spirit and provisions of law, the protectors of law acting to support the things totally against the law.

Such campaigns against inter-religion, inter-caste marriages are not only against the spirit of national integration they also aim to control the lives of girls in the patriarchal mode. In addition the bogey against a minority is whipped up to aid the divisive politics. It is a double bonus for divisive politics. Since in patriarchal norms, women are regarded as property of man and are made to live in the control structure defined by men, such an issue rouses high emotions. Communal politics targets to subjugate Muslims and to promote patriarchal norms. And for achieving this they have succeeded in roping in another victim minority to ally in the communal project. It kills so many birds with one stone.

The committed social organizations have a long list of issues related to women. In Kerala, in particular the psychological problems of women are immense. Women all around are victims of gender discrimination. The social organisations falling under the trap in the name of Love Jihad need to wake up and address the real issues of women rather than becoming an ally in a communal project.

It is a pity that the courts rather than clamping on Khap Panchayats, which are taking arbitrary decisions to separate the couples marrying in the same gotra, rather than clamping on Shri Ram Senas and Babu Bajrangis, they are snubbing the girls for their choices and letting the anti Muslim tirade grow through another of a make believe myth, a falsity with dangerous portents.

One recalls that it was during the freedom movement, that different communities started interacting more and inter-religion, inter-caste, inter-region marriages started taking place. These are the cement for Indian nationalism. The propagators of Religion based nationalism, any way are against the Secular Indian Nation so this one more fabrication to intimidate the society!

38

Maa Tujhe Salaam: Vande Matram Controversy to the Fore Again

Jamiat-Ulema-e-Hind on 2nd Nov. 2009 passed a resolution asking Muslims not to recite Vande Mataram on the ground that some verses of the national song are against the tenets of Islam. Similar fatwa was also passed by Darul Ulum Deoband three years ago, when the controversy began afresh. These organisations have also passed the fatwa that violence, terrorism is against the concept of Islam.

Hell broke loose, with the fatwa on Vande Matram. The self appointed custodians of nationalism and section of media asserted that this fatwa is anti National. RSS Chief Mohan Bhagwat, said that '*Vande Matram Kahna Hoga*' (One will have to say Vande Matram). Earlier Shiv Sena in particular, had dictated that '*Is Desh Mein Rahna hai to Vande Matram Kahna Hoga*' (If one has to live in this country they must say-sing Vande Matram.

There is a vast middle ground. Most of the Muslim participants in the television talk shows and many other Muslim leaders and intellectuals said that this fatwa is unacceptable and not worth giving any importance as Indian Constitution has settled the matter. The first two stanzas of the song, which are free from the Hindu imagery is to be sung. Many a commentators also pointed out that the singing of any song cannot be imposed as that violates the freedom of religion as guaranteed by the constitution.

So we have three major streams of opinion on the Song issue. On one extreme, Muslim orthodox-conservatives like from Jamiat-Ulema-e-Hind are opposing it. Middle ground from amongst Muslims and Hindus not making a big issue of someone's singing or not singing it. As a matter of fact, majority of Muslims are stating that they have no problem in singing the song and that they will sing it. On the other extreme is the RSS fatwa, intimidating and assertive, that the song must be sung.

This song has a complex history. It was written by Bankim Chandra Chatterjee and, later was made a part of his novel *Anand Math*. This novel has strong anti Muslim rhetoric. This song was very popular with a section of society, but Muslim League strongly objected to the song, as the song compares India with Goddess Durga. Islam being monotheistic religion does not recognize any other God-Goddess than Allah. Many others belonging to monotheistic religions also had problem with the song. In 1937, the Song committee of the Indian National Congress with Nehru and Maulana Abul Kalam amongst others as members selected Jana Gana Mana as the national anthem and picked up first two stanzas of Vande Matram as national song.

Supreme Court had also to deal with this issue. School-children from the 'Jehovah's Witnesses faith' had refused to sing the national anthem because their religion forbade them to sing it. School expelled the students. The matter went to Supreme Court, which observed that a secular court cannot enquire into the correctness or otherwise of religious beliefs. The ground on which court gave its verdict was the assessment whether the belief is genuinely and conscientiously held by a sizable section of the community, and that the belief is not opposed to public order and morality. The Supreme Court struck down the students' expulsion as violative of their freedom of religion guaranteed by Article 25 of the Constitution and students were taken back.

Soli Sorabjee one of our celebrated legal luminary takes the cue from Justice Chinnappa Reddy to explain the rational of the judgment, "Our tradition teaches tolerance; our philosophy preaches tolerance; our constitution practices tolerance; let us not dilute it". The controversy has been raging since 2006 when the UPA Government called for singing of the song in schools.

Interestingly even the Shiromani Gurudwara Prabandhak Committee had asked Sikhs not to sing Vande Matram, but most of the Sikhs defied that and continued singing the song. One of the most touching rendition of Vande Matram has come from none other than A.R. Rehman, the celebrated Indian music maestro.

To use general labels as anti national are very misplaced and oppressive. Same Jamat-I-Islami Hind is the one which stood solidly with the concept of composite Indian nationalism. And there are shades and shades of opinions amongst Muslims. Maulana Abul Kalam Azad, Maulana Hussain Ahmad Madni and many other Muslim clerics went along with the idea of singing first two stanzas of the song. Legally while Constitution recognizes Vande Matram as a National Song, it also gives us the freedom of religion, and the Supreme Court judgments have struck down the extreme position that Anthem-Song must be sung.

Father of the nation, the heart and soul of Indian Nationalism, who united all the people cutting across religion, caste and gender, Mahatma Gandhi, also came to the same conclusion that Jana Gana Mana, should be the Anthem. But this conclusion of Gandhi was not acceptable to Nathuram Godse who made this as one of the points of anger against the father of the nation leading to Godse's assassinating the father of the nation. (http://www.outlookindia.com/articles.aspx?232358).

So how does one reconcile to differences in a democratic society? Dr. Ambedkar pointed out that in a democracy the minority should gradually try to overcome its separate 'minority identity' and the majority should create a situation where minority does not feel insecure to retreat inside the shell of its minority identity. One feels the more we create a situation where minorities can live with security and equity, such fatwas will be totally ignored by the minority community, as has been the case with Sikh community ignoring the mandate of SPGC. And even now amongst Muslims most of them are against this fatwa, so it is time that the other extremists stop sticking anti national label to these conservative groups and more so to the community involved.

Minorities can either be brow beaten to submit to the wish of those claiming to be representing the majority, or the situations should be created where minorities feel equally safe and confident in this country to voluntarily and comprehensively overcome such types of dictates, fatwas from one or other section of conservative groups.

SECTION–IX

CROSS BORDER ISSUES

39

Taliban's Terror-Jizya on Sikhs

Pakistan is going through dangerous turmoil. The Taliban's capturing of Swat valley (April 2009) and other parts of Pakistan are accompanied by the news of their atrocities in the region, which not only include the brutal killing of innocent citizens, mostly Muslims, on the ground of their belonging to different sub-sect of Islam, but also there has been imposition of Jizya, on non Muslims, Sikhs. While many Muslims have been killed and abducted on various flimsy grounds, many a Sikhs have fled from the area. The failure to pay the full Jizya has caused Sikhs dear, while some of them have been kidnapped and others' households-properties have been confiscated. Taliban's logic is that they are imposing this as per the tenets of Islam.

What is the place of Jizya in Islam and is it relevant today? There is a mention of Jizya in Koran, the tax levied on non Muslims, in the conquered territories. Interestingly there was no such tax in Medina where Prophet lived for long years. The logic of Jizya on non Muslims in the conquered areas was that the non Muslims are to be exempted from military services, they are under the protection of the rule of Muslims so this tax. It was a negotiable tax to be paid at the end of the year; it was levied only on the earning population in exchange for state protection. There was the parallel tax, Zakat on Muslims, which in many cases was more than the Jizya. There are instances when the Jizya levied by Muslim conquerors on non Muslim population turned out to be lower than the earlier taxation. It was more than clear that Jizya is not amongst eternal norms of Islam, it is something which has to be decided on social and political circumstances of the place and time.

We see that in later times with emergence of different political systems, Jizya was not much heard of. In India some Mughal rulers imposed this on non Muslims with the similar intention.

The aim of this was neither to punish the subjects nor to convert them. Mischievously the communal historiography in India tries to project that Aurangzeb and some other Muslim rulers imposed this as a means to convert the people. This argument does not hold any water. If Jizya was dished out as a threat to make people to convert to Islam then with conversion one will have to pay Zakat, which is no less. But any way the communal forces have made a good use of this to project the Muslim rulers in bad light and to demonise Muslims in current times.

Taliban is one of the most retrograde tendencies of Islam, bordering on insanity. Its action of atrocities on women, on other Muslims is most reprehensible. Jizya on Sikhs is the latest in the series of such barbaric acts. If we go slightly back in time we see that Taliban was also responsible for destruction of Buddha statues in Bamiyan. Who are Taliban and do they represent Islam?

Taliban has to be seen as a part of the politics in the name of religion, based on extremist Islamic streams, emerging in the oil rich zone, in countries like Saudi Arabia, Kuwait e.g., where the rulers have been making merry by playing hand maiden to the US designs of control on the oil wealth of the region. They have used Wahabi-Salafi, and other retrograde versions of Islam to keep their population subjugated and to ward off the democratic transformation of society. Their export of these fanatic versions to other countries got support in the areas at a time when United States was scheming to fight the occupation of Soviet troops by Russian armies.

The goal of US policy was to fight the Russian army by using the Asian Muslim youth. They achieved this by picking up meanings of Kafir and Jihad from these retrograde versions of Islam, where by the original meanings and the context is sacrificed, and Kafir comes to stand for every non Muslim and Jihad stands for killing the Kafirs. The systematic syllabus to train and indoctrinate the Muslim youth was developed in the strategy rooms of Washington and implemented in the specially opened Madrassas in Pakistan. It is the students of these Madrassas who were the fodder for Al Qaeda, led by Osama bin Laden. Osama was richly funded by US, through CIA and lot of this money was raised by encouraging the opium trade. While a decade ago this might have been a revelation, today all this has come out through various scholarly researches. Even Asif Ali Zardari confessed so much in his *New York Times* article, the article was reproduced by many major papers in India.

Osama not only received the monetary aid, he also received the armaments in huge quantities, with the help of which he defeated the Russian armies. With the power vacuum coming up in Afghanistan, the less known Taliban, duly supported by US came up to be the major force in Afghanistan, later to be undermined after the post 9/11 US invasion of Afghanistan. They resurfaced again with time. This cancer sowed by the US to fulfill its oil thirst survived the invasion and is currently tormenting the region, more particularly the Pakistan society. Hillary Clinton conceded as much when she said lot of the problems in the area are outcome of US policy in the region.

One should not jump to demonise Islam by the actions of Taliban or Al Qaeda. Many rulers have used the identity of religion for expansion of their empires, to launch brutal wars, Crusades, Jihads, and Dharmyudhas. The beneficiary of this version of 'religion at the service of rulers', is Kings and the clergy, while average people suffer. The common theme of use of religion in politics is that such a use, nay abuse, of religion revolves around the identity related things of that religion and not to the morality of the religion. And Taliban or Al Qaeda are not alone in this category, there are others from other religions who commit similar atrocities on people of other religions, in the name of their religion. Religion is not an abstract phenomenon as such. On one hand, it reflects the social and political reality, and on the other shapes the same forces. There are different streams in every religion, depending on which social reality it reflects.

One fully stands with the Sikh community in condemning the brutality of Taliban. One also stands with the leaders of Indian Muslim community who have whole heartedly condemned this act of Taliban. The social and religious leaders of Indian Muslim community in their joint statement have not only condemned this act of Taliban, they also point out that Jizya has no place in modern world. As the region in the neighbourhood of India has been infested with the poisonous seeds of Al Qaeda and Taliban, one must recall the dangerous role played by the US Empire and local collaborators the Pakistan army. It is not its moral obligation that

US compensates the region for the mess it has created here? Is it not time that United Nations ensures the preservation of Human rights of those living in this area? The local Muslim leaders have already condemned the Taliban-Al Qaeda atrocities. The fanatics wearing the garb of Islam must be dealt with firmly and human rights of all must be upheld to the fullest extent.

40

Pakistan: Victim of Imperialist Designs

The tragic events of 26/11, the Mumbai terror attack, have brought forward different responses from diverse sections of society. One most common is that since the terror groups are based in Pakistan, the attack should be launched on Pakistan to wipe out the training centers located in there. The popular yoga guru, Baba Ramdeo with massive following expressed that this is the right time to teach a lesson to Pakistan.

Pakistan President, Asif Ali Zardari in an article in *New York Times*, argues that the terror training camps located in Pakistan were propped up and supported by United States to train the terrorist to fight against the Soviet occupation of Afghanistan during the cold war era. It is clear that these bases and the indoctrinated terrorists, who are a product of these camps have been brain washed into violence on the misplace notions of Kafir, enemy, and this concept of kafir was instilled amongst the youth in these US supported madrassas.

Will attacking Pakistan help the matters? The Frankenstein's monsters created for pursuance of political goals are easy to produce and difficult to control and eradicate once their political utility is over. Khalistanis were similarly promoted to go more and more into extremism, Sikhism was invoked as a cloak for this politics. Later the same monster turned against the forces which aided in their creation. Not surprisingly Al Qaeda clones later turned their guns against their creators and others.

With Zardari stating the truth about the US designs in floating Al Qaeda, the researchers/activists working in the area who have been saying this, the truth of this phenomenon is reinforced. The truth is that the US imperialism is capable of creating monsters for its political goals and then these elements continue to do the dirty tricks in times to come. The biggest harm due to US couching its political-economic ambitions in religious language has been demonisation of a religion and a religious community with tragic consequence for the community.

So much paper has been blackend likening terrorism with Islam and Muslims. But the average common sense stopped short of the truth of US involvement in the whole game. Our social common sense is reflected by what saffron robed Swami has said.

The state of Pakistan as such has been a victim of the Colonial power's design in the pre-independence era and later it has been mauled and used by US for maintaining its hegemony in the oil rich zone. Most of the political commentators will equate formation of Pakistan as the result of Muslim separatism. The fact is that British policy of divide and rule encouraged the Muslim and Hindu elites to put up Two Nation theory, which was initially theorised by Savarkar. Handful of elite was behind the idea of Pakistan and Hindu nation respectively, but British gave them importance out of proportion to their social base. The politics of Hate propagated by these communal formations intensified the communal violence, resulting in severe cracks in the concept of composite Indian nationalism leading to partition of the country. More than Muslim League it was British design of having a long term control in the region that resulted in formation of Pakistan. Hindu communalists have to share the equal blame as they also said that nationalism is based on religion, that there are two nations within the country and that Muslims have to be subordinate to Hindu nation.

US empire substituted the declining British empire and turned Pakistan in to a semi vassal state, using it as its military base, to control the whole oil zone. In Pakistan the US hegemony is as much responsible for stifling the democratic process as the hold of Mullahs and Army. We have to recognize that today a very positive process of rise of democracy is going on in Pakistan. The elements which will benefit by attacking Pakistan are those opposed to democracy, the mullahs and the army. US seems to have milked Pakistan as much as it needed and now is looking for shifting its base in South Asia, and also blaming Pakistan for terror groups, forgetting its major role in the same.

Attacking Pakistan at this point is what the fanatic elements in Pakistan and India want. The response to 26/11 has been cleverly modulated into becoming anti Pakistan hysteria. The demand for attack on Pakistan will well serve the fanatics in Pakistan and the fanatics in India both. Their interests match most of the times. While it is sheer insanity to think of attacking a nuclear weapons armed country, and it also means strengthening the arms of Pakistan army and mullahs.

The need is that of a joint endeavor by both the democratic governments to honestly investigate the Mumbai terror attacks, to punish the guilty. If possible India should take steps which strengthen Pakistani government in its own battle against the army and Mullahs. This strengthening of democratic process will help India as much as Pakistan, if not more. One can see the change in the language of Pakistan Government since the military is cooling its heels in the barracks and democratic process has taken over the centers of power. One hopes the Indian government does not fall into the trap laid by Pakistani fundamentalists and is able to overcome the exhortation-hysteria of sections calling for blood of Pakistan in the act of blind revenge, while ensuring the terror acts are controlled.

41

Indo-Pak Peace Talks and Taliban Provocations

There are reports (February 23, 2010) in Indian media that two Sikhs were killed by Pakistan based Taliban militants in Khyber and Orakzi areas near Peshawar. These Sikhs were part of a group of many Sikhs who had been kidnapped by the Taliban over a month ago. The Taliban had demanded Rs. 30 million as ransom for the release of this group and killed two of them after the expiry of the deadline for the payment of the ransom, Jizya. Two persons, Gurvinder Singh and Gurjit Singh amongst others are still believed to be in the custody of the militants.

Some reports suggest that these Sikhs were killed after their refusal to convert to Islam. Indian Government has reacted strongly to this mindless act by Taliban. Many an Indian political groups and a group of Muslim intellectual activists have also condemned this barbaric act in no uncertain terms. The group of Muslim intellectuals/activists in their statement point out, "The inhuman and un-Islamic act of killing innocent civilians has once again exposed the true face of the terrorists whose only aim is to use the name of Islam, the religion of peace and mercy, for their nefarious designs, ulterior motives and worldly pleasures. These are the people who denigrate the name of Islam and bring disrepute to all Muslims of the world. No civilized Muslim would accept the logic of killing innocents in the name of religion. Safeguarding the lives of its minorities from lawlessness, mayhem and protecting their lives and property is the paramount duty of an Islamic State. The continuous pressure on the Sikh community in Pakistan is alarming and demands urgent attention of civil society, religious leadership and the establishment in Pakistan."

The other aspect of this brutal act is that it is coming just in the wake of the Secretary level talks between India and Pakistan to begin this 25th (Thursday). Earlier also there has been a correlation between the improving Pak-India relations and such acts of insanity which put a great amount of pressure on Indian Government to put off the talks. There are numerous such incidents which one recalls. The first such major incident was the Kargil occupation by Pakistan army under Pervez Musharraf in the wake of Atal Bihari Vajpayee's Bus Yatra which aimed to break the ice of coldness between the two neighbours. This was done without the knowledge of Nawaz Sharif, the President.

The second major act had been the Mumbai 26/11, 2008, before which Asif Ali Zardari had been giving positive signals of improving the relations between India and Pakistan. Today one is clear that there are multiple power centers in Pakistan. The democratic Government is trying to establish its writ, but the army and Taliban are doing their best to thwart the return of democracy, democratization process in Pakistan and betterment of Pak-India relations. One must compliment the Indian Government to keep its cool, and firmness in the face of these deliberate provocations. The need to distinguish between the civilian Governments, army-mullah-Taliban complex is mandatory if we want to understand Pakistan today.

From the decades of 1980s multiple processes have gripped Pakistan and these had adverse impact on the whole of South Asia, India in particular. One recalls the rise of Zia Ul Haq with the support of US and Maulanas, led by Maulana Maududi. The formulations of Maulana Maududi provided ideal foil to the military dictatorship in Pakistan. At the same time US could merrily support Madrassa's which were training Muslim youth as its cannon fodder for its plans to boost anti Soviet forces in Afghanistan, which was occupied by Russian army. Since US army was deeply humiliated due to its defeat in Vietnam, US masterminded to indoctrinate Muslim youth to be trained as terrorists. These were the one's who joined anti Russian forces, which got defeated and since then these Taliban's/Al Qaeda are creating havoc. Not only in India, they have also wrecked the life in Pakistan, several terrorist attacks, one of which killed the Pakistan ex-Prime Minister Benazir Bhutto. Today Taliban/Al Qaeda types are like cancer eating into the vitals of Pakistan. Their impact is also felt here in India. Pakistan in a way is caught in a pincer movement, on one hand, the Al Qaeda-Taliban creating havoc, and on the other, Army trying to remain as the major power center. India has a tough task to remain calm and firm in the face of this massive turmoil in the region.

We must see clearly that in this situation Pakistan civil government's hand must be strengthened so that it can deal effectively against the army highhandedness and terrorist nuisance in the region. One also must make it clear that what Taliban is doing has nothing to do with Islamic teachings as such. As per Islam, there can't be force or compulsion in matters of religion. To force somebody to convert by force is not acceptable as per Islamic teachings. Also to kill the innocent people also goes against teachings of Koran.

As far a Jizya is concerned it was a tax levied on non Muslims in Muslim rule. This was in lieu of exemption from military duties and was a small proportion of the income of the person. It was mostly lesser than the Zakat, which is mandatory in Islam. Today to talk of Jizya is a political abuse of worst order; those using this language need to be restrained in the democratic society. The million rupee question remains, will civilian rule prevail over the fissiparous forces operating within Pakistan. Indian Government must take up the issue of protection of minorities in Pakistan without any compromise.

SECTION–X
NATIVE TERROR

42

Blasting a Myth: Two Bajarang Dal Activists Killed While Making a Bomb

By now the acts of terror, Islam and Muslims have become synonymous terms in popular imagination, propagated by US media globally and supplemented by Hindu right wing here at home. A large section of the media has added to the manufacturing of this stereotype. Most of the times the alleged terrorists are shot after the incident and their pockets very obligingly produce a letter of their identity and the intentions which are accepted without any probe. Generally the questions raised about the holes in the official version are ignored and forgotten over a period of time. Many a times the blasts come in handy for BJP to sweep the elections as happened in the aftermath of Akshardham attack in Gujarat. No doubt investigating the acts of terror are not easy these terrorists are the left over of Al Qaeda and many other groups still carrying on their agenda of creating terror and rift in the society, and some of these groups have bases in Pakistan or Banlga desh. But is that the end of the tally?

On 6th April (2006) in the middle of the night, a powerful bomb exploded in a remote place in Maharashtra, Nanded. The house where it exploded belongs to the RSS sympathiser with Bajarang Dal flag flying atop the house. The impact of the blast could be felt in the whole town, in the perimeter of two kilometers, some people felt as if it is an earthquake. The house where the blast took place, all the furniture was blown apart and two members of Bajarang Dal were killed on the spot and three others were seriously injured. It was a single explosion, not multiple one as happens with crackers.

Next day the local Superintendent of police was prompt to offer a cover to the Bajrang Dal and its activists by declaring that it was due to crackers, which have accidentally been exploded.

The house search revealed the powerful bomb, I.E.D. with timer and remote control, after which the Inspector General of police had to concede that it was a bomb blast and that those involved in the blast are the members of Bajrang Dal. Local papers reported that a diary has been found at the spot, which has the details of bomb making techniques and other relevant information. The local BJP MP started dishing out the subtle instructions by saying that innocent should not be implicated and that it was a minor incident.

The police, despite the severe implications of the incident are dealing with this blast with kid gloves. They did arrest some fourteen people, who were close to the one's who died. But they all have been released as the charges framed, deliberately or by default, were under the minor clauses and not adequate to reflect the seriousness of the crime so accordingly court granted the bail. Also the police/state pleader had no objections if the bail is granted to the arrested ones. Police is working on the theory as if such a massive exercise could have been done by a bunch of youth in an isolated manner. The Bajrang Dal chief and other activists of the Bajrang Dal are roaming freely. Apart from the overall intentions of the bomb makers, one has also to examine the intentions of the bomb making in the context of the local events and the profile of Nanded events. Nanded is a city where the major Sikh Gurudwra is located and Sikhs are present in substantial number. Just a month ago one Sikh girl and a Muslim youth eloped and got married. This incident left bitter feelings and tensions amongst the two communities. At the site of the bomb making false beard and moustache has been recovered. One has to recall that during last two years three major incidents of bomb blasts have taken place in the nearby towns of Parbhani, Purna and Jalna.

The surprising aspects of the episode is, the soft peddling of the incident by the local police, the apathy of the guardian minister and the home minister of the state, the non cognizance of the event by the Central government and the national media, print and electronic both. Congress ruling coalition has its own calculations and it has never shown the will power to take the Hindutva forces on democratic grounds. There is nothing new about its showing disinterest in investigating the incident properly and bringing to book the volunteers of RSS, Bajrang Dal and other associates of this multi-headed hydra. Barring two investigations, one by a Nagpur based team of Secular Citizens Forum with PUCL and other by Mumbai based Forum against War and Terror, not much has been done to take the implications of the events seriously. Of course a section of local media has done good job but it has failed to attract the national attention. The contrasting scenario can very well be imagined. If by chance any Muslim would have been a part of the ghastly incident, by now hundreds of Muslims and their organizations would have been rotting in the jail and all the national media and the concerned authorities would have swooped down the city and apprehended the culprits and detected/discovered the links with Al Qaeda/ISI and what not. No such probability exists here as by now state administrations and social common sense has associated terrorism and blasts with a particular religious community. The RSS and its affiliates who began with the lathi drill have come a long way, from lathi wielding to the making of the bomb and giving the training to its volunteers in using knives, disguised as Trishuls, guns and lately the bomb as this incident shows. At what time to use which of the weapons through which of the volunteers and then to disown the volunteer is nothing new for this outfit. Nathuram Godse, the killer of father of the nation was disowned, so was Dara Singh, the killer of Pastor Graham Stains. No wonder this episode in the remote interior of Maharashtra may get suppressed, forgotten and a major source of terrorism will go uninvestigated with guilty remaining unpunished and the organisation behind that continuing its divisive journey as before.

43

Ishrat Jahan: Murder in Cold Blood

In the aftermath of Gujarat carnage the then Prime Minister, Atal Bihari Vajpayee subtly reprimanded Modi Government that Raj Dharma should have been followed. The implication was that state should have actively intervened to protect the innocents who were killed during the violence. What will one say if the same state selectively picks up innocent citizens, kills them and presents false stories to save its skin? While taking the oath, while joining the state one is supposed to treat all citizens as equal irrespective of their religion, caste and gender. What do we say about the state, which goes on to kill its innocent citizens who happen to belong to minority community?

As the Citizen's Tribunal pointed out in the aftermath of Godhra train burning, Gujarat State machinery was told to sit back when the rioters were unleashed to kill and maim, to loot and to rape during the carnage. Now we know that in the same state, police officers have become emboldened enough to pick up minority elements, kill them in cold blood and proclaim that it is an encounter! The repeated cry of terrorists planning to kill Modi has been a favourite ploy of the police officers for killing innocents to please the CM, to seek promotions. It also helps to create a larger than life picture of Modi.

When Ishrat Jahan was killed in June 2005, along with three others, the police officers boasted of their success that they have ably averted the attack on Modi by killing four terrorists of Lashkar-e-Tayyaba. Forensic and post mortem reports confirm that they were killed in cold blood on 14th June, shot at close range in police custody and then, taken in a car, then put in a row on the road on the outskirts of Ahmedabad. To show that it was encounter, arms-ammunition was kept on their body. At this point of time National Human Rights Commission asked for magisterial inquiry. Later state Government also confirmed of magisterial inquiry going on. At the same time the police investigation was also started.

Justice Tamang has come out with his report that it was not an encounter and that the four killed in cold blood by police were not having any terrorist links. In response the Gujarat government is leaving no stones unturned to say that Justice Tamang had no business to release his report, the Gujarat high court has brought a stay on the report. But already the contents of the report are known through the media reports and Gujarat Government is finding no place to hide its face, also Supreme Court has seen nothing wrong in what Justice Tamang did. The total lack of remorse on the part of Gujarat Government is not surprising at all!

The officer, D.G.Vanjara, who killed these four, was also the one who had brutally killed Sohrabbudin and his wife Kauserbi, and is now behind the bars. There is a section of Gujarat people, who are very appreciative of what Vanjara has done, and the situation which Modi Government has brought in. Now the Gujarat Government asks that when the police inquiry was going on, what is the legality of magisterial inquiry? On the contrary, as per the law after the death of a person in police custody, or due to police action of this type, inquest, magisterial inquiry and police inquiry all these have to be done.

It is not that it is the first time that an encounter, fake encounter killings, are taking place. The difference here is the total identification and defense of such acts by the political leadership of state. The difference is that a section of people are being made to believe such dastardly acts are needed to make the society safe. The effort of Gujarat Government is just to show a brave face in the light of exposure of its brutality in killing the innocents. Incidentally Ishrat was wearing her college, Khalsa College Mumbai, Identity Card around her neck when she was killed in cold blood. Legal nuances and nitty gritty apart where are we heading in the Twenty-first Century?

Nearly an year ago in the face of police arrest of many Muslim youth in the aftermath of bomb blasts citizens tribunals were held in Hyderabad and then in Jaipur. Legal luminaries and social activists formed the jury of these tribunals. Both tribunals pointed out that the attitude of police is very biased and many a Muslim youth are being arrested without any proof whatsoever. Will such actions by state, will such a defense of killing of innocents, not intensify the sense of injustice amongst a section of Indian citizens?

Where are we heading to? On one hand, there are inquiry commission reports showing as to how communal organizations orchestrate crimes and the section of police and part of state administration colludes. On the other plane, there is the phenomenon of terrorism, which has many factors contributing to it but it is only Muslims who are blamed for that. We are also witnessing a serious and by now inbuilt discrimination leading to exclusion of minorities from the social facilities. In such an atmosphere what will happen to the psyche of the youth and others from minority community? The social disparities we are creating due to such policies are there for all of us to see. The tragedy is that a section of people have started asserting the correctness of these happenings. The situation which is being created due to all this is further used to blame minorities for it. The Modi-Vanjara duo, which is becoming a law unto them, is the symptom of deeper malaise of Gujarat.

44

Jehadi and Sadhvi

The arrest of Sadhvi Pragya Singh Thakur as the alleged culprit of Malegaon blast of September 29, 2008 has opened the can of worms. Sadhvi, daughter of an RSS sympathiser, was an active member of RSS affiliates, Akhil Bhartiya Vidyarthi Parishad and Durga Vahini before adorning the cloak of Sadhvi. Word Sadhvi stands for the woman who is pursuing the path of truth and renunciation. Needless to say she is totally steeped in the political ideology and values of RSS, which must have been her staple diet from her childhood.

Currently another word has been made very popular in the context of repeatedly occurring terror attacks. The word is Jehadi. While this word is not there in Koran, this was constructed by the US Administration and picked up by media in the aftermath of 9/11 attack on WTC and the consequent death of nearly 3000 innocent lives. At the same time the words Jihad and Kafir appeared with a newer meaning. Later these words became the part of social common sense and were associated with the Muslims, associated with acts of terror. While terrorists are not born, they become one due to political, social and economic cause. It was the formation of Al Qaeda by the CIA, via ISI of Pakistan that number of Madrassas were opened in Pakistan to indoctrinate the Muslim youth who were made to believe that killing of non believers is Jihad. This indoctrination was aimed to create Al Qaeda which was to take on the Russian army occupying Afghanistan.

The indoctrination module developed in Washington and applied through the Madrassas in Pakistan went like this: Ours is the best religion, our Muslim Afghanistan has been occupied by Russian army, the communists. These communists don't believe in our Allah so they are kafirs and killing these kafirs is Jihad, the sacrifice, Qurbani, for Jihad will pave the way for your going to

Jannat (heaven), with 72 Virgins waiting for you has been the incentive preached.

This political battle was couched in religious language and the same indoctrinated youth later went on to spread the terror in other parts of South Asia in the name of Islam. Later initial political goals of US administration got masked in the language of religion and the indoctrinated minds created havoc. As such in Koran, Jihad means to strive, to struggle to be better human beings and to fight against injustice. But this clever political manipulation led to the rise of the dreaded form of terrorism which is bane of our society even today.

Sadhvi Pragya Singh Thakur's source of seeing the world had been the RSS ideology of Hindutva, goal of Hindu nation. RSS has its own indoctrination module operated through its Shakha (Branch) *baudhiks* (intellectual sessions). The affiliates of this organisation are also indoctrinated into a module which says that Hindus and Hindus alone constitute this nation, Hinduism is superior to all other faiths since it is tolerant. Unfortunately this tolerance has been misunderstood as weakness by the foreign aggressors the Muslims and Christians. To quell their threats Hindus need to organise as a political body. We are a Hindu Nation. Muslims and Christians are foreigners, and a threat to Hindu nation. Secular people have created an impression as if this nation belongs to all the people. To this core indoctrination, many a additions have been made, that Hindu society is facing the threat from Jihadi terrorists who are killing through terrorist acts and the Christian missionaries who are converting by force, fraud and allurement. The latest addition to this was seen in the propaganda of Hindu Jagran Samiti, which was involved in the blasts in Thane (June 2008), Panvel and Vashi. This organisation draws its inspiration from RSS founder Hedgewar and Hindutva ideologue Savarkar. According to this organisation, in the present Kaliyug, we Hindus are facing the threat of Danavs (the demons) who are taking birth as Muslims and Christians. So they need to be punished to save Hindu society.

One is struck by the parallelism of the two 'ideologies, which are used as indoctrination modules. What is common is the claim of superiority of one's religion, the real or imaginary threat to the particular society, looking down upon the 'other' as the threat and the need to protect one's society by killing 'other'. What separates a 'Jihadi' from Sadhvi is no fundamental idea but the label of religion, the content remains the same. One is not talking of different other terrorist groups, which come up due, deep injustice, like the LTTE, the ULFA or Adivasi National Liberation Front, which fall in different socio-psycho-dynamics of their formation. This indoctrination variety of terrorism rests on the political interests of a global power and on a set of local social layers, and their vested interests.

So a section of population also looks at them as the embodiment of all the virtues, sacrifice for the sake of their religion, and even worships them. In 2005 US based terrorism research center had categorised RSS as the terrorist organisation. This was in the context of violence in Gujarat and anti Christian violence. Interestingly Pastor Graham Steward Stain's murderer, Dara Singh also was associated with Bajrang Dal. While he did this dastardly crime and has been given life imprisonment, the RSS family calls him Hindu *dharma rakshak*; their affiliates raised all the resources to fight the legal battle for him. No wonder RSS is gearing up to protect the Sadhvi and army officers involved in the acts of terror, as for them these people are the biggest protectors of 'our' religion.

45

Malegaon Blast Accused Get a Respite

Eleven suspects of Malegaon blast, September 9, 2008, got a breather (August 01, 2009) when the special court dropped the charges under MCOCA against 11 suspects of the crime. Prosecution failed to show that all accused were members of a single organised crime syndicate. This MCOCA Act also requires that there should be two previous charge sheets against one of them. Since the case prepared by police could not prove these, the charges have been dropped. The ATS and Maharashtra Chief Minister have stated that they will ensure that they will go to the higher courts, against the order of this court's decision. In past Congress has not undertaken any serious efforts to punish the guilty, so this statement of the authorities has to be taken with a pinch of salt.

MCOCA apart, the overall scenario and line of investigation followed by police has left lot of ground uncovered which can come handy for the culprits getting away lightly if the police does not do its home work well. There may also be deeper political dimensions to the issue as well. The first point which struck the observers so far was that for a long time police line of investigation in the blast cases was based on the premise that some Muslim group is involved in the crime. This created two problems. One was that the innocents kept getting arrested and tortured and second that the real culprits could hide under the cover provided by the popular perception about terrorism. The vicious cycle was broken by Hemant Karakre with the impeccable evidence in the form of the Motor cycle of Sadhvi Pragya Singh Thakur from the crowded lane of Malegaon. Her link led to several people and many organizations. The people involved were Swami Dayanand Pandey, Lt Col Prasad Shrikant Purohit, Ajay Rahirar, retired Major Ramesh Upadhayay, Rakesh Dhawade and many others. The connections with Abhinav Bharat, Hindu Jagran Samiti, Army units, Bhonsala Military School (Nagpur and Nashik), Akanksha Resort Sinhgad, all emerged and the picture of a broad conspiracy became clear.

The investigating officer, Hemant Karkare, about whose death in 26/11 terror attack, Antulay raised certain questions, faced immense pressure due to criticism from Hindu right wingers, Thackeray's paper *Saamana* went on to say that they spit on the face of such an anti-national person like Karkare, and some others also called him as Deshdrohi. One does not know what direct/indirect impact all this had on the future drafting of the charge sheet. Human Rights activist Teesta Setalvad in her articles in *Communalism Combat* Feb 2009 raised several questions about the charge sheet, which remain unanswered.

One recalls that the Nanded blast (April 2006) case investigation itself was very much muted and it was only the pressure of campaign from Rights activists that the investigation was pursued. Rakesh Dhawade, one of the accused in the Malegaon charge sheet had confessed to his involvement in the training of few youth, for the preparation and detonation of bombs. The training was done near the Sinhgad Fort, Pune, in July-August 2003. Despite this he was allowed to be discharged from the Purbea masjid blast case on July 27, 2009! ATS says it was because the local police did not file a strong enough charge sheet! One does not know whether it is a lack of coordination or there is something deeper to this?

It is beyond one's comprehension as to why Section 125, waging war against the Indian Nation, has not been applied to these accused. In this case the involvement of the serving military officers and the retired ones has not been probed. It has ramifications far deeper then can be seen from the surface. These military officers had the background of Bhonsla Military School, which is practically controlled by RSS. The RSS has its wing for retired military personnel and has a lot of emphasis on cultivating connections with men in uniform. The theft of 60 kilograms of RDX by Purohit is a pointer of what the serving and military officers can do once they are ideologically indoctrinated by the notions other than that of secular democratic India. Purohit in his narco analysis on 9th November 2008 had revealed about his role in Samjhauta Express blast and a possible role in Mecca Masjid blast.

There are multiple aspects of the case involved. One does not support MCOCA at all, it is not only arbitrary and draconian; it also is a refuge for police not to undertake the trouble for deeper investigation and doing its home work properly. Even if one does not trust the narco analysis, there are enough other evidences to link up all those accused indoctrinated by RSS ideology. The point is why so many links which are there for all to see are not followed? Why resort to the short cut of MCOCA, or Narco analysis.

The core point is the biases of the state apparatus, political, bureaucratic and that of police in particular which have resulted in evolution of two sets of justice delivery systems. One is for the affluent and privileged that can get away with whatever they want and the second is for the weaker sections, including minorities. Here right from the police investigation to the charge sheeting, the political influence and biases which influence the process of justice delivery (or the lack of it) and the final verdict all are having a tinge of bias.

The political policys do determine the whole process. It is such outcomes which make a section of population feel that they are used merely as vote banks and when the time of justice comes they are not considered at all. If the culprits of Malegaon are treated with kid gloves under the theory that violence from Hindu fold is retaliatory that will be the travesty of justice of the worst order.

46

Terrorism: Scapegoats and Holy Cows

I

India has been tragically witnessing many acts of terror. These acts have occurred more so from last two decades, to be precise after the Mumbai Carnage of 1992-93 and later have been occurring at regular intervals in different cities. There is a long list of these tragic acts but some of these which have tormented the society and are permanently etched in our memory are, March 1993: Mumbai serial bombings, which killed 257 people and injured more than 1,100; December 13th, 2001: More than a dozen people, including five gunmen, killed in an attack on Parliament in New Delhi; May 14th, 2002 Militants attack an army camp near Kashmir's winter capital, Jammu, killing more than 30, including wives and children of soldiers; September 24th 2002: Militants with guns and explosives attack the Akshardham Hindu temple in the western state of Gujarat, 31 killed, more than 80 injured; August 2003: Two taxis packed with explosives blow up outside a Mumbai tourist attraction and a busy market, killing 52 and wounding more than 100; October 2005: Three bombs placed in busy New Delhi markets a day before kill 62 people and injure hundreds; March 2006: Twin bombings at a train station and Sankatmochan temple in Varanasi killing 20 people.

July 2006: Seven bombs on Mumbai's trains kill over 200 and injure 700 others; September 8th 2006: 30 dead and 100 hurt in twin blasts at a mosque in Malegaon; February 19th 2007: Two bombs explode aboard a train bound from India to Pakistan, Samjhauta Express, burning to death at least 66 passengers, most of them Pakistanis; May 18th 2007: A bomb explodes during Friday prayers at a historic mosque, Mecca Masjid Hyderabad, killing 14, people, of which five died in the police firing later. Police later shot dead five people in clashes with hundreds of enraged Muslims who protest against the attack. August 25th 2007: Three explosions within minutes at an amusement park and a street-side food stall in Hyderabad kills 40 people. May 13 2008: Seven blasts strike Jaipur killing at least 63 people and wounding hundreds of people. July 25th 2008: Nine explosions in Bangalore create terror killing two people and injuring twelve. July 26 2008: 21 blasts hit Ahmedabad killing 55 and injuring 100. Meanwhile, 24 live bombs were claimed to be recovered from Surat. September 13th 2008: Five blasts rock busy markets of New Delhi killing 25 and injuring over 100. And three live bombs were defused in India Gate, Regal Cinema and Central Park.

Many of these blasts took place just before some election; some in the aftermath of communal clashes and some took place on the Friday afternoon prayers. The pattern was so diverse a single description of these blasts is out of question. Still there were some common factors in the aftermath of the tragic events. First of all the police machinery most of the times came up with the theory that the Pakistan based terrorist groups or local Muslim groups have been involved in the blasts, Harkat Ul-Ansar, Lashkar-e-Tayyaba, Noor-Ul–Hooda, Harkat-Ul-Jihad, Hijb-ul-Mujahiddin, Indian Mujahuddin, figured most of the times. The claims, that SIMI is involved as a mastermind, or as associate was generally put forward on most occasions.

The usual police claims have been that the culprits have been caught with the laptops, Identity cards and other information which led police to come to these conclusions. For a large section of media, these were either poor Muslims trapped in the terror net for the longing for Jannat or Technology savvy young men, out to create mayhem in India. While no investigation barring the one of single case Malegaon proceeded to any meaningful direction, most of the times Muslims, mostly youth were arrested tortured and later on after weeks-months released for the lack of any credible evidence. Two of these cases need pondering at slightly greater depth.

A blast occurred in Malegaon in the Kabristan, which is near a mosque. It was Friday, 8th September 2008, at 1.15 PM, just after the prayers. This was a Shab-e- Barat holiday so there was bigger crowd. In this blast 37 people died and 125 got injured. Most of the people who died were Muslim pilgrims. The police investigators blamed SIMI for the blast. One person Noor-Ul-

Hooda was blamed to be a part of SIMI, and he was arrested for the act of terror. By and by other usual suspects were also named, Shabbir Batterywala was named as part of dreaded Lashkar-e-Tayyaba, and Raees Ahmad was arrested as co conspirator, he was tagged with SIMI. While there was a murmur that Hindutva organisations may be involved, the authorities ruled it out on the ground that the type of explosives, RDX, are not available with Bajrang Dal, etc. and that the type of bomb used in Malegaon was too sophisticated for Bajrang Dal type organisation. Also that they do not have such organisational capability. While police pointed out that the pattern of these blasts is similar to the one which occurred in other mosques in Maharashtra, still Bajrang dal was not suspected. From the accused confessions were elicited under coercion, they denied the charges in front of magistrates and no further headway could be made, there was no concrete proof.

In same Malegaon, another blast took place two years later. The low intensity blast took place in the crowded Bhikku Chowk in Malegaon, at a time when people were breaking their ramzan fast. Initially police thought that it was blast of gas cylinder, but later confirmed that the blast took place due to the device tied to the Hero Honda motorcycle. This investigation was conducted by Hemant Karkare of Maharashtra ATS, who was later killed in the Mumbai 27/11 attack. The investigation led to Sadhvi Pragaya Singh Thakur, Swami Dayanand Pandey, serving army officer Lt Col. Prasad Shrikant Purohit and retired army officer Maj. Upadhyay. They are behind the bars.

The second case is that of Mecca Mosque blast in Hyderabad on May 18th 2007, at the time of Namaz prayers in the afternoon. At that time thousands of people were in the mosque. Further, police as usual put the fingers at Harkat-ul-Jihad-al-Islami or HUJI and the Students' Islamic Movement of India (SIMI) as the main suspects behind the Friday Mecca mosque blast. Nearly 25 Muslim youth were arrested alleging different affiliations, but all of them were released after six months, for the lack of evidence. In both Malegaon and Hyderabad Mecca Masjid, like many other places, what is evident is that Muslims had been the main victims and later the main suspects, showing the track followed by the officials that all terrorists are Muslims, which has been their line of thinking in all cases of blasts.

II

The perception that"All Terrorists are Muslims" has been the underlying guiding factor of investigating authorities in India. While there are lot of other misconceptions about minorities, perceptions which form the base of communal politics, this one about terrorism got intensified after the 9/11 incident. It was after that that the US media manufactured a word Islamic Terrorism, which for the first time indicated to Islam as the cause of terrorism and created a situation Worldwide whereby demonisation of Muslims began. This process in India was many times worse as already during freedom movement the communal streams came up due to the British policy of divide and rule. The communal politics was rooted in the social and economic factors, but due to communal historiography and other factors the expression of class differences started assuming communal form. This later on went on to become a big monster, the myths about the other communities; it was from both the sides, Muslim and Hindus. The elite of the community and the landlord-Kings began the process to save their privileged position in the society, later middle class intellectuals not only joined it but some of them went on to form the ideology of communalism, and religion based nationalism, Hindu Rashtra and Islamic state.

In India the majority of Muslims came from the poor shudras, who were victims of the caste system and responded to the Humanistic teachings of Sufi saints to embrace Islam. With partition of the country the elite sections left for Pakistan and this part of the country was left with large section of poor Muslims, who were subjected to gross discrimination in all fields of life, and the process of their exclusion from economic arena, jobs and other social opportunities worsened by the day.

With the change in the global scenario, decline of Socialist states, the world became unpopular and the process of globalisation became much adverse for weaker nation and for the poor sections of society. At this point the sections of society, the affluent middle classes, gripped by their insecurity longed for status quo, wanted to even push back the process of social transformation of caste and gender. And now they came up as the big supporters of the divisive politics in the name of religion. This poisoned the social atmosphere; the social communal sense became very adverse to minorities. All sorts of biases started becoming more and more popular amongst broad sections of society and this was the fertile ground on which the communal violence came up, forming the base of communal politics and leading the emotional ghettoisation and later physical ghettoisation of religious communities.

In this backdrop the 9/11 came as a bolt from the blue and worsened the already distorted perception widely prevalent in the society. As such terrorism, which is primarily due to social, economic and political reasons, started being perceived as due to one particular religion executed through that community.

III

It is in this context that the formulation'all Terrorists are Muslims' became part of social common sense and the guiding thesis of the investigators and state officials who posed as 'experts' of terrorism. Not only that the impact of this formulation on the popular psyche has been immensely negative.

After all what is terrorism? As such it is difficult to define terrorism, as some people whom we regard as terrorists, others may regard as freedom fighters, those fighting for a particular cause. LTTE a terrorist organisation is looked up as fighting for the cause of rights of Tamils by some. Roughly one can say terrorism is an act which may be done by a state, a group or an individual for a political motive and due to this innocent people get killed. This act is a part of political statement or political purpose. Those acts where there are no deaths but people feel intimidated can also be called as terrorism.

Terrorism is different from communal violence. In communal violence a communal group spreads hatred against a community, and average layers of society are mobilised to attack the minority groups. The Gujarat carnage, Mumbai violence, the Orissa violence (2008) fall in this category. Terrorism is planned secretly and its execution comes as a surprise, communal violence is built up and its perpetrators are easy to locate. In case of Mumbai violence an intense hate atmosphere against minorities was built up through section of media and by word of mouth and then average people were made to believe that minorities are a threat to them and so they should be attacked. In Mumbai it happened in the wake of Babri demolition and in Gujarat it happened after the Godhra train burning. Simply speaking in the latter those guilty of train burning should have been punished but an atmosphere was created against the whole community and poor sections were mobilised to attack them.

Currently in Orissa, the make believe perception that Christian missionaries are converting by force and fraud is ruling the popular mind. As such if we see there is not a single case in the police record where the complaint against missionaries for conversion are registered. Christianity is a very old religion in India and today there population is a mere 2.30%. This population of Christians has been on decline from the 2.60% of 1971 to today's 2.30%. Wadhva Committee report which went into the killing of Pastor Graham Stains in 1999, showed that the Pastor was not involved in the acts of conversion and that the Christian population in his area of work was fairly stable. This perception about missionary work has been used to instigate the violence against a tiny minority of the country.

As such terrorists have come from all the religions. Let's recall the killer of Mahatma Gandhi, Indira Gandhi and Rajiv Gandhi. Similarly yesteryears biggest terrorist organisation has been Liberation Tiger of Tamil Elam. The Irish republican Army constituted mainly by Christians has been indulging in the acts of terror in Ireland for long time.

Terrorists are not born. Some youth take to the path of terror due to gross injustice or perception of injustice, done to them or their community. This is associated with a feeling that society-state will not give them justice. This was witnessed in Guwahati, in November 2007. A group of Adivasis had come to city for demanding their rights over land and forest resources. They were not only beaten up, also one girl accompanying them was molested. A week later an Adivasi National Liberation front was formed which planted bombs in Guwahati Rajdhani express and in this 7 people were killed. We remember that after the Mumbai violence a group of frustrated-dejected people took help of underworld to plant the bombs in Mumbai train. In Afghanistan, US in order to fight back the Russian army and to control the oil wells, set up Madrassas in Pakistan to indoctrinate the Muslim youth. The indoctrination module was made in Washington. According to this the youth were made to believe that Russians/every Non Muslim is a kafir, killing kafirs is Jihad and sacrifice for Jihad will take you to Jannat (heaven) where 72 virgins will be welcoming you. After defeating the Russian armies the Al Qaeda turned against other South Asian countries and also against US itself. India is a victim of the offshoots of this in particular as they now firmly believe in what was taught to them in the Madrasssas, specially set up to indoctrinate them, in the territory of Pakistan by the US.

The other major cause of terrorism is ethno-national, like Sri lanka-Jaffna where LTTE came up, in Kashmir, where the issue of autonomy of Kashmir turned to become ethno national one's, the North East where the integration of NE into Indian stream gave the hiccups of terrorism. Similarly Irish Republican army also came up due to ethnic injustices.

Lately we saw the involvement of some Hindutva elements, Sadhvi Pragya Singh Thakur and others in the acts of terror related to the blasts in front of the mosques, Malegaon, Ajmer Dargah etc. This again is due to the indoctrination of the mind by the political process, by ideologies which are totally anti democratic and look at politics in the colors of religion. Here the indoctrination has been done that a particular community is under threat due to another community. One knows that the threat is not due to religious community, but since this politics is based on communal principles they attribute all the reasons to religion and so the misconception are deliberately produced resulting in violence.

The type of terrorism which we witnessed in Mumbai (Nov 2008) is the left over of the Al Qaeda type groups, the indoctrinated one's. Let's remember that once a person is indoctrinated for the political goals, the reversal of such process is practically impossible. Toady the country is the victim of this insane process, which has been the result of various global and local political an economic processes.

IV

For India investigating authorities of all types after every act of blast joint act at a foreign link (i.e. Pakistan) Harkat ul Jihad,

Lashkar-e-Tayyba, Mujahidin etc. This has been the most instant response as to who the culprit has been? While some places it may have been true, but beyond a point it became a knee jerk understanding after the terror act. And as an accomplice or as the executer in its own right SIMI kept figuring most of the times.

Many a youth were arrested under this label as the old member of SIMI, after SIMI was banned in 2001. It became a matter of routine after every blast, Malegaon; Mecca Masjid in Hyderabad, Jaipur and other places was broken with the impeccable proof of Sadhvi Pragya Singh Thakur's motor cycle being found in Malegaon. The trace of motorcycle link led to Swami Dayanand Pandey, Lt Col Shrikant Purohit and many others associated with Hindu right wing organisations, offshoots of or inspired by RSS ideology.

Society witnessed that after most of the blasts so far, Muslim youth were arrested on the charge of being behind the blasts, were harassed for months and then released for the lack of evidence. This was more or less a routine pattern and it frightened the whole Muslim community to no end. Many a Muslim youths' careers were crushed due to these reckless and baseless arrests. Many a minority families under went severe problems, were ostracized from their own community once they were dragged into the net on the charges which were guided more by the prevalent biases or stereotypes than any substance. SIMI came to be regarded as the core organization responsible for fomenting trouble through youth. Despite the ban on SIMI in 2001, the Muslim youth kept on being labeled as SIMI activists and were put behind the bar.

It's not to say that SIMI was holding ideology which was talking of democracy and secularism. One knows that SIMI, which began as a student front of Jamat-e-Islami Hind gradually, came out of its control and became radical in the decade of 1990s in particular. Yoginder Sikand, an Islamic scholar of repute gives a very crisp history of this organisation (/www.countercurrents.org/comm-sikand150706.htm). SIMI was founded on the ideology propounded by Maulana Maududi, according to whom all non Muslims are kafirs and man made systems like democracy are false and Shariah is the only way. It kept the goal of spreading Islamic consciousness amongst Muslim students and peaceful missionary work amongst non Muslims. Some events in the decade of 1990 were to shape its ideology in a radical and militant direction. These events were Soviet Russia's invasion of Afghanistan and Islamisation of Pakistan in particular.

SIMI after coming out from the control of its parent organisation started talking in a different language. The demolition of Babri Mosque and the post demolition violence gave it a fillip in the negative direction. It said that Democracy has failed to protect Muslims so there is a need for some one like Mohammed Gazni, the destroyer of Somanth. This was also the theme of the poster released by them in the aftermath of Babri demolition. It was alleged that SIMI has links with Sikh and Kashmiri militants. It was alleged that they have links with Osama and ISI. At the same time SIMI claimed that it wants to work through peaceful methods, while the worsening communal situation made it to say that Muslims are a belabored community. Under these circumstances SIMI was banned in 2001.

The ban on SIMI was challenged, so a tribunal had to be appointed to review the ban. Ajit Sahi of Tehelka in his painstaking investigation, followed the tribunal's sitting all through (Tehelka, SIMI Fictions, 12th August 2008), the tribunal did not find any evidence of the charges put against the organisation for banning it. The ban could not be upheld. About this investigation Ajit Sahi said, "... his investigation is no dry story rising from lifeless court documents. It has been an emotional rollercoaster to sit across young boys barely into manhood, their foreheads creased by sleepless nights worried stiff over the jailing of a father, a brother, wondering endlessly, "Will this end? Is this for real? What do I do now? Where do I go now? Will I survive this?" He further says "as I interviewed countless Muslims, so weathered, I couldn't but ask myself, What if this was me? What if it was my brother, my father in jail?" Ajit Sahi presented his travails to find out about SIMI at the tribunal. It was one of the peak points of tribunal.

With the world scenario tilting against the Islam and Muslims, courtesy the radical Islamists trained in the Madrassas set up in Pakistan with US aid, the popular psyche perceived an average Muslim as a terrorist and police machinery operated on this understanding. Even when scores of lives were shattered and the community came under the intimidation of highest order, the

Government did not put any corrective to this pattern of investigation with which police was pursuing its work.

The names of HUJI and SIMI have been bandied about by the police as the perpetrators of the blasts without any evidence. A number of former members of SIMI have been arrested and detained without any basis or evidence against them. The media has also been uncritically repeating and amplifying the baseless allegations and innuendoes of the police mentioning persons and organisations belonging to the Muslim community, thus resulting in ethnic profiling and feeding into the Islamophobia being sought to be created and reinforced in the minds of the Hindu community by the Hindutva organisations. In Jaipur this has resulted in the vilification of the entire Bengali Muslim community who has been victimised by the Hindutva organisations in complicity with the police.

Thousands of them have been picked up after the blasts and forcibly transported to New Jalpaiguri and then Bangladesh without any due process of law and without giving them an opportunity to show their Indian Citizenship. This has resulted in the ethnic cleansing of Jaipur.

V

If one keeps looking at one side, if that happens to wrong there are two implications of that. One, the innocents are tortured and two, the real culprits get away, to merrily keep doing their job. One cannot say that it is true for all the cases of terrorism, but it seems to be true for most of the cases of blasts near mosques, probably in Samjhauta express also. So making a scapegoat also is accompanied by elevation of some other criminals to the status of Holy cows, who cannot be touched despite their acts of terror.

This came to light with the Nanded bomb blast in the house of Bajrang Dal workers who were making bombs.

1. On 6th April 2006 two Bajrang Dal workers died when making the bombs. The place where they died belonged to the RSS worker and saffron flag was hoisted atop the house. There was also a board of Bajrang Dal Nanded Branch on the wall of the house.

Police recovered the materials for making IED devices, a dairy and fake beard, moustache and Payjama Kurta. The Anti

Terrorist Squad established that the place was used for making bombs The house search revealed the powerful bomb, I.E.D. with timer and remote control, after which the Inspector General of police conceded that it was a bomb blast and that those involved in the blast are the members of Bajrang Dal. Local papers reported that a diary has the details of bomb making techniques and other relevant information.

On 11th April, Special IG Police Mr. Surya Prakash Gupta declared that it was not an isolated event; rather a bomb-manufacturing center (Bomb Nirmiti Kendra) was functional at the house of Rajkondwar. He said this center was working since many days. He said one of the injured, Rahul Pande had categorically confessed to have made many such bombs earlier.

Incidents of bomb blasts were witnessed in many places around that time, Parabhani, Jalna and Aurangabad in Maharashtra. Most of these were in front of the mosques. The Nanded investigation 'leads' were not pursued. The attitude of police in this investigation has been totally lax. Social activists made the complaint about this to Human Rights commission. The SP failed to turn up for hearing!

Beyond the geographical similarities, the details of the attacks which took place in the nearby areas were uncanny: each took place between 1:45 and 2:00 in the afternoon, just after Friday prayers, at the most prominent mosque in town. The bomb that went off in Nanded in 2006 on 6 April, a Thursday, was apparently meant to be set off at an Aurangabad masjid the following day.

In same Nanded, on February 10, 2007, 28-year-old Pandurang Bhagwan Amilkanthwar died on the spot. *"Amol Biscuits"*, a bakery shop, was run by the deceased, at Shastrinagar, Nanded. Shop was closed from outside. He was a Shiv Sena Shakha Pramukh.

2. In Thane on 4th June 2008, two Hindu Jagran Samiti workers were arrested for planting the bombs in the basement of Gadkari Rangayatan, due to which 7 people got injured. The same group was involved in the blasts in Vashi, Panvel also.

3. In Goa a bomb kept in a scooter went off on the eve of Diwali (17th Oct 2009) in Margao. It killed Malgonda Patil and seriously injured Yogesh Naik. Another bomb was detected in

Sancoale in a truck carrying 40 youth for Narkasur competition. Both the activists belonged to Sanatan Sanstha. The second aim of this blast was to create communal tension in Margao, which has a history of communal violence. This group takes inspiration from Savarkar (Hindu Mahasabha) and Hedgewar (RSS) and indoctrinates its members into hating Christians and Muslims.

While investigating the Malegaon bomb blasts Hemant Karkare found that the motor cycle Hero Honda which was used for the purpose belonged to Sadhvi Pragya Singh Thakur, whose connections extended to different Hindutva organisations. Swami Dayanand Pandey, Lt Col Prasad Shrikant Purohit, Retd Major Upadhayay and many others were part of a gang who were behind Malegaon and probably other such acts of terror. Only when the irrefutable evidence of motor cycle was found, the investigation could make some headway, which till that time was not giving any importance to this angle of the investigation despite so many leads in this direction.

4. On 24th August 2008 two Bajrang Dal activists died in Kanpur, while making bombs. The Kanpur zone IGP S.N. Singh stated that their investigations have revealed that this group was planning massive explosions all over the state.

5. Indian Express, 23 Oct 2008 reports that those involved in the bomb blast in Malegaon and Modasa (Sept 2008) had links with Akhil Bhartiya Vidyarthi Parishad.

Similarly in Tenkasi, Tamil Nadu pipe bomb attack on RSS office (Jan. 2008) was projected to have been done by Jehadi Muslims. The investigation revealed many a Hindu names and later the investigations was frozen. In an alleged Fidayin attack it was claimed that in the attack on RSS office in Nagpur (June 1, 2006) three of them were killed in the police encounter, as per the police version. Citizens Inquiry report, headed by Justice Kolse Patil doubted the police version in a serious way; the clarifications did not come through from the authorities.

By now a pattern is emerging where not only that, Bajrang Dal activists are carrying guns and swords in the public display of the arms but are also active in undertaking the acts of terror. It is likely that in many cases their role has remained uninvestigated. There is a deliberate cover up of these incidents. Some of these leads are not being pursued while the police are hyperactive in cases where suspected Muslim youth seem to be involved. And that too just on the basis of their confessions. This is a biased attitude of the authorities involved.

VI

A tribunal was organized by Anhad and associated human rights organisations in Hyderabad (2007). It had a very demanding task of hearing and going to the truth of the various alleged culprits. What was surprising, the gross violation of laws which the police indulged in freely? Not only that, alleged culprits were kept in custody and denied all their rights, their relatives were not informed, their date of arrest was shown to be much later than the real time they were picked up. The torture which they were subjected to is beyond words, the wrecking of poor families which took place due to the whole process is shattering. The careers of many a promising young men was totally ruined due to such arrests without any proof what so ever. Is all this reflective of the poor norms, poor professional training of the officers? Is it rank inefficiency couched in this cruelty, or the tormentors are acting like this due to the prevalent biases which have gone deep into the whole society including these officers?

The pattern observed in most of the cases was that there were illegal detentions. Following the torture, if the person is to be released it seems to be a norm that police takes the signature on a blank paper and also threats with dire consequences if the person goes to human rights activists or lawyers. At times they are made to shout Jai Shri Ram just to humiliate them. Sometimes even possession of Urdu literature is taken as a proof of terrorist links. Third degree torture to the accused and severe torture to the relatives of the accused to elicit confession is employed very widely. The accused and their relatives are taken to the police station or other places of detention on false pretexts and the elementary needs of water and food are not looked at. Bribe is extracted most of the times. For permitting the families to see the accused under custody.

What happens to the future of those who are accused and released later? The students loose their career-track, at times colleges don't take them back until court ruling is brought to that effect. The families of accused get ostracised from the community out of fear. Others stop relating to them. The business gets a severe setback and at these times banks refuse to give them loans etc. Some of the accused are also tempted to become approvers with the carrot dangled in front of them that they will be released. The powers vested with the police seem to be present only through there misuse, most of the times.

A two way impression operates in the society. One, amongst the larger sections of society, that Muslim terrorists are a big threat to the nation. Two amongst Muslims the feeling is that state is totally partisan and deliberate injustice is being done to them since they are Muslims. Two set of mechanisms of investigation norms are coming to be rooted. One, Muslim youth are picked up after every blast and are subjected to torture till courts pronounce them non-guilty. And two, to treat the blasts accused who are Hindus, with kid gloves.

VII

This seems to be a dark phase of human society. In this era religion has been used as the cover for the political goals of the imperial power, and the dominant social sections. In the earlier era, Cold war, Communism was projected by propaganda mills, as the major threat to democracy and freedom. Today, communism has been substituted by Islam and Muslims. The communalisation of society at large and that of state apparatus leads to the double standards in matters of justice and control of law and order.

The impact of this policy of state and stigmatisation by society is distorting the psyche of large sections of Muslim minority. Perverse fears generated by political goals, propagated at social level are a big obstacle to amity in society and tramples upon the notions of justice and peace.

47

In the Name of SIMI

In third week of July (2009) Maharashtra police arrested several Muslims in Pusad, Akola and neighbouring regions on the charge that they are reviving SIMI under a new name. It is after a fairly long time that one has heard of arrests in the name of SIMI. The earlier cycle of arrest of Muslim youth which was a matter of routine after every blast, Malegaon, Mecca Masjid in Hyderabad, Jaipur and other places was broken with the impeccable proof of Sadhvi Pragya Singh Thakur's motor cycle being found in Malegaon. The trace of motorcycle link led to Swami Dayanand Pandey, Lt Col Shrikant Purohit and many others associated with Hindu right wing organisations, offshoots of or inspired by RSS ideology.

Society witnessed that after most of the blasts so far, Muslim youth were arrested on the charge of being behind the blasts, were harassed for months and then released for the lack of evidence. This was more or less a routine pattern and it frightened the whole Muslim community to no end. Many a Muslim youths' careers were crushed due to these reckless and baseless arrests. Many a minority families under went severe problems, were ostracized from their own community once they were dragged into the net on the charges which were guided more by the prevalent biases or stereotypes than any substance. SIMI came to be regarded as the core organisation responsible for fomenting trouble through youth. Despite the ban on SIMI in 2001, the Muslim youth kept on being labeled as SIMI activists and were put behind the bar.

It's not to say that SIMI was holding ideology which was talking of democracy and secularism. One knows that SIMI, which began as a student front of Jamat-e-Islami Hind gradually, came out of its control and became radical in the decade of 1990s in particular. Yoginder Sikand, an Islamic scholar of repute gives a very crisp history of this organization (/www.countercurrents.org/comm-sikand150706.htm). SIMI was founded on the ideology propounded by Maulana Maududi, according to whom all non Muslims are kafirs and man made systems like democracy are false and Shariah is the only way. It kept the goal of spreading Islamic consciousness amongst Muslim students and peaceful missionary work amongst non Muslims. Some events in the decade of 1990 were to shape its ideology in a radical and militant direction. These events were Soviet Russia's invasion of Afghanistan and Islamisation of Pakistan in particular.

Meanwhile Jamat-e-Islami came to accept democracy and secularism as its guiding ideology. SIMI came out from the control of its parent organization to talk in a different language. The demolition of Babri Mosque and the post demolition violence gave it a fillip in the negative direction. It said that democracy has failed to protect Muslims so there is a need for some one like Mohammed Gazni, the destroyer of Somnath. This was also the theme of the poster released by them in the aftermath of Babri demolition. It was alleged that SIMI has links with Sikh and Kashmiri militants. It was alleged that they have links with Osama and ISI. At the same time SIMI claimed that it wants to work through peaceful methods, while the worsening communal situation made it to say that Muslims are a belabored community. Under these circumstances SIMI was banned in 2001.

The ban on SIMI was challenged, so a tribunal had to be appointed to review the ban. Ajit Sahi of Tehelka in his painstaking investigation, followed the tribunal's sitting all through (Tehelka, SIMI Fictions, 12th August 2008), the tribunal did not find any evidence of the charges put against the organisation for banning it. The ban could not be upheld. About this investigation Ajit Sahi said, "... his investigation is no dry story rising from lifeless court documents. It has been an emotional rollercoaster to sit across young boys barely into manhood, their foreheads creased by sleepless nights worried stiff over the jailing of a father, a brother, wondering endlessly, "Will this end? Is this for real? What do I do now? Where do I go now? Will I survive this?" He further says "as I interviewed countless Muslims, so weathered, I couldn't but ask myself, What if this was me? What if it was my brother, my father in jail?"

With the world scenario tilting against the Islam and Muslims, courtesy the radical Islamists trained in the Madrassas set up in Pakistan with US aid, the popular psyche perceived an average Muslim as a terrorist and police machinery operated on this understanding. Even when scores of lives were shattered and the community came under the intimidation of highest order, the Government did not put any corrective to this pattern of investigation with which police was pursuing its work.

Disturbed by this situation, two people's tribunal were set up by the Human Rights groups. The report and recommendations of both the tribunals are similar and overlapping. The first one was headed by Justices (Retd) Bhargava and Sardar Ali Khan, with prominent social activists like Asghar Ali Engineer and Prashant Bhushan as the jury. The testimonies showed that a large number of innocent young Muslims have been and are being victimized by the police on the charge of being involved in various terrorist acts across the country. This is particularly so in Maharashtra, Gujarat, Madhya Pradesh, Andhra Pradesh and Rajasthan, though not limited to these States. This victimization and demonisation of Muslims in the guise of investigation of terror offences, is having a very serious psychological impact on the minds of not only the families of the victims but also other members of the community. It is leading to a very strong sense of insecurity and alienation which may lead to frightful consequences for the nation.

The second tribunal set up by different set of organisations of Rajasthan worked under the leadership of Justice (Retd) Bhargava. One of its pertinent observation was that the police authorities investigating the terror offences appear to be violating all the laws of the land and directions of the Supreme Court during the conduct of the investigations. In particular, many persons have been detained for days or weeks, without showing them to be arrested and without producing them before any Magistrate. They have been sometimes tortured and humiliated by the police officers. They have not been allowed to meet their relatives and lawyers, who have often not even been informed of their detention. The investigation of the blasts by the police also appears to be communally motivated and only persons belonging to the Muslim community have been the target of the investigations.

The names of HUJI and SIMI have been bandied about by the police as the perpetrators of the blasts without any evidence. A number of former members of SIMI have been arrested and detained without any basis or evidence against them. The media has also been uncritically repeating and amplifying the baseless allegations and innuendoes of the police mentioning persons and organisations belonging to the Muslim community, thus resulting in ethnic profiling and feeding into the Islamophobia being sought to be created and reinforced in the minds of the Hindu community by the Hindutva organizations. In Jaipur this has resulted in the vilification of the entire Bengali Muslim community who has been victimised by the Hindutva organisations in complicity with the police.

Thousands of them have been picked up after the blasts and forcibly transported to New Jalpaiguri and then Bangladesh without any due process of law and without giving them an opportunity to show their Indian Citizenship. This has resulted in the ethnic cleansing of Jaipur.

One does not know with what seriousness the administration looks at these people's tribunal, the fact is they have put forward profound realities of the society. It is imperative that the Government takes a serious look at these reports and instructs the investigation authorities to be more professional in their approach and sheds its biases while dealing with minority community.

48

Is it a Crime to be Born a Muslim in India?

The rising tide of communal violence from the decade of 1980 has consolidated the communal politics, politics in the name of religion. The party riding on the chariot of religious nationalism became the second largest party and tasted power at center for six long years and is now entrenched in few states and is knocking at the door of power in few other states. The hope that its recent defeat in Lok Sabha elections will reduce the impact of communal politics in society or will ensure that all communities can breathe the air of civil rights and equal citizenship rights with ease, seems to be like distant drums!

The impact of the rise of this politics and accompanying effect on minorities has resulted in worsening their lot. This downward slide in the condition of minorities is very obvious, going from bad to worse, to worst. It has resulted in the conditions for minorities where they have to live in fear, alienation and the impact of constant profiling in different walks of life. This communal politics has been talking of Hindu nation, it has been spreading hate against minorities, against Muslims in particular. The Muslim community has been the major target of attack and has been bearing a huge brunt of the divisive politics being spearheaded by RSS, its progeny and by those influenced by the RSS ideology. They are not only there in the state machinery and media but also in other crucial spots of Indian social, economic and political life. The worsening plight of Muslim community got reconfirmed in the recently held national meet on 'What it means to be a Muslim in India Today', organised by Anhad in Delhi (Oct 3-5).

The meeting was addressed by the victims and social activists working in the area of human rights particularly of minorities. The pain and anguish of the Muslim community was heart rending, coming through different narrations of illegal arrests, tortures, detentions and adverse judgments. The latest trick is to implicate the Muslim youth in multiple cases in different states. This will ensure their being behind the bars for good. The communal violence which has broken the back of the Indian community is being supplemented by the intense and blind police action against innocent Muslim youth, in the name of terror attacks. While the communal violence is now being orchestrated at low intensity and is scattered far and wide, in the post 9/11 period another front for torturing the community has been opened. Here the modus operandi is simple enough, there is 'Intelligence' tip and that makes our efficient police machinery to arrest the Muslim youth, being Muslim is the major 'tip' for arresting and torturing innocent youth by the guardians of law. Many a youth in the middle of their education for professional lives face immense obstacles, their illegal arrests are never compensated for and nor are they supported to complete their education despite being proved innocents.

There had been many such arrests followed by all sort of illegal steps by the police. Using cars without number plates, taking victims blindfolded to farm houses for third degree tortures are new addition to the 'efficient methods' of the police machinery. There are enough grounds of doubts in Batla House encounter, but it will not be taken up for honest investigation. The argument to avoid honest investigation is that it will demoralize the police force. Can we have such a police force whose morale depends on hiding truth?

Following Mecca Masjid blast, there was a shooting by the police which killed more people than the number killed by blast. The pretext was that the crowd was menacing, which it was not. Truth of Ishrat Jahan case is out in the open but the perpetrators will remain in the seats of power unscathed, barring an odd official living in jail. While such enthusiasm in arresting Muslim youth is there for all to see, those arrested by Hemant Karkare's ATS in Malegaon blast case, are currently being treated with kid gloves. The apprehension is that these guilty gang against whom evidence was collected by late Hemant Karkare may not get the punishment it deserves.

The families battered by such brutal police actions and the families shattered by communal violence are on the streets unattended, marginalized and neglected by society and state. Those Muslims having successful business have been targeted to ensure breaking their economic backbone. This is not only in Gujarat but also in other BJP ruled states. This economically marginalized community is practically boycotted by financial institutions, telephone companies and others. There are many cases where the community is being denied space for graveyards, which are either being taken away or not allowed to expand where there is need for more space. The plight of Shabana Azmi or Imraan Hashmi not getting the house in desired locality is not isolated; this phenomenon is becoming more widespread. The walls of separation along religious community lines are becoming stronger. The Sachar Commission and the Prime Minister's 15 point programme remain a showpiece for purposes best known to the state!

The myths and stereotypes in the media and social space are very much there. The large section of school text-books reinforces the stereotypes and myths about the community. So where does all this lead us to? In a democracy, in a secular state the minorities should be provided safety and dignity irrespective of their religion. The present condition of Muslims in India is nothing but abysmal from the point of view of security, economic condition and social life. A large section has started feeling the deprivations in a very painful manner.

One recalls under the domination of Brahmanical values, caste based exclusionary social-political-system, the caste of Shudras was systematically denied the life of dignity and made to live in subjugation and ghettoization. The efforts of 'Brahmanical ideology based politics', the one of RSS and its progeny, is achieving the same pattern with some difference. Now Muslims are being reduced to second class citizens. This is precisely what RSS wants, this is what is coming to be practiced at all the levels in the country. RSS progeny being in power or out of it does not matter as far as the life of Muslim community is concerned. The RSS workers and ideology have infiltrated the 'social common sense' through media and education. It has infiltrated the state machinery. The limit of this can be seen that RSS controlled Bhonsla Military School in Nasik is supplying large number of recruits for Indian army one of them being Lt Col Prasad Shrikant Purohit, an accomplice of Pragya Singh Thakur, alleged culprits of Malegaon blast. If RSS, a fascist organisation is wrapping its politics in the cloak of Hindu religion, Swaymsevaks can infiltrate army, which institution in the society is safe from slow communal fascist infiltration? Which institution can be trusted for upholding Indian Constitution?

It is with this gloomy scenario around that many a victims deposing in the meeting said with pain and anguish, "Is it a crime to be born a Muslim in India?"

49

Eradicating Terrorism: Groping in the Dark

November 26 (2008) terror attack on Mumbai shook the whole nation like never before. The society and state have been putting up their best to see that measures are taken whereby the terror acts don't repeat. So traumatised has been the nation that every conceivable measure is being given a serious thought for the safety and security of society.

To begin with the condolence for the dead was expressed through number of events, candle light march, human chain, all religion prayer meetings etc. Citizen area networking has come up in a very visible fashion. In many of these protests the anger against politicians had a 'free for all' expression, at places sometimes overtly and sometimes covertly the fear of Pakistan and 'Jehadi' terrorists has been the running thread of the protests. The misplaced call for war against Pakistan is the part of this phenomenon only. The state, the central Government in order respond effectively has passed a law, empowering the state as if that will deter terrorists, who generally come with the full readiness to die. The state is blowing hot and cold, sometimes threatening war and at others talking tough and less often also saying that war is no option.

At another level state is reviewing the quality of bullet proof jackets, increasing airport security and the security of coast line. Civic society groups have been undertaking workshops for disaster management, a university went on to declare a two year course against terrorism. The best amongst these have been the Mohalla committee initiative to cement peace between different communities.

One recalls that after most of the severe phenomenon of violence, the civic society has responded with great concern earlier also. Be it the post Babri demolition, Mumbai riots or the Gujarat carnage 2002, for a good bit of time socially oriented and concerned individuals and groups sprang into the relief, rehabilitation and intercommunity amity work. This time around there is a lot of social churning, ferment throwing up initiatives and opinions. Large sections of people hold Pakistan as the culprit of the attacks of terror. The activities of civic society groups, particularly related to intercommunity amity, are very valuable. But how far will they go?

It seems that the knee jerk reaction after the spectacular event; tragedy, is generally focused on the symptoms of the phenomenon. Tighten security, have better bullet proof jackets and have stringent laws is the most immediate response. Teach Pakistan a lesson is the common advice. As such there is not much attempt to go beyond the obvious to unravel the truth of sectarian or terrorist violence. Surely sectarian violence is due to some political groups baking their bread in the fire of divisive politics, the ground for which is prepared by the hate ideology, spread of misconceptions and distorted view of the minorities, their history, their present. So as lot of groups and individuals correctly talk about peace, about need for amity, their attempts do not reach to the core issue of fighting against divisive politics, the attempt to unravel the truth about minorities, their present, their past.

The communal violence and emotive issues give strength to the communal parties, who in turn give bigger space to their affiliates who work at cultural and religious level to increase the communal divides and weaken national integration, further paving way to worse violence in time to come. The vicious cycle of Hate propaganda, violence, communal polarisation, strengthening of communal parties goes on unabated. Not only that, their intensity has been worsening every next time communal violence has been occurring. Gujarat was worse than Mumbai and Orissa has been more horrific than Dangs. The trajectory of communal violence has clearly shown that all the efforts by state to curb it have been misdirected; the social initiatives have been serious but probably the cause has not been addressed effectively. One means by that the underlying demonisation of minorities, the base of communal organisation has been going up and in turn communalisation of society has worsened and in turn the fertile base for future communal violence remains intact.

As far as terrorist attacks are concerned, the formulation that 'All Terrorists are Muslims', has been the understanding on which policies are made and implemented. The second parallel thought to perceive that terror attacks are due to Pakistan. With the result that the real causes of terror are not taken up for treatment they deserve. From 1993 onwards terror attacks have been wrecking havoc in our region, our country. The feeling that tough laws will eradicate terror attacks has been proved wrong historically. Even when draconian laws were in use, terror attacks went on merrily. Laws are not deterrent to those who are indoctrinated to lay down their lives for a particular cause, wrong or right.

Amongst various other factors, a sense of deeper injustice, has also been providing *'raison dietve'* to the repetition of these attacks. If we want to see the real causes of terrorism we will have to go beyond blaming Pakistan or believing that 'All Terrorists are Muslims'. The popular perceptions stops at Al Qaeda, Lashkar-e-Tayyaba being the real cause obviates the need to see that beyond Al Qaeda etc. There is a role of US imperialism in bringing them up and using these terror outfits for US' political and economic gains. So all anger, protest against Pakistan and accompanying factors is not going to yield any results beyond a point. One misses the point that terrorism of Al Qaeda variety has roots in US policies of propping up these groups to fight Russian armies occupying Afghanistan (1979). One has to see beyond the obvious to realise that this type terrorism has its genesis from the deeper political designs of controlling the oil wells in the Gulf region. The indoctrination of the radical groups which began due to this policy of US can not be fought against merely by strengthening some laws and by new set of weapons.

Pakistani society is as much a victim of this dastardly phenomenon as India is. Terrorists always are looking for the holes in security through which they operate and their biggest advantage is that they are indoctrinated to the extent that they are willing to stake their all, including their lives to do what they have been doing. On similar wave length operates the terror attacks by Sadhvi Pragya Singh Thakur and others of her group. So where do we go, what direction we give to our concerns to ensure that terror attacks do not occur.

First and foremost is that all places where injustice breeds, where democracy is stifled in a shortsighted way, becomes a rich fertile ground for breeding of terrorism. The one planted by US, Al Qaeda type, needs to be fought at global level. US is to be made accountable for much of this cancer which has spread in the area. While firmly dealing with the present terror set ups, democracy also needs to be made strong in Pakistan itself. One sees the subtle difference in the utterances of democratic elements in Pakistan and the Army-Mullah combine. The global peace movement has to ensure that the United Nations comes to the fore and stops the hegemony, the imperial behavior of US in particular. No measure short of restoring UN, making US follow the wishes of global community, a more democratised United Nations, which is made to take up the global issue of terrorism, will be adequate. US war on terror, and those who go by that, need to be put on the margins and charge taken up by UN to eradicate it.

While draconian laws are no solution to the problem, it is likely they create and intensify the problem. The mantra to tighten the security has not yielded any success in preventing it. The core point is to see that the concerned civic society makes its stand clear, that terrorism's roots lie in injustice on one hand and US policies on the other. We need to raise our voices against injustice and US hegemony both to see that over a period of time the terror menace is eliminated by and by.

The recent ferment and turmoil in the wake of Mumbai terror attack, the extremely positive attitude of citizens needs to address itself against the deeper causes of terrorism. Necessarily we begin with identifying the symptoms, but remaining stuck at that will let the real disease go undetected and will make it stronger over a period of time. It is time that civic response undertakes the awareness programs to propagate the whole truth of terrorism, and to channelise its energies against those causes.

SECTION–XI
STRUGGLE FOR PEACE

50

Peace for the Planet: Prophet Muhammad

This February 28 (2010) the world will be celebrating the birth day of Prophet Muhammad (Prophet). Currently it is ironical that a messiah who preached for Peace in the society is being projected as being founder of a religion of violence. It is a tragedy of our times that global politics for control of oil has devised a language which targets and demonizes Islam. At the same time in India the 'social common sense' propagated through communal politics also demonised Muslims and Islam. Various distortions are presented as being the character of Islam and so of the Muslims.

Prophet Muhammad was born in year 570 in Mecca, Saudi Arabia. At the age of forty he started preaching the values which laid the foundation of the religion called Islam. The background of his preaching, the teachings were centred around the tribal society where the prevalent values were primitive. The concept of revenge, an eye for an eye, suppression of women's rights was rampant. Prophet's teaching came to cover the whole range of human relationship at familial, social and political level. In his personal conduct and preaching he set very high human standards and was able to unify the society on the basis of these teachings and their application in practice.

The core concepts preached by him relate to *Adl* (justice), *ihsan* (benevolence), *rahmah* (compassion) amongst others. The idea was to bring peace in the strife ridden society. The tribals were quarreling on material issues and had many Gods, each as a symbol of one tribe. In this background he came up with the concept of Allah (Single God), and elaborated the brotherhood of society, talked of peace through surrender to the will of Allah. Most of his concepts were for peace and justice to all, including justice to women. It is because of these contributions that he is regarded as messenger of Allah.

He also focused on issues like struggle against *julm* (injustice) through jihad (striving). He realised that *Jahl* (ignorance) is the root of strife in the society so he focused a lot on acquiring knowledge. For social upliftment he urged upon people to strive (Jihad) to fight against their own evils and evils prevalent in the society. A new term also came to be coined, *Kafir* (from the root word Kufr, for hiding truth) for those who were opposing the new converts to Islam.

These values gave a lot of peace in the region and the community also organised politically around these principles for sometime. Later many different interpretations of his preaching's came. Much later many well demarcated sects within Islam, each claiming to be the only true inheritance of the Prophet, came into being. Many a versions of Islam are currently prevalent, some of these are very conservative and orthodox while others are fairly liberal and in keeping with the times. The conservative and orthodox versions are more due to orthodox sections, especially close to the rulers, and are imposed on the communities where the feeling of insecurity is very strong. Today the conservative versions are going up as globally Islam and Muslims are being demonized by diverse political interests.

The teachings of Prophet Muhammad are a major landmark in the history of mankind. His emphasis on various values and concern for the women, poor and deprived is high point of Islam as a religion.

Currently with the onslaught of politics of vested interests, various misconceptions have been deliberately propagated. One such misconception is that Islam spread on the strength of sword as it encourages violence. The truth is that in India in particular many people embraced Islam to escape the tyranny of caste system. There is a clear mandate in Islam that force cannot be applied in matters of faith. 'To you your religion; to me mine' is the basic dictum. Similarly the perception is that Muslims keep their women under greater bondage. This perception has resulted in communal violence where the minorities have to suffer a lot and Muslim women are the target of attack on their bodies in various despicable forms. Such stereotypes get reinforced due to the policies like those of Taliban who have totally banned women from coming out of the house. While Prophet was amongst the initial preachers who emphasized on the being sensitive to gender and giving better status to women than was prevalent at that time.

Even polygamy (Four wives) is totally misrepresented. Due to tribal wars the number of war orphans and widows was high. Also due to feudal society men were marrying number of times, so to ensure that women get decent home and also dignity the restriction to four wives came as a contextual value, with a proviso that each wife must be treated on par. This too was not supposed to be applicable for all the times, and in Muslim countries where Muslim women can live without fear, the concept of polygamy is under severe criticism.

The worst distortion of Prophets teaching is seen when US, after 9/11, popularised the word, Islamic Terrorism. Terrorism is an act in which many innocents loose their lives. The mandate of Koran's teaching is that killing of even a single innocent person tantamounts to killing the whole humanity. In the same game of bringing up Al Qaeda through Madrassas set up with US assistance through CIA, the terms Kafir and Jihad were mutilated. While in Koran, Prophets teaching, word kafir stood for those hiding truth; the CIA inspired Madrassas presented it for those not believing in Allah. Jihad which stood for striving came to be distorted as war or killing, which it is not. As such Jihad is the striving to fight against internal and external evil, today it has been presented as killing of non Muslims. This is the biggest travesty of truth.

It is one of the big paradox of history that Islam, the religion which stands for peace, has been demonised as the one standing for violence. Prophet Muhammad has been a noble being standing for humanism of highest order. It is because of teaching of prophets like him and Bhagwan Mahavir, Mahatma Gautam Buddha, Jesus Christ, Guru Nanak and others like them that Humanity has enriched its values. There is an urgent need to understand Prophet Muhammad in correct perspective for betterment of global scenario.

51

Civilisations: Clash or Alliance

During last two decades the world has seen the rise of politics based on religious identity. Particularly after the 9/11 2001 WTC disaster there is a widespread feeling that Samuel Huntington's thesis, that after the end of cold war the current time is the one of Clash of Civilisations (Clash), is true. One has witnessed many a controversies where religion has been dragged into the murky world of politics. Osama bin Laden talked of Jihad and George Bush responded to the WTC attack by uttering that it is going to be Crusade for him. He and his associate Blair both gave divine reasons for attack on Iraq. Multitude of controversies veered around Danish cartoons, Pope's statement about Islam, the banning of burqa in some Western countries, the rise of acts of terror in the name of Islam with the epithet coming that all terrorists are Muslims, has become popular in the social thinking at broad layers. Superficially it is projected as if it is the clash between the Islamic culture and the Western civilization. Here in India also attempts were made and are underway to project Islam as a religion of violence and Muslims being fanatics out to stick to the medieval social norms. The overall impact of the events and acceptance of this clash thesis by Huntington has worsened the problem and is widening the intercommunity rifts.

As such the term clash of civilization was put forward by Bernard Lewis and later on converted into a thesis by Samuel Huntington, whose essay in a journal, *Foreign Affairs* 1993, became more popular after the 9/11 2001. At the end of cold war Francis Fukuyama postulated 'End of History', which stood for "What we may be witnessing is not just the end of the Cold War, or the passing of a particular period of post-war history, but the end of history as such: that is, the end point of mankind's ideological evolution and the universalization of Western liberal democracy as the final form of human government." (quoted from "The End of History?", 1989) This was in response to the philosophy of Karl Marx, whose Historical materialism propounded that the struggle between the classes is the cause of progress of society, leading to the classless society and end of History, i.e. beginning of classless, commune based society, communism

In the backdrop of Fukuyama's 'End of History', Huntington postulated that while the age of ideology (Marxism, classless society) has ended with the collapse of Soviet system, the World has only reverted to the state of cultural conflicts. According to him the primary axis of conflict will be along cultural religious lines. The principal conflicts of global politics will occur between nations and groups of different civilisations. The clash of civilisation will dominate global politics and fault lines between civilisations are the battle lines of future. According to, "It is my hypothesis that the fundamental source of conflict in this new world will not be primarily ideological or primarily economic. The great divisions among humankind and the dominating source of conflict, will be that the cultural nation states will remain the most powerful actors in world affairs, but the principal conflicts of global politics will occur between nations and groups of different civilisations. The clash of civilisations will dominate global politics. The fault lines between civilisations will be the battle lines of the future."

Many did approve of this thesis and the accompanying classification, whose main criterion is religion. This thesis did create an anxiety and confusion adding to the problems of the nations all around. It is in this context that Kofi Annan, Secretary General of UN launched an initiative co-sponsored by Prime Ministers of Spain and Turkey for an Alliance of Civilisation in August 2005. This initiative nominated a high level group cutting across different religions and nations to come up with an understanding of the world today and to recommend the measures to restore the amity of civilisations, cultures and people of the world. The report has been (Mid Nov 2006) submitted to the Secretary-General (http://www.unaoc.org/repository/report.htm)and it's a landmark in more ways than one.

It debunks the Clash thesis to bring our attention to the alliance between different cultures, nations and people at all the levels, social, political and economic. It is not only in current times but since the times people started migrating and interacting that the alliance has been the undercurrent of the societal life. The report points out that Clash theory has distorted the terms of discourse on the real nature of predicament the world is facing. The history of relations between cultures is not only one of wars and confrontations; it is also based on centuries of constructive exchanges, cross fertilisations and peaceful co-existence. One is reminded here that India's ex-president, Dr. K.R. Narayanan, in response to the Clash thesis, said that civilisations don't clash, it is barbarisms which clash. In Clash thesis, cultures and religions are identified with the religions of the kings and their wars are presented as clash between religions or civilisations. The Hate ideology spread by communal group's right here in South Asia also bases itself on the wars between Kings of different religions and these kings are presented as symbols of that religion. The whole aspect of cultural interaction is missing in this discourse. For example, in India while the atrocities of Aurangzeb are the core of building the Hate ideology, the confluence articulated by Dara Shikoh as one can glean through his book *Majma Ul Bahrain,* India being a confluence of different cultures, is missing in this mindset. Similarly the rule of Muslim Kings in the subcontinent is taken as the point for legitimisation of Islamic nation.

The worst part of this Clash thesis is that by propagating that cultures are set on collision course, it helps in turning the negotiable disputes into seemingly intractable, identity based conflicts and this is what has taken control of popular imagination. The report is based on the multipolar perspective and the UN Charter of Human rights. Significantly it points out that there is no hierarchy amongst cultures as each of them has contributed to the evolution of mankind. While the core problem remains poverty and deprivation of vast sections of mankind, the rising trend of terrorism cannot be dealt with by seeing it as a mere law and order problem or having its roots in religion. On the contrary, terrorism itself is a product of political circumstances, which need to be solved on urgent basis. In societies if some groups are discriminated against the violent repercussions come up and are perceived as libratory by a section of people while the same is seen as anti national by the state and other set of people. The durable solution to the causes of terrorism does not lie in attacking some countries or increasing the role of armed personnel in that area but in addressing the roots of resentment.

It traces the roots of current violent responses in the partition of Palestine and formation of Israel, and latter's occupation of part of Palestine and other Arab territories, which has come to be seen as a sort of colonialism by vast mass of people. While Jerusalem remains Holy for Jews, Christians and Muslims, the support of Western powers to Israel's highhandedness is perceived as the collusion of West with the expansionism of Israel. The committee is very clear on the point that no cause can justify the killing of civilians, non combatants. It does call for freedom of religions and takes a strong stand against desecration of holy places, irrespective of the majority minority religions. The report does recommend several measures in the arena of education, youth programmes, community actions aimed to promote alliance, peaking it with the recommendation that a forum of alliance of civilization under the auspices of UN should be established and this should be promoted at all the levels, national, societal and what have you.

The humane spirit of the report is visible all through. However the point is, in current times when the very authority of UN has been undermined by the powers that are arrogant, can we look forward to the era of alliance and amity so that the real problems gnawing the vast numbers of human kinds are properly addressed to, i.e. march in the direction of better world, i.e. struggle for human rights. To put it in another way, is it possible to think positively, to think that 'another world is possible', a world where human rights of all of us are adhered to.

52

Dialogue for Peace in Action: Violence Threatening Social Peace and Need for Amity

Last two decades have seen a very negative trend world over. Immense violence has been unleashed, and that too in the name of religion. When two planes strike the World Trade Center and 3000 innocent persons die, Osama bin Laden expresses his joy and declares that what is going on is Jihad. In the name of Crusade, George Bush President of US launched an attack on Afghanistan. In this attack over 60000 innocent people get killed. In India, on December 6, 1992 the rampaging mob of three Lakh people led by Lal Krishna Advani, mobilised by RSS combine (RSS combine word stands for RSS and all those organisations which are driven by the political ideology in the name of Hindu religion, whose volunteers are trained by RSS for the goal of Hindu Nation). This demolition of Babri mosque has been regarded as the glory to Hindu religion by them. In Orissa (July, December 2007) a massive aggression is launched on the Christian community on the pretext of the murder of Swami Laxmanand. All through the name of religion is in the forefront of the violence.

Accompanying the violence a thesis "Clash of Civilizations", that the present era is the one where civilizations, religions are clashing is supposed to be describing the present phenomenon. This thesis propounded by Samuel Huntington, sees the current state of global affairs as one of conflict between civilisations, unmindful of the fact that civilizations don't clash it is barbarisms which clash. This thesis is also unmindful of the fact of history that while Kings and colonial powers have launched wars for their vested interests, the people of different regions and religions have interacted amicably resulting in the growth of human culture and civilizations. In India the dominant political discourse presumes that Christians and Muslims are foreigners and that they are not having equal rights! This ignores the fact that Indian culture is a plural one, that people of different religions have lived amicably with each other and that it is due to the participation of people of all the regions and religions that we got Independence, and that the concept of India as a nation is all inclusive.

Violence in the name of Religion

The communal violence, more so from last two decades is leading to polarisation of communities, strengthening of communal politics, and in turn ghettoization of minorities. The social links between communities are snapping fast and religion based localities are coming up in big number. In US and many other places Muslims are being looked at with suspicion and the gulf between religious communities is widening.

After the decades of 1950s to 1980s, when people from all religions came together for national liberation struggles and for marching towards democratic norms, the process seems to have been reversed and the aggressive slant of political and social powers is creating a situation where it seems that religious differences are the cause of problem.

Religion or Politics

The worst part of present social language is the abuse of religious identity for political goals. None of what is going on has any thing to do with the morality of religions. As a matter of fact the moral values of religions do supplement each other for a better world. What has happened is that the global super power has in a shortsighted way promoted Radical Muslim groups and trained them in an insane ideology, which resulted in growth of terrorism. In India the RSS combine has similarly used the identity of Hindu religion to promote their agenda of Hindu nation, an agenda which is opposed to democratic values of society. The global scene due to this twin phenomenon is affecting the atmosphere of peace and is creating an impression of clash between religions.

Terrorism: Clash of Civilisations!

The main group which has created the impression that terrorism is due to religion is Al Qaeda. This group was propped up by Unite States to counter the Russian occupation of Afghanistan, in the decade of 1980s. To ensure the participation of Muslim youth in the battle, Madrassas were opened in Pakistan with the help of US money. The syllabus taught in these Madrassas was designed in US and it distorted the meaning of word Jihad and Kafir. In Koran, Kafir stands for the hidden person, who attacks the people of faith. The US designed syllabus presented Kafir as one who does not believe in Allah, a non Muslim. Jihad which means 'striving' effort for betterment was presented as war against non Muslims. In this direction Osama was brought in to lead the Al Qaeda and was supported by US with 8000 Million Dollars and 7000 tons of armaments, with the help of which he defeated Russian armies. The same Al Qaeda and its offshoots sprung up and survived over a period of time. Later in popular perception all acts committed by this group got associated with Islam and Muslims.

US media after the 9/11/2001, popularised the word Islamic terrorism for the acts of the group which they helped bringing up and which later turned against them. The demonization of Muslims worldwide went on unchallenged, major sections of media propagated the word Islamic Terrorism and the whole community came under intimidation. Here the theory of Clash of Civilisations also presented Muslims as backward and aggressive, ignoring the fact that Muslims are as good or bad as any other religious community.

RSS Combine

In India RSS which began with the agenda of Hindu rashtra (Nation) began with the ideology that Muslims, Christians and Communists are a threat to 'our' Hindu nation. In pursuance of its politics RSS gave rise to many communal organisations, BJP, VHP, Vanvasi Kalyan Ashram, Bajrang Dal etc. These organisations built on the communal historiography introduced by British and went on adding more to it. They spread the canards that Muslim kings destroyed Hindus temples and insulted Hindu religion, converted people by force, did atrocities on Hindus, are eating beef while Hindu regard cow as her mother, are aggressive, are terrorists, have four wives and twenty children and the like. All this has been demonstrated to be totally false and based on half truths.

One knows that holy places were destroyed by the Kings of all religions for wealth and as a symbol of their victory over the defeated king. They also built holy places to respect the feelings of their subjects. The religions have not been spread by Kings, barring the exception of King Ashok and that religions spread by multiple mechanisms, interaction, influence of saints, expectation of reward, etc. Also that, the victor King used to humiliate the defeated king by imposing various conditions on him, one of them being conversion to victor's religion. Kings' atrocities on their subjects, their humiliation of women in the areas defeated by them was done by all armies. Here selective presentation of such acts only by Muslim Kings was done by the British to win over people's loyalty to woo them away from the loyalty to Muslim kings.

Beef eating is a global phenomenon; also beef was the food item during the Vedic times is well known by now. Emperor Babur in his will to Humayun advices him to desist from cow slaughter in deference to wishes of the Hindu subjects. Today the question of four wives does not arise as the sex ratio is adverse as far as number of women are concerned (All India average 932, amongst Muslims 936). The number of children depends on the level of literacy and social development. This number of children amongst Muslims is more a sign of their being marginalized from social development processes. Terrorism is not a religious phenomenon; it is due to political, economic and social reasons. Liberation Tigers of Tamil Elam, Irish Republican army, ULFA and 'Sadhvi Pragya-Dayanand Pande and associates' tell us that terrorists have come from all religions. The result of this propaganda has been demonization of Muslims and laying the ground for communal violence.

Religion: Dialogue and Current Times

Before we engage in dialogue we have to make two basic points clear. One, what are the issues involved, are they of religious nature or political nature. Second what is the implication of primary process on the intercommunity relations? Starting from this then we go on to explore as to how intercommunity relations can be improved, and bridges built for better and more amicable society.

As we have seen above globally it is the lust for oil which is the major cause of terrorism. It is not due to Islam. At home, in India it is the political outfit working for Hindu nation, which is spreading the lies and is doing propaganda against minorities. So we have to make it clear that the moral values of Islam, Hinduism and Christianity are not hostile to each other, they as a matter of fact complement each other. One is not talking of the theological, mythological issues, one is talking about the moral values propagated by these, like *Vasudhaiv Kutumbkam*, (Hinduism), Love thy neighbor (Christianity) or take care of your neighbor's needs (Islam). To re-emphasise the present problem is not with religions, it is the political interests of section of society which are being presented as being related to religion, the dialogue process has to make it clear that divisive force do not lie in domain of religion but in the arena of political interests. The problem has been imposed on societal, cultural and ideological spheres of society.

The moral content of religions has to be projected along the lines of the human rights of all in the society, and we have to help each other in enhancing the concept of morality and human rights. At the same time we can leave the issues related to identity, holy books, rituals and festivals to each religion, as their private-social matters. Here also one can encourage the participation in others' festivals and celebrations as far as the social aspect of festivals is concerned. Theological matters of the other religions should be left to them for sorting it out. Others should not pontificate on such matters except of their own.

Political-Social Dialogue

The tragedy of communal violence has been creating the walls of separation amongst the communities. A dialogue is needed to overcome these artificial barriers created by the political phenomenon. For this, the social workers and religious workers do form starting point of interaction where the matters are discussed from the point of community, keeping the politics aside. The basis of this interaction has to be three fold.

One, the moral values of religion, the syncretic values and traditions of people, to recapture the essence of that practice and to bring it back as the basis of social relationship. Second, we have to rededicate ourselves, to reaffirm proactively to the values of Indian freedom struggle. These values came to be enshrined in the Constitution of India. These are the values of Liberty, Equality and Fraternity. By equality one means the similar status as citizens, irrespective of one's religion, caste and gender. To reaffirm that ours' is a secular democracy. To recommit that these values are the ground on which people of different faith will stand. Fraternity (community) teaches us that irrespective of our caste, religion or gender we are an Indian community. And that is the basis of our interaction. While picking this up we need to keep in mind that United Nations Charter of Human Rights is our guiding principle, which ordains for a dignified life as the right of all of us.

Promoting Affinity

With these in mind we realise that negative propaganda is the root of hatred and it is the ground for violence. We need to work proactively to dispel the misconceptions and wrong perceptions about other communities. The bridges between communities are to be made stronger. Many a social effort is needed in this direction. To make ourselves aware of the truth about the history and the communities, we have to develop platforms through which the truth is disseminated. It may be workshops, seminars, lectures, films or other cultural expressions.

The community leaders have to reach out to Human rights workers and those striving for plural values. Currently not much effort is being put to highlight their work. The major victims of the present attack on plural values of the society are dalits, women, workers, Adivasis and minorities. These sections have to be provided a platform where they exchange their ideas and grievances and raise forums for interaction and dialogue. It is through the dialogue of these sections that a positive force against the violence and retrograde politics can be made strong.

The country is continuing to be plural and secular because secular and liberal elements are much more in number. The problem is that they stand fragmented, and their voice remains in the background due to lack of cohesion. We have to talk in the terms of humane voices coming together and struggling for a composite society.

Since the society is in crisis of identity, let us define as to what is our primary identity, religious or national? We need to reassert our primary national identity at this juncture. Our efforts of dialogue have to be multilayered, starting from the school to the community, we have to spread the message of peace. The misconceptions about other communities/religions have to be negated by propagating the essential values of religions, the values related to love, compassion, peace and non-violence. We also need to intervene at cultural level. For this, the specially designed programms involving people of the community, cutting across religions need urgent attention. The moral value classes in schools have to be enriched with the content of inter-religious understanding.

The prophets could inspire people as they stood for truth in a non compromising way. There cannot be peace without justice. Today the major section of population is unaware of the richness of Indian culture and plural ethos and has been frightened in the name of religion. Those doing politics in the name of religion or religious identity need to be re-educated in the norms of human values, with the focus that it is the goodness of different people which has kept human society on the path of progress.

Way to Humane Future

The responsible people of different faiths do realise that this is not in tune with the spirit of their religion. They are watching helplessly this whole process of demonisation of certain religious communities and the social rifts being created due to that. Faith in the values of humanism is paramount in the values of religion. This current scenario is pushing back the aspirations of poor people and so it is needed that the situation is overcome for the sake of better world, for the sake of peace and amity. While the political forces bent upon creating this mayhem are very powerful and almighty, having control over resources of different types and on media, the people with genuine faith in human values need to come forward to ensure that this dark phase of human history is overcome in the spirit of dialogue. The need for inter community relations and dialogue was never needed more than at present times.

The isolation due to this political process is not only creating emotional walls amongst different communities, it is also resulting in the retardation of social development. The kernel of present efforts for peace lies in the process of building bridges amongst communities and that process can be started only by a genuine dialogue amongst people of different faiths, by coming close to each other by abolishing the artificial boundaries created by the politics of hate being practiced by various forces, globally and locally.

These dialogues amongst different religious communities are needed at all the levels, starting from the *basti* and *mohalla* to the leadership of religions, scholars of religions, the activists engaged in dispelling hate from the society, and those working for human rights, all of them need to be involved in this process of dialogue. The present impasse which is presenting religions as the separating points need to be overcome and the understanding that religious differences and plural ways of life are a strength and not an obstacle to peace. The dialogue amongst religions needs to be supplemented by the cooperation in the field of social work to alleviate the pain and misery of the mankind, there is a need to encourage and coordinate in the field of struggles for the human rights of deprived sections of society. We aspire for peace and we remind ourselves that the peace desired by us can not be achieved without justice for the people. Justice is a mandatory pre-requisite for peace. The spirit of service to mankind has to prevail over the current assault on the basic human values in the name of religion.

We need to look into the high level committee of UN which went on to counter the thesis of Clash of civilisations put forward by the US professor Samuel Huntington. This thesis forms the cover for US ambitions for its aggressions in West Asia. The UN committee (http://www.unaoc.org/repository/report.htm) has put forward that there is no clash between civilisations, as a matter of fact civilisation have an alliance for a better tomorrow. On the similar lines one will like to say that there is no clash between the moral values of religions, it is the alliance between these values that the human race can look forward to a better future, a future which will eliminate poverty, hunger, disease and misery from the world. Religions should be standing for love and peace. One posits that there cannot be peace without justice and so the implication is that religions should address the issues not only of poverty but also of the system which creates poverty, it just does not talk of superficial manifestation of the problems but to go to the root of prevalent problems and to raise the voice against perpetrators of injustices. Religions have to raise the issues of human rights of all people of the world. It is this alliance which will ensure that the focus of world policies has to be brought back to the issue of Human rights of weaker sections of society. Nothing short of a genuine dialogue amongst people of different faiths can overcome the obstacles created by the political forces misusing the religious identity for their political goals.

India is essentially a plural, multicultural, multi-religious nation. The tasks for secular movement are huge, we need to retrieve the values of freedom movement from the clutches of communal politics, politics in the name of religion. We need to reconnect with the plural, mixed heritage and cultural diversity of the country. We need to strengthen the syncretic aspects of religious traditions, the traditions which look at religion as a uniting force, not a divisive disrupter.

Index